Other Titles by
New York Times Bestselling Author
JEN LANCASTER

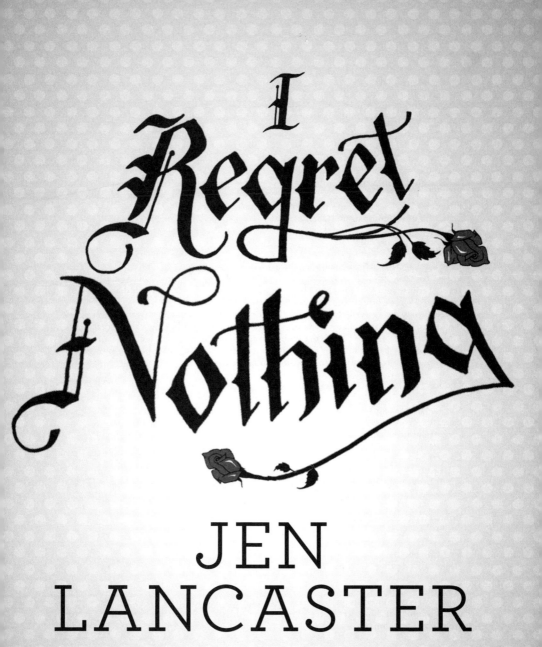

I Regret Nothing

JEN LANCASTER

NEW AMERICAN LIBRARY

New American Library
Published by the Penguin Group
Penguin Group (USA) LLC, 375 Hudson Street,
New York, New York 10014

USA | Canada | UK | Ireland | Australia | New Zealand | India | South Africa | China
penguin.com
A Penguin Random House Company

First published by Signet, an imprint of New American Library,
a division of Penguin Group (USA) LLC

First Printing, May 2015

LIBRARY OF CONGRESS CATALOGING-IN-PUBLICATION DATA:
Lancaster, Jen, 1967–
I regret nothing/Jen Lancaster.
p. cm.
ISBN 978-0-451-47107-9
I. Title.
PS3612.A54748I2 2015
813'.6—dc23   2014042354

Printed in the United States of America
10 9 8 7 6 5 4 3 2 1

Set in Bembo
Designed by Spring Hoteling

PUBLISHER'S NOTE
Penguin is committed to publishing works of quality and integrity. In that spirit, we are
proud to offer this book to our readers; however, the story, the experiences and the words
are the author's alone.

For Tau Delta Beta, because we were in the shit,
and for Ed Lover, for providing the backspin

CONTENTS

For of all sad words of tongue and pen, the saddest
are these: "It might have been!"

—John Greenleaf Whittier

The past is a great place and I don't want to erase it
or regret it but I don't want to be its prisoner either.

—Mick Jagger

My biggest regret . . . is that I didn't hit John Denver
in the mouth while I had the chance.

—Denis Leary

I Regret Nothing

1.

IT'S NOT SPRING BREAK, OKAY?

"Don't get a tattoo."

I glance over at my husband, Fletch, who's grudgingly agreed to ferry me to the airport at this ungodly hour. We left the house so early that it's still basically night outside, with only the palest streaks of pink on the eastern horizon. In the dimness of the driver's seat, his features are barely illuminated by the dashboard lights. Still, even in the dark, I can detect his smirk and I'm aggravated. "How do you figure tattoos are likely with this crew?"

"Because you're going on Adult Spring Break." He says this all matter-of-factly, as though it's already a fait accompli and the artist will begin inking as soon as I decide between the shoulder tat of Calvin whizzing on a Chevy logo or the rainbow-hued butterfly across my butt cheek.

I'd choose neither, obviously.

(Sidebar: I'd especially not choose the butterfly. To keep proportionate with the rest of the real estate back there, that thing would have to be the size of a pigeon, which . . . no.)

Anyway, I don't want to lose my patience with him because

he's doing me a favor. Still, I'm offended he feels he has to issue warnings. "If this trip's considered Adult Spring Break, then I'm pretty sure we're doing it wrong. Julia had us all read *Midnight in the Garden of Good and Evil* in anticipation of our trip. No one delves into what critics call 'a lyrical work of nonfiction' to get ready for Spring Break."

He snorts. "Yeah, you say that now. Talk to me in forty-eight hours."

Argh.

"This is going to be a bona fide grown-up girls' weekend. We specifically rented a place with a veranda, where we'll drink *modest* amounts of excellent wine. Rachel's husband's an oenophile and he's sent along a few of his favorites, which we plan to savor. When was the last time you heard anyone say 'oenophile' in reference to Spring Break, Fletch? Hmm? No answer? Didn't *think* so."

Fletch flips his blinker and glances over his shoulder before merging into the right-hand lane. His silence speaks volumes.

"Whatever you do, don't get the tattoo somewhere visible. Nothing reads '*I make minimum wage*' like neck art. You're never going to run into an allergist with THUG LIFE stenciled over his Adam's apple. You don't meet a lot of investment bankers inked up Henry Rollins–style."

For all our years together, sometimes it's like he's never even met me. "Why so danger-danger-Will-Robinson here? If you were to say, '*Avoid eating a bowl of cheese grits larger than your head,*' or '*Maybe you have enough handbags,*' I'd be all, '*You're right. Yeah, gonna be better about that,*' but this is nonsensical! From a logistics standpoint, when do you propose we hit these mythical tattoo shops, anyway? After we tour historical sites? Before our tasting dinner? Between jaunts to antique stores? I haven't been one tequila sunrise away from *Girls Gone Wild* in almost two decades. I guarantee none of the women coming plan to party like it's 1999. Or, considering most of us are mid-forties, 1989."

"Mark my words: Trouble's a-brewing."

I begin to fume in earnest. "You're infuriating! Which of us is Ferris Bueller here, making the good kids do bad things? *Joanna?* You mean, the kindest, most gentle person to ever send a hand-written thank-you note? You know at three out of the last three weddings she's attended, she and her husband were purposefully seated next to the minister at dinner? Ladies selected to buttress the clergy aren't ladies who'd willingly give their undies to a geek. I assure you, there's no Ferris in this group."

"You're mixing your John Hughes metaphors. All I'm saying is every time you and Joanna get together, you're both eighteen-year-old freshmen again, spilling trash-can punch all over your Keds. Be careful."

(Sidebar: I miss my old Keds.)

As we get closer to O'Hare, the sky lightens, but the pinkness morphs into gray. Looks like something's about to blow in, but hopefully not until after we're in the air. Julia has a full day of activities planned for our nine thirty a.m. arrival, starting with a group bike ride, of which I've opted out. Supposedly, the bike's more like a big trolley with a table and everyone pedals and apparently you're encouraged to bring your own snacks and libations. I told her I refused to be part of a hydra-headed jackass, careening down the streets of Savannah in the sweltering heat, even with the benefit of my own sandwich. (Also, I sort of don't know how to ride a bike, but that's not the point.) Instead, I plan to take the convertible I've rented to the grocery store to stock up on healthy snacks.

You know where they don't worry about providing healthy snacks? Spring Break.

Then I remember the argument that would win this case if we were in front of a judge. "You realize Joanna holds our medical power of attorney, right?"

"Trouble."

Unfair! The rest of our holiday crew is equally sane and staid, particularly since most of them have kids. I mean, Julia tries so hard to maintain a balance between motherhood and a career that she doesn't have time to watch television. She'd never even heard of *The Bachelor* before I told her about it! As for Rachel, she's Joanna's cousin and they're both so beatifically calm it's uncanny. (I wonder what it's like to come from families where yelling isn't the default mode?) I haven't met Julia's friend Trenna, but hear she has a master's degree in theology.

You know who didn't have a master's degree in theology?

Sid Vicious.

Kathleen's the only participant besides me who's not a mom, but she and her husband are actively trying to adopt. Plus, she's so organized and savvy that she once mentioned how she's able to subtract dry-cleaning costs and museum entrance fees from her income taxes.

You know what doesn't scream punk rock?

Itemized deductions.

"What about my Girls Gone Mild life leads you to believe I'm a body shot shy of debauchery? Is it the pearls? Is it my vintage trophy collection? Is it the knitting? Are they just throwing down way too hard for you at the Three Bags Full yarn store?"

"You're like that line from *Men in Black*," he says. "Remember the part where Tommy Lee Jones complains about how unpredictable people are?"

I reply, "Obviously. It's only one of the five finest films ever made."

(Sidebar: I'm not kidding. Will Smith is my spirit animal. From "You Saw My Blinker, Bitch" to *I Am Legend*, I celebrate his entire body of work.)

"Remember when Will Smith says something like, *'How can you say folks will do stupid things? People are smart.'* And Tommy Lee replies, '*No, a person is smart. People are dumb, panicky, dangerous animals and you know it.*' You are a person who's smart. In a group, you're a panicky, dangerous animal. And that's my thesis statement."

"You know where they don't say 'thesis statement'? Spring Break."

"Let me ask you this—when was the last time you went away for this long with this many women?"

It's . . . been a while. Outside of traveling to book events, I haven't been much of anywhere in the past few years. From 2009 when our pit bull Maisy was diagnosed with cancer to when we lost her in 2012, Fletch and I spent a total of only one night together away from her. We rearranged our entire lives around that magnificent little girl, from buying our first house within ten miles of the specialty clinic where she was treated to limiting the number of tour cities I'd visit. I even figured out how to make my previous book take place entirely under the roof of my own home so that I'd stay close.

I wouldn't change a single action in caring for Maisy and I'd have gladly kept that schedule for many more years. However, as sad as I am to have lost her, there's something liberating about finally leaving the house without worrying the entire time.

Come to think of it, it's been a while since anyone in the group's cut loose. A couple of the women have special-needs children and they're busy being advocates on top of their other duties as wives and professionals and moms to all of their children. Between IEPs and therapy sessions, there's not a ton of time for fun.

You'd think that as we get older, our lives would become easier because we've had the chance to master the learning curve, but that's not the case. Our issues have grown *more* rather than *less* complex, especially when you add in factors like health and aging family members and planning for the future during an economic downturn. A couple of my friends are at the age where they thought they'd be empty nesters, only to find their adult children living back at home with them.

Ain't nobody got time for that.

We all have a million different demands on our days, like Kathleen, who's starting a new business while pursuing adoption. Each of us is busy going in ten directions at once. We realize that it's easy to get so weighed down by the minutiae of the day that we forget to take time to recharge our batteries. All of us need a hard reset to come back to our lives refreshed and that's what we believe this trip will do.

Not long ago, I went to lunch with some of my other girl-friends. Each of us had some small mid-forties malady that day, like a stiff back or a sore knee. As we went around the table comparing notes on our favorite brand of ibuprofen, we had to laugh at how far we've all come from whatever our version of *Sex and the City* was back in the day.

"How sad is it we're talking about NSAIDS and not hook-ups?" Gina had laughed.

I'm lost in thought when Fletch prompts me. "Well? Do you remember? Let me give you a hint—*'I licky boom-boom down.'*"

"Huh?" The nonsensical words seem familiar but it takes me a second to connect the dots. He's referring to how the song "Informer" played nonstop for the whole spring semester of 1993.

(Sidebar: I actually still giggle about the Canadian reggae band's entendre-ridden album title—*12 Inches of Snow.* Get it? Snow was the guy who sang it and he was saying he had twelve—oh, fine. Forget it. Only funny to me.)

"That song was *everywhere* in Clearwater that year. I loved how all the kids in the bars wanted to sing along, but no one could get any of the words right. Kind of like how the only lyrics of *The End of the World as We Know It* anyone nails is the 'Leo-nard Bernstein!' part."

Fletch continues with his smug nodding.

I ask, "Wait, is this what you mean? Is your point that the last time I went away with this many girls was in 1993?"

"Spring Break, baby."

I exhale loudly. "You're not going to let this theme die, are you?"

"Let's discuss what happened while you were in Florida."

Demonstrating more patience than I feel, I reply, "Um . . . I slept eight to a room, I got a great tan, and I hooked up with a guy from some really random college, like Southeast Missouri State University. FYI, I'm still bitter that Purdue's break was always so early in March. We were back in class long before MTV's coverage began. I never got to meet Ed Lover. I feel I was gypped. By the way, making out on the beach is overrated. I was rinsing off sand for days. I mean it. DAYS."

"What else happened?"

Exasperated, I look over at him. "Why don't you simply tell me what you're driving at and save us both the aggravation?"

"You'll figure it out."

I scan my other memories of that trip. Let's see, my friend Penny lost one of her K-Swiss sneakers at a gas station and demanded we drive back to Tennessee to see if we could find it. Our collective response to that was, "Tenne-*see* you in Hell!" Also, the guy from SMSU wanted to hang out with me the whole week and I kept trying to ditch him, exclaiming, "One-night stand means one night!" Come to think of it, we packed a lot in those five days that accidentally turned into eight.

Oh, wait, I get it.

I ask, "Is it The Storm of the Century? It took us two extra days to make it home. Total nightmare."

"And?"

"And what? And I should have taken a cab to the airport this morning?"

"You're so close. Keep trying."

"I give up."

He crows, "You got a tattoo. You went on Spring Break and you came home with a tattoo."

That? That's only significant in that in 1993, collegiate women who weren't art majors didn't get tattoos. I was so proud of myself for being an iconoclast.

I was a trendsetter.

I was a tastemaker.

I was very pleased with myself.

Turns out, I was the drop that preceded the deluge, because within a year, everyone was inked up, their bodies turned into so many canvases, covered from head to toe like Maori warriors. Suddenly, my silly little above-the-ankle sorority letters weren't quite so evocative. Rather, they looked like something I'd done myself with a ballpoint pen.

In prison.

In my thirties, I was still vaguely amused by my tattoo, laughing about my tangible reminder to not make rash decisions. But in my forties, I realized the thrill was gone the day I crossed my legs in front of my banker when discussing a business line of credit, leaving nothing but Greek-alphabet-shaped regret in its place.

I consulted a plastic surgeon about having that tattoo lasered off and discovered that a session runs about $250. I'd need somewhere between eight and ten sessions to make the whole thing finally disappear like so many Southeast Missouri State University hookups.

Let's do the math—the ink that cost me twenty-five dollars to put on could now run up to three thousand to take off.

This is why I wasn't an economics major.

Tattoo removal has become a huge growth industry in the past few years. Makes sense. Kurt Cobain's been dead for two decades, Snow's now writing hold-music jingles for Yahoo, and a healthy portion of Generation X desperately wishes they could finally wear arm-band-revealing short sleeves to the company Cubs outing without some wiseass commenting, "Hey, what tribe were you in, Skip?"

So, getting re-inked on this trip? Not going to be an issue.

In the most serene tone of voice I can muster, I say, "Honey, I'm on the wrong side of forty, I own a home, I buy season tickets for the opera, and one of my dearest friends has her AARP card. My days of going on Spring Break are over. Don't worry, I'm not doing anything stupid in Savannah."

Grudgingly, he replies, "If you say so."

Somehow I don't feel he's convinced, but I'll delight in proving him wrong when I come home on Sunday. Given all that I've learned about myself/others/life in general in the twenty years since that fateful trip, I'm done making bad decisions. Fortified with the knowledge of my forty-six years, I'd have certainly approached my youth differently, starting with making out with guys from better colleges and ending with not getting a tattoo.

Am I glad I lived through what I call *The Wonder Years*, as in *I Wonder What the Hell I Was Thinking*? Of course, and I'm grateful for having made the kind of game-changing mistakes that led me to my current path. Doesn't mean I don't still cringe when I look back at my choices, like The Birkenstock Semester or the time I got into a shouting match with a now ex-friend over my passionate love for Wham! and its clearly heterosexual front man, George Michael.

(Sidebar: I wanted to apply to law school after graduation, so I used to practice arguing in bars.)

(Additional sidebar: I clearly wasn't smart enough for law school as evidenced by my exceptionally shitty taste in music and lack of gaydar.)

Given the choice, I'm not sure many of my generation would go back and do it all again. Sure, if you told me I could have my twenty-year-old body again, I'd jump at the chance, but if it came with my twenty-year-old mind?

Not for all the Prada bags in the universe.

If I may, I'd like to take a moment to praise Mark Zucker-berg's parents for not procreating sooner. Praise be to all that is holy that Facebook didn't exist when I was that age and the Inter-net then was but a Usenet group for *Star Trek* fans. I feel like the luckiest person in the world to have grown up when cameras used actual film because the only thing that stood between infamy and me was the clerk who developed photos at Walgreens.

Thank God for him.

In fact, photo developers everywhere are likely the reason my entire generation didn't devolve into total chaos.

I often consider the line in the movie *The Social Network* that goes, "The Internet's not written in pencil, Mark—it's written in ink." That's the message I'd give to the younger generations today, but I doubt they'd listen to some middle-aged lady with opera tick-ets and snow tires.

Seems like the youth of America believes that having the sum total of all human existence at their fingertips equates to knowing everything. Truth is, they're no more or less clueless than we were at that age, only they'll have the pictures to prove it.

But my generation figured it out, as did all of those who came before us. Today's kids will, too, because that's the natural cycle.

Someday soon those in their twenties will discover on their own exactly how expensive it is to remove that ironic rasher of bacon or can of PBR inked on their sternum, probably around the time they shop for their first set of snow tires.

Welcome to the dark side; we have Bridgestone.

Fletch and I arrive at the United terminal and wait for a hotel shuttle to move so we can park closer to the curb, as it looks like it's about to pour. My phone chimes and I glance at a text from Julia.

"Julia and Trenna are on the road," I say. "They're driving up from Atlanta." We all could have flown into Atlanta instead and ridden with them, saving two hundred dollars off our airfare, but we figured direct was the most expedient route. And honestly, spending five hours each way crammed six to a car really did seem a bit too Spring Break-y.

While we wait to pull into our spot, Fletch notices what the rest of the text says. Julia's compiled a shopping list of all the liquor for me to pick up while I'm running errands.

"Fifteen bottles of wine? *Fifteen?* Plus, she's bringing the moonshine you were given in Atlanta, but you should still pick up gin, tequila, and vodka?"

"Organic vodka," I offer, as if that makes a difference.

He reaches over to kiss me good-bye, his hand lingering on my shoulder. He looks me straight in the eyes and says, "When you come back with your dead dog's name inked on your neck, you can't say I didn't warn you."

2.

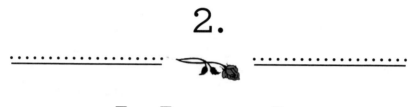

THE TAO OF THE DO

Kathleen, Joanna, Rachel, and I meet up for a leisurely breakfast before our flight since we're all early-arriving airport nerds. We're set to land in Savannah around nine thirty, pick up our convertible Mustang, and drive ourselves to the house by ten o'clock. At that point, everyone else will take their hideous self-powered trolley ride, while I peruse the local Whole Foods because nothing makes me happier than seeing how much paper towels and ground beef cost in other sections of the country.

In the past, I'd have just gone along with the group and grudgingly participated in the stupid bike ride, but I feel like I'm finally at the age where it's okay to say, "Sorry, that doesn't work for me." At my age, I feel like I'm halfway to the finish line and life's too short to do what I'm sure to hate.

My friend Gina agrees. She says we're at the beginning of our second act in life and it's up to us to make the most of it. While I'm still trying to figure out exactly what my second act looks like, I know now's the time to take action, to make a bold move, to forge a new path, which is probably why Fletch is so worried that I'll get inked again.

This whole second act business feels like it came out of nowhere, though. I mean, wasn't I in my twenties, like, *last week*? Maybe it's that I spent so long in a state of arrested development that I feel like I've barely had time to be a grown-up, let alone come to terms with middle age.

Laurie, a dear pal who's a decade older than me, says that at a certain point in a woman's life, likely when she transitions from being called "Miss" to "Ma'am," she becomes invisible. A part of me wants to mourn for my lost youth and gravity-defying rear end, and yet a larger portion wonders exactly what it is I can do with all this newfound freedom during my second act.

While we're eating our eggs, the storm hits hard, so we check our phones for flight delays. We don't receive any messages until we arrive at the gate, which is now empty because our flight's been canceled. Damn it! Now the two hundred people who were also on our flight are in line at the United service counter, trying to rebook.

The scene is, in a word, pandemonium.

You know what's great about being over forty? Finally having more than twenty-six dollars available on my credit card. In 1993, I barely had enough scratch for Arby's, much less a plane ticket home in lieu of driving through the snow for three days. But today? Today I have options. Today I happily bypass the line, instead going to the United Club where for the price of a day pass, we'll find four customer service agents for every passenger, instead of two agents for two hundred passengers. Also? Free cappuccino and all the Biscoff cookies I can cram in my carry-on. Win, win.

The club's agent is able to place Rachel on a one p.m. direct flight to Savannah, but can't do the same for us. Kathleen, Joanna, and I have to take an eleven thirty to Atlanta first, but then we should all arrive in Savannah at the same time. The only casualty from the delay will be the scheduled bike ride, which everyone else agreed to do because they're polite. (Clearly, I'm the first to discover the "sorry, that doesn't work for me" mantra.) The general mood is that of relief.

Sure, we're a few hours off track, but it's no problem. Shit happens when you travel, and no one wants to fly in dangerous weather. We're just going to enjoy one another's company here on the ground and drink our free cappuccinos.

This is going to be great!

But this is *not* going to be Spring Break. I can't stress that enough.

Fourteen hours after arriving at the airport, we land in Savannah.

Fourteen hours.

Rather, *three* of us land in Savannah. We're now a man down. Rachel's headed back to Grand Rapids because her one p.m. flight was canceled and United couldn't get her on another plane until Saturday, which is *three days from now.*

(Sidebar: That's right, United. We in a fight.)

We're overcome by the general WTF-ery of the situation and devastated to have lost Rachel, but she has a fine attitude—her anniversary is this weekend and she says that maybe this was the universe's way of saying she should spend it with her thoughtful, wine-loving husband.

We could have easily and quickly devolved into three very cranky travelers, or maybe trashed the lounge Axl Rose–style in protest, but Kathleen, Joanna, and I make the best of the situation. We more than compensate for the cost of club entry in gratis snack and drink consumption.

The minute I learn of our flight snafu, I call the national number for Hertz to tell them we're delayed. I still very much want the convertible and ask for it to be held. I should have predicted there'd be trouble when the customer service agent has me spell the words "Savannah" and "Georgia," as he's never heard of either place before.

(Sidebar: Did I mention he was in an American call center? I weep for the state of our public education.)

I also check in with the local Hertz branch at the airport to make sure our car will be waiting. The agent assures me again and again that the Mustang is indeed ours and that no one can touch it because I've already paid for it. With a delightfully rich and melodious accent, he says, "Really, ma'am, we do this every day and y'all needn't be so worried."

I'm telling you, the Ma'am-ing is beginning to take over.

This is why, after fourteen hours that included an O. J. Simpson–worthy sprint through Hartsfield to make a ten-minute connection time, the Yankee in me finally comes out when the slack-jawed, teased-haired, gum-chomping lady-clerk explains she's "gone ahead and given away your Mustang 'cause someone else wanted it somethin' awful" but instead has a "real nice new Buick for y'all."

As I stand there, silently seething, she adds, "The best part is, it's not a convertible so it won't mess up your do!"

(Sidebar: Hertz, we in a fight now, too.)

Joanna catches me before I lunge across the desk and she and Kathleen wrestle me to the car that's housed in a pitch-black parking lot. We stow our gear in the dark, grumbling about the stupid Buick the entire time, and as we're climbing in, Kathleen can't see the line of the car's roof and ends up whacking her head so solidly against the doorjamb that the entire vehicle shakes.

"Oh, my God, are you okay?" I ask.

Joanna rushes back to check for blood. She uses her iPhone flashlight app to determine that Kathleen's not bleeding, but an enormous goose egg has already begun to form.

"I . . . I don't think I can spell anymore," she finally says.

"Should we find a hospital?" I ask.

"No, no, I'll be okay," she replies stoically, yet I can practically see the little cartoon exclamation points and ampersands circling her head.

If we were still in college, there's no way we wouldn't have sought emergency care immediately. Everything seemed so much more life and death back then, particularly since we weren't concerned with the cost of health care; none of us was paying for our own insurance. (If we even had it.) Of course, the only other people in the ER would have been testosterone-charged fraternity boys who'd broken their wrists punching walls and the whole place would take on a party atmosphere as we tried to determine which of our friends was there for the dumbest reason. Chances were good that we would come home with a cast *and* a date.

"Are you sure, Kathleen?" I ask.

"I think so."

"Then spell Buick for me."

"B-U-I-C-K."

"Shit! We have to go to the ER!" Joanna exclaims.

Joanna has too many positive qualities to name and she perpetually amazes me with her abilities, like when she replaced a leaking U-joint on her powder room's sink. However, she is to spelling what I am to math. At Purdue, we used to help each other compensate for our weaknesses. I'd proof her papers and she'd explain my geoscience homework. That's why we became so close so fast—she excelled in areas where I lagged and vice versa. Alone, we were fine, but together we were invincible.

I ask, "Are you good, Kat? Do we need to seek medical advice or are you fine being the walking wounded?"

"Get us the hell away from this airport," she replied, digging in her carry-on for aspirin.

"Hey, Joanna, can you grab my phone and ask Siri directions to the house?" I request.

"I can navigate," she insists. Joanna firmly believes there's nothing she can't do better herself, even though there was a slight problem on her second go-round with a U-joint and her husband confiscated her wrench. (She has a second one hidden in the ceiling tiles of her basement, though. Shh, don't tell.) Joanna puts the address in Google Maps and tells me to take a left to exit out of the parking lot.

"You don't have to do that—you can just ask Siri," I explain, trying to familiarize myself with the unfamiliar car.

(Sidebar: The Buick is actually really nice. We not in a fight.)

Joanna is resolute. "No one can read maps anymore. It's a lost art and I plan to bring it back."

"Maybe you could bring cartography back after we get to the house, when I'm not having a brain bleed back here," Kathleen suggests.

"I can read a map better than Siri," Joanna insists.

I say, "I'm willing to wager that's not true."

"Please, I'm highly competent. Oh, wait, you were supposed to turn back there," Joanna says, as we whiz past the exit on the right.

"I thought you said we should turn left."

"I must have had the map upside down," she admits.

"Siri, get directions to EAST JONES STREET," I shout in the direction of my phone.

Joanna clutches the device to her chest. "No, Siri, don't listen to her! We're doing this ourselves, like the pioneers did!"

"Siri, what does it mean when I can't feel my molars? And how important is a functioning frontal lobe?" Kathleen asks. "Also, Siri, are there two sets of headlights over there, or do I have double vision?"

"Whoops, wait, turn here right now!" Joanna exclaims, and I barely have time to cut across two lanes of traffic to make it. "Now veer right and stay on this road."

"For how long?"

"Um . . . this long." She holds her thumb and forefinger an inch apart to demonstrate the distance on the map.

"Is that an hour? A minute? A mile?"

"Do you guys hear sleigh bells? I hear sleigh bells," Kathleen says.

"You, lie down," I call over my shoulder. I turn to Joanna. "And you, either tell me how far in actual distance or *please ask Siri.*"

"You're going to want to . . . exit back there!"

I have to swerve again and I'm really glad there are no other cars on the road. "You're not making your case, Joanna. You can't give me turns in retrospect. Now you have to let me know how long we're on this portion of the road or I'm pulling over."

She squints at her screen. "You're going to travel on this road for . . . three times longer than you were on the last road."

"And how the fuck long is that?" I've been trying to curtail my use of f-bombs because once I arrived in Ma'amsylvania, swearing lost its charm. Well-groomed sorority girl spouting profanity? Totes adorbs. Middle-aged woman doing the same? Next stop, the Springer show.

However, swearing in this case is wholly necessary.

"This much." She holds up her thumb and forefinger again, as though she's about to pinch someone.

"Do you want me to solve for X? Is that what you're telling me? These aren't directions, Joanna. This is Euclidian geometry!"

From the backseat Kathleen is quietly singing to herself. "Just hear those sleigh bells jingling, ring-ting-tingling, oooh."

Joanna slips on her reading glasses and examines the phone some more. "In exactly one and one-tenths mile, you will turn right. How's that for accurate?"

"That's perfect," I admit. "Thank you. Kat, how we doing back there?"

"Ring-ting-tingling?"

I assure her, "Don't worry, we'll be at the house soon."

I make the turn and only then do I read the name of the street we're merging onto. "Joanna, are you aware you're having us take Martin Luther King Jr. Boulevard? Now, I don't know how to say this without sounding like an a-hole, but, um, traditionally this very good man's name is not always attached to very good neighborhoods."

"But it's a shortcut," she insists.

"Ring-ting-tingly!" Kathleen offers.

I grit my teeth. "Then I'm sure in no way will we regret this route."

However, Joanna's right on this one and it's the most expedient way to get where we're going.

"I told you so," she offers, a bit too smugly for one who not sixty seconds ago sent us the wrong way down a one-way street.

"And we didn't mess up our dos," Kathleen adds.

We arrive at the house minutes later. I wish Fletch could see this place so he'd understand how Not Spring Break this stunning wedding cake of a home is. Our new digs are a Victorian town house in the middle of a picturesque neighborhood where the trees are all draped with moss.

We can gather in the antique-strewn living rooms on the first or second floors and there's plenty of space for us all to hang out on one of the multiple verandas. And, instead of sleeping on a blow-up raft like I did in Clearwater, we each have our own bedroom. Trenna and I have our own bathrooms—hers with a claw-foot tub—and there's a whole separate dressing room for those sharing the other baths. I can't imagine any place more grown-up or civilized. The best part is that Julia's a bargain shopper and the house costs less than if we'd booked our own rooms at a budget hotel.

Julia hands us each a glass of wine when we walk in and once we unpack and have a moment to decompress, we finally begin to relax and enjoy our grown-up girls' weekend.

Everything is going to be great!

"Remember to set your alarm clocks, girls—we're doing Zumba first thing in the morning," Trenna says.

With a clear commitment to my own convictions and with zero regrets, I reply, "Sorry, that doesn't work for me."

3.

I Am the One Who Knocks

"How's Adult Spring Break?"

"When are you going to stop asking me that?"

"When it stops being funny. Hey, you realize I can see you rolling your eyes, right?"

Damn you, FaceTime, foiled again!

Perhaps threats will cease Fletcher's endless mockery. "Do you want me to spoil the next episode for you? Because I will." Almost five years late to the party, Fletch and I have started watching *Breaking Bad*. Our goal is to catch up with everyone before the series finale, so we're currently ODing on all things Walter White.

We've since discovered that binge-watching is the new binge-drinking, at least for us. I'm sure College Jen and Fletch would call us pathetic for subbing TV for cocktails, but College Jen and Fletch also sat on a couch they found by a Dumpster and ate Beefaroni straight out of the can. Besides, *Breaking Bad* is masterful and I just want to take Jesse home to hug him and make him a nice stew.

(Sidebar: Why do we hate Skyler so damn much?)

Also, between this show and having plowed through *Weeds* earlier this year, I'm now secretly convinced that everyone sells drugs. EVERY. ONE. Whenever I see a weird business like a still-operating video rental store, I swear up and down that it's actually a grow house. I have no reason to ever enter one of these stores, save for making a citizen's arrest, but I always shake my fist at them when we drive past, like, *I'm onto you.*

"No! I want to be surprised," Fletch pleads. "New subject, are you having fun?"

"Yes, this was such a good idea," I tell him. "Thank you for encouraging me to come." Fletch was the one who helped motivate me to shift my plan-canceling, sticking-close-to-home, why-don't-you-all-just-come-stay-here paradigm and I'm so glad that I did. The last couple of years have been nothing but stress and tours and due dates and I'm wound pretty tightly right now. He's been very conscious of my needing some kind of outlet, lest I explode.

The fact that he now gets to spend a number of days sitting on the big couch alone, not watching endless episodes of *Big Brother,* likely motivated him as well. Still, I appreciate how he's almost better that I am at gauging my moods, and inevitably, he helps push me to make the right decisions.

Since I've been in Savannah, I've started to ponder what else I might have been missing over the past few years of being a deadline-ridden semihermit. For all my "seize the day" resolve, I've too often allowed myself to be bogged down by boring household bullshit, like spending countless hours trying to figure out what kind of tile I wanted in the upstairs bath. In fact, the funds for this trip were originally earmarked for said new tile, but Fletch asked me what was going to be more important when I looked back on my life—creating new memories with people I love or upgrading to travertine. Put like that, the choice was clear.

There's an expression about how there's what you know, what you don't know, and what you don't know you don't know.

I have a feeling my second act should be all about exploring what I don't know I don't know.

Again, I need to forge a new path.

The time has come to make a bold move and I may have just figured out the way to make one.

"Hey, I had an idea, but it might be dumb. What do you think about bucket lists?"

Hambone, Maisy's sequel, suddenly appears on-screen. This extraordinarily silly red pit bull has planted herself next to Fletch and keeps trying to lick his brain by way of his ear.

(Sidebar: No matter how much you might love *Breakin' 2: Electric Boogaloo*, it's never quite as good as the original, is it?)

"Augh, this dog. She's been glued to my side ever since you left."

Her enormous monochromatic melon takes up the whole screen and the picture quality is so clear I can see the tiny dimple in the middle of her nose. As always, she makes me melt.

(Sidebar: Wait, what about *Godfather II*? Perhaps there's hope for her yet.)

"Aw, Hammy misses her mumma! You miss your mumma, sweetie? See? This is why I stay home; it's too hard to be away from her precious widdle face. Hello, Hammy! Hello, Hammy baby! Give your mumma some sugar!!"

"You have the world of technology at your fingertips and you use it to talk to the dogs." He sighs and positions the Ham away from him on the couch. She sits up next to him on her haunches, with her back pressed into the couch, aw . . . just like people!

"What about lists now?"

"Bucket lists—the things you want to do before you die."

"Are you dying?"

"Eventually, but hopefully not on this trip. Bucket list items are stuff you want to achieve, like write a book or be on television."

"You've already done both."

"So those won't go on my list, but there's plenty other stuff I've always wanted to do but put off until later. Maybe *now* is my later." I shift on the bed so now I'm facing the fireplace. My room has a fireplace! Sure, it's twelve-hundred degrees outside right now, but nothing beats the *option* of having a fire.

Technically, I suspect this whole place may be flammable. As luxurious as our rental looked online, clearly we received the deal we did because the homeowners are borderline hoarders. We're finding really weird stuff crammed into every nook and cranny. For example, we noticed that one of the big Chinese vases on the landing between the second and third floor is packed with dirty men's shirts. There are fifteen different types of cutting boards in the kitchen, so many that there's not actually any counter space left to *use* a cutting board. And the dresser in the front hallway has what looks like a Steve Buscemi doll nestled in a tiny coffin among tons of junk.

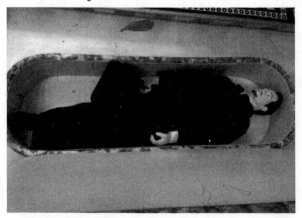

I opened one of the bedside tables and it is stacked full of hundreds of old copies of *Entertainment Weekly.* Mind you, I love *EW,* but the point of the magazine is timeliness. Is it really necessary to save the fall preview guide from 2008? (Although, is that when *Breaking Bad* debuted? Maybe I actually should read that issue for other viewing suggestions. Otherwise, though, no.) We've been having little treasure hunts for the weirdest stuff we can find squirreled away. Thus far Dead Steve Buscemi wins, but the trip is still in its early stages.

From his spot on the big couch at home, Fletch teases me. "*'Now is my later'*? Is that like *'How babby is formed'*? You sound like an Internet meme."

"All I'm saying is I'd have put 'rent a house with friends' on my list if I'd had a bucket list previously."

"Well, you do love a list."

He's right. Nothing makes me happier than putting pen to paper when it comes to what I want to accomplish. One of the things I learned from my year of attempting to live by Martha Stewart's dictates is that not only am I perfectly capable of cleaning my own house, but I like doing it. So, every week I make a big list of all the housekeeping tasks and I take great delight in systematically scratching them off when complete. And when I end up scouring something that wasn't on my list, like bleaching the grout in the bathroom or lemon-oiling the wood paneling in the living room, I write the item down just so I can immediately cross it off.

I did the job, it counts, and I want credit, even though the fact that it's done should be credit enough.

For years, I've been marveling at the brilliance of writer/director Mike Judge. From *Office Space* and *Idiocracy* to *Beavis and Butt-Head*, no one has a keener eye on society. I've been doing the retroactive list cross-out for years, but it wasn't until I saw *King of the Hill*'s Peggy do the same in regard to teaching a bird to talk that I truly recognized his genius. My only regret now is that Peggy Hill (my other spirit animal) is gone from the airwaves because I'd have liked to see how she coped with middle age, largely so I could copy her.

I keep coming back to Gina's notion that we're starting our

second act in life. I've dreaded acknowledging the whole aging thing, inoculating myself with as much botulism and filler as my face can hold in an attempt to hold back time. But I wonder if instead of avoiding the inevitable, maybe I should be embracing this time in my life?

I tell Fletch, "I'm going to do it! As soon as I get home—after I clean out our closets, that is, because *damn*. Hoarding really is a *thing*." I hear footsteps and I begin to panic. "Shit, they're coming for me. I've got to sign off and hide in the bathroom."

"What, why?"

"Because Trenna wants to teach us to do The Wobble and I'm not sure how many more times I can tell her, 'Sorry, that doesn't work for me.'"

We're having the most marvelous time together, even though the house has inadvertently divided itself into two factions that I've dubbed Team Butter and Team Lettuce. Team Lettuce (Julia and Trenna) do indeed rise at dawn to Zumba (I assume this is a verb but refuse to ask for fear that it might come across as enthusiasm), which they follow up with kickboxing, and then some light yoga. In the meantime, Team Butter prefers to start the day eating chocolate croissants and drinking cappuccino on the veranda.

Fortunately, we can all agree that it's wine o'clock right now, so we gather under the Haint Blue ceiling of the veranda. On the Mercer House tour, we learned that the Lowcountry Gullah believed ghosts couldn't travel over water, so they'd paint this color of blue on ceilings and under furniture to prevent the spirits' passage. As we look down East Jones Street, we note that every other porch's ceiling is the exact same shade of pale, cloudy blue. I so love this all-encompassing nod to tradition and wish we had more of this in the North. (Also, more cheese grits.)

"What's the plan for tonight?" Kathleen asks.

"Ghost tour!" Julia our cruise director exclaims.

"Savannah's supposed to be one of the most haunted cities," Trenna adds.

"Then it's a good thing we have our Haint Paint to keep us safe," Joanna says.

"Are we taking one of those hearses we've seen around town?" I ask. "How fun does that look?"

"No," says Julia. "This one's a walking tour."

"As in *outside*?" I ask. "We're walking outside? In this weather? Are you kidding? I'm on my third shirt of the day because I keep sweating out all my spray tan. It's going to be a thousand degrees."

Team Butter perspires more than Team Lettuce.

There.

I've said it.

Perhaps taking better care of myself will be a part of my eventual bucket list.

Until then, I plan on swimming in a pool full of shrimp and grits.

"No worries, it'll get dark fast and cool off," Julia assures me. "Plus, we have tons of cold wine!"

Outside of Vegas, I've never been in a city with such lax open container laws. You're literally allowed to drink in the streets here. This kind of access would likely have ended me in college.

(Sidebar: Julia says that Savannah is what would happen if New Orleans and Charleston had a baby.)

For our evening's festivities, Julia's toting a huge thermal bag full of vino for the tour. As a surprise, she bought each of us a large plastic wineglass-shaped sippy cup, monogrammed with our initials.

I chose not to mention this fact to Fletch. I finally convinced him this isn't Spring Break, so rolling five-deep with travelers wouldn't exactly strengthen my case.

"Cab's here!" Kathleen calls. "Let's go!"

Team Butter begins to file outside, but Julia says she and Trenna plan to hoof it.

"You're going to walk *to* the walking tour? It's like three miles away and ninety-percent humidity! What, did we lose a war or something?" I ask.

"We'll meet you there!" Julia chirps. "Does everyone have their cups?" We all hold them up for inspection and Julia tops them off before we get in the cab.

"I never drank wine through a straw before," Kathleen says.

"Eh, when in Rome," Joanna replies, gamely taking a sip. "What's the worst that can happen?"

"Quick! To the firehouse!"

"Firefighters are heroes—they have to help us!"

Joanna and I stumble through the sultry night air to our salvation.

Something went horribly awry on the ghost tour.

By horribly awry, I mean we were bored. The tour had far too much walk-y and talk-y and far too few ghosts. We just kept moving from spot to spot in this park, looking at various trees because they somehow related to something. I mean, where my haints at? Can we unpaint a ceiling so that something supernatural can finally happen? Could someone at least hire college students to cut a couple of eyeholes in some sheets and jump out at us?

Team Lettuce seemed fairly engaged on the tour, but Team Butter just wasn't into it, largely because we were hot on top of bored.

And thirsty.

Which was a problem.

Because it led to our getting shit-housed.

While on the seemingly endless tour, Julia kept telling us we needed to "respect the straw," but what does that even mean? I don't live in a universe where fermented beverages are consumed through narrow plastic tubes, so how was I to know how to offer a modicum of respect toward it?

I'm the more sober of the two of us—although that's a relative term—so it's on me to approach the firemen.

I clear my throat, determined to make our case as eloquently as possible. Despite the straws, Joanna and I are both gentlewomen and scholars, here in this fine city as upstanding representatives of the North. I've also determined that in Ferris Bueller terms, I'm the Cameron of our group, so it's important to me to follow rules and respect decorum and make sure no one drives my dad's Ferrari through a glass wall.

With every bit of Yankee gravitas I can muster, I say, "We have to use your bathroom real bad and no foolin'! We were drinking wine with straws and it's hot here—it's so hot, Jesus Christ is it hot—why is it so hot, did you lose a war or something, oh, wait, heh, scratch that, sorry, I know you're still sensitive about The War of Northern Aggression, damn you, Ulysses S. Grant and your hipster beard, and we were dehydrated so Julia kept giving us more wine and you should never drink with straws because it's a BAD idea and I don't know how she's so healthy because she's hashtag Team Lettuce and now we're here representing hashtag Team Butter because we have to pee, and is your house like the one on *Chicago Fire* and if so, which of you is Severide because he's my favorite."

The young firefighter appraises us with a gimlet eye.

(Ooh, gimlets!)

The younger firefighter, probably the Peter Mills of the group, says, "I'm afraid we don't have a ladies' room."

Joanna fields this one. She steps up, throwing her mom–seat-belt-arm in front of me for protection. She tells them, "That's okay—we're not ladies today."

He points to the bathroom across the engine bay, and clutching each other for balance and comfort, we make our way over there only to discover our next obstacle. "Oh, no, Joanna, there's only one stall! Can I go first? Please? I can't hold it anymore. I already ruined three shirts today sweating out spray tan and I don't want to wreck my pants, too."

And then Joanna, the minister's dining companion, the fixer of plumbing, the navigator of maps, and the person who began saving for a down payment on her first home when she was a freshman in college, utters the best words I've ever heard her speak over the twenty-eight years of our friendship.

"You go ahead, Jen. I'm going to pee in the urinal."

I share my shame with Fletch over FaceTime the next morning. He's still on the big couch, all sprawled out, blanketed in dogs.

"You're why the South hates Yankees," Fletch says. "Nice job."

"Listen, those firefighters thought we were cute," I reply.

"No, they thought you were cute twenty years ago."

"Ouch." Seriously, *ouch*. "I'd argue, except you're not wrong."

"And you're sure you didn't get a tattoo."

In the haughtiest voice I can muster considering my wicked

headache, I say, "I most certainly did not. Julia and I did climb the Death Stairs to see a psychic but she was already booked. She told us to return in twenty minutes but we didn't go back. Julia and I agreed that if she were a real psychic, she'd have known we were coming and budgeted her time accordingly."

What I don't mention is that we didn't run across a tattoo shop, which is the only reason I'm not currently sporting the newly inscribed name of my dead dog.

The good news is that I've decided that when I get home, I'm definitely starting a bucket list, if for no other reason than to put **convince Joanna to use a firehouse urinal** at the very top of it before crossing it off. Technically, bucket list items should be my own accomplishment, but I'm willing to overlook that rule here.

Regardless, this trip has been exactly what I needed. In shifting my paradigm and leaving the house, I made a new friend (Trenna did forgive me for not trying Zumba) and I forged more lasting bonds with my old friends. I not only remembered what it was like to be in my twenties, but I gained an appreciation for living in the now. I've discovered that although I'm at the end of the beginning, in no way am I at the beginning of the end.

Truly, I'm in the middle of my life now and we're all agreed that the middle is the sweetest part of anything. (Please refer to Exhibit A: Twinkies, Oreos, *and* Reese's Cups.)

And if the price of discovering all of the above is spending the morning after hugging the toilet? So be it.

As I lie back on the cool hexagon tiles of the bathroom floor, I realize there's a distinct possibility that within our group, I'm actually the Ferris here.

Which is fine.

Because I bet Ferris would totally embrace Adult Spring Break.

4.

IS IT CLICHÉ TO SAY
I'M CHECKING IT TWICE?

I finally get what drives the "midlife" crisis, largely because I suspect I'm having one.

As I sit at Command Central (otherwise known as the kitchen table), pen in hand, contemplating my bucket list, I feel unexpected surges of panic.

As enamored as I am with the idea of listing and then finally scratching some long-standing itches, a part of this idea feels off. Essentially, I'm figuring out what I'd like to accomplish before I "kick the bucket," which means I'm definitely going to die.

Not a fan.

I realize the end is inevitable for all things, but I hate even considering it. There's no scenario in which I'm ready to check out. I believe that one of the reasons I'm a writer is because I desperately want some part of me to live on, even though I'm pretty sure no one's going to read *Bitter Is the New Black* in a comparative lit class a hundred years from now.

*"Class, how does Lancaster present the theme of 'asshattery' through-
out the text and how does this theme relate to the larger portion of American society in 2001?"*

And yet in having written, the possibility exists, which is enough.

When I got home from Savannah, I ran the idea of a bucket
list past my lunch buddies and they all thought this was a fine idea.
A lot of my friends have been grappling with their own mortality
lately, because ours is a tricky age. The freedom that comes with
our forties exacts a price.

Throughout the fun of the twenties it's easy to feel invincible,
like life will go on forever, while the thirties are one new beginning after another.

These two decades are chock-full of rites of passage—gradu-
ations, professional responsibilities, acquiring furniture that wasn't
Dumpster-dived, china patterns, weddings, babies, white picket
fences in neighborhoods no longer stumbling-distance from a bar
by design, and minivans.

But in the forties? There are new milestones, and most of them
suck. This is when the majority of us begin to deal with aches and
pains that won't go away, with increased professional responsibilities, with the challenges that having elderly relatives bring, and with
teenage children who absolutely understand how to work around
every parental control on their iPhones. And, P.S., get ready to
write a check with many zeroes for their college educations.

Fortunately, the forties often allow the means and wherewithal to occasionally treat oneself, so I fully support every
middle-aged man's sports car purchase. Go ahead and buy that
Viper—you've earned it, pal. Purchasing a zippy convertible
doesn't necessarily mean your man's cruising for a bimbo. A lot of
times, it's because he has so little hair left to mess up that driving
with the top down no longer matters. And ladies? It's just fine to
love your kids but hate what they did to your rack, so there's no

time like the present to nip and tuck your way into the figure you want.

Or not.

Because it's your choice.

I believe how we approach middle age determines the second half of our lives, so I plan to start off right. I intend to make changes and achieve some goals because I want to reframe the *midlife crisis*, making it into the *midlife opportunity*.

As we talked about this over breakfast burritos at Lula Cafe, I realized I've specifically chosen the friends in my life because all of them embrace the concept of "what's next." Gina's headed into her second act by starting a holistic skin care line with a product called Kiss My Ash, a venture that'll succeed based on the name alone. Stacey's learning how to play tennis and recently bought her first home, which she'll spend the next two years rehabbing from the studs. Tracey's just booked her first solo vacation, to explore the Grand Canyon on her own. Joanna recently toured the Holy Land and floated in the Dead Sea with her mother, because neither one of them is ready to stop and stagnate.

Their message is clear: It's not too late.

No one's giving up. No one's done. Sure, the tread on our tires is a little more worn than when brand-new, but that doesn't mean we can't get where we want to go. There's a real danger of hitting this age and just . . . petering out. I always find it disconcerting to walk into people's houses where literally nothing has changed in thirty years, not the pictures in the frames, not the kinds of groceries in the fridge, not the styles of clothes in their closets, and not the music on their turntables. (Yes, I mean actual record players, and not the cool-hipster kind.)

Of course I'm a fan of tradition, yet I don't appreciate stasis. Whatever it is that makes people say, "Welp, this is as far as I'm going," I prefer to avoid; ergo, I'm making my bucket list.

Wait a minute. I just realized *I've* been listening to the same music for thirty years. Perhaps that's where I should start. Is there life after Wham!'s *Make It Big*? I should probably find out.

Okay, we have our first bucket list item and it's an easy one! How about I:

Discover an entirely new playlist.

This isn't 1978 anymore where I had to use a tape recorder to capture the songs I liked when they played on the radio. Technology has made it possible to listen to any piece of music, anytime, anywhere. We're light-years ahead of when I needed a pencil to spool the tape back into the cassette in order to play R.E.M.'s seminal work on *Document*, so it's time to see what else I might like.

(Sidebar: I used to have a huge R.E.M. poster in my bedroom. I'd look at the band members with their crazy unibrows, pasty bodies, and terrible glasses every night and think to myself, "They started this band because they knew it was the only way any of them would ever get laid.")

Finding a small niche that I dig and then never diverge from is a bad habit I perpetually need to break. I'm the same with music as the spots I visit on the Web. In the morning, I check my news feed, a handful of blogs, and Cute Overload and then I'm done because that's essentially the entire Internet for me.

Closing myself off to what's new or different without ever even giving it a chance seems . . . unhealthy and limiting. A plant will never thrive if it's not systematically refreshed, so I need to fertilize, water, and mix up the soil that is me; ergo, I should:

Find a new hobby.

I don't know what this might entail, but suspect I'll find one organically. Preferably, this hobby will occasionally take me outside of the house, because I'm basically two Kleenex-box-slippers away from going all Howard Hughes. Plus, if I had a hobby, I'd have something entirely new to discuss and who knows what kinds of adventures I might stumble into in pursuit?

Okay, this list is starting to flow. If my goal's to expand what I know and what I do, I definitely want to:

Learn to speak a new language.

There's something so elegant and continental about being able to converse with people of another culture. One of my favorite stories Fletch tells is one day he and his boss were walking back to the Sears Tower (NEVER the Willis Tower) after lunch and a tourist approached them, asking for directions to Navy Pier in German. They'd spotted the tourist trying to talk to others, but everyone else had shrugged and walked away. It just so happened that Fletch spoke German and his boss/buddy Wes was fluent in Danish, and between the two of them, they easily directed the man where he needed to go. Fletch said his initial thought was, "Good luck finding someone who speaks your language, pal," immediately followed by, "Hey, *I'm* a guy who speaks your language!"

While I've had a number of years of French and I used to be fairly proficient, I discovered that no French person actually wants to hear their gorgeous language coming out of my cheeseburger hole, no matter how much phlegm I incorporate, so trying to recapture what I knew of French would be no fun.

Spanish would be useful, but I fear I'd go all Peggy Hill, rolling my Rs at busboys, and I suspect that would insult all involved.

I'm probably most interested in speaking Italian. I had a semester in college and I absolutely fell in love. When I was little, my grandparents occasionally conversed in Italian and it was magically melodious. Only years later did I realize they were insulting each other and that *"Tua nonna e la puttana del diavolo"* ("your grandmother is the whore of the devil") and *"Tuo nonno e un asino"* ("your grandfather is a jackass") aren't exactly terms of endearment. Yet there's something appealing about being able to express my displeasure in an entirely new tongue, so you can see my dilemma.

What else would I like to do?

When Fletch and I talked about bucket lists, he suggested a lot of adrenaline-pumping activities, like skydiving or fire-walking or swimming with manta rays, which, no, no, and no. I don't want to try anything adrenaline-spiked because I'm not one of those folks who have to face death to live life. I don't care for terror; I find it terrible. I'd rather pursue the useful or the enjoyable. Like, I want to learn a language so that if I ever went to, say, Italy, I could converse.

Hold the phone! I should:

Travel to Italy.

I've long suspected that Italy is Disneyland for adults, because there's so much to see and do (and eat) there. I'd love to visit the Roman Forum and see the Vatican and float down the Grand Canal of Venice in a gondola, then tour the museums in Florence, and see street fashion in Milan. While I'm there, I'd want to sit on a cliff on the Amalfi Coast with a glass of local wine and look out at the water. I'd kill to learn to make pasta properly in Tuscany.

No matter where I were to go in Italy, I'd want to eat dinner alfresco where the waiters are in no hurry because too many pretty girls are walking by. I'd want to sip cappuccino in a little café every day, just soaking up the feel of the country. I'd like to bargain with street vendors. I'd taste new foods and discover new styles. I'd have my picture taken in front of something iconic and historical so we could frame it to start a cool wall of black-and-white photos of the places we've been. I'd buy a pair of glasses there because then when people asked where my badass frames came from, I could shrug and say, "Italy," like, where else would I have gotten them?

Bragging rights aside, I'm half Italian, so more than anything, I'd like to witness where my ancestors came from and try to discover if there's any part of me that harkens back to my Italian heritage.

In terms of international travel, I'm suddenly game to go everywhere. I'm dying to ride mopeds in Greece. I want to hit Turkey and Morocco if for no reason other than my deep and abiding love of Mediterranean food. (I'll eat pretty much anything if it's stuffed inside a date. Fact.) I'd like to see all the neon in Tokyo and find out if the dirty underwear vending machines are actually real, largely so I can stand next to one and cluck in dismay every time some perv looks to make a purchase. I mean, that's all kinds of wrong . . . unless the sellers are (a) not exploited, and (b) receiving top dollar, in which case I have baskets full of that stuff in my laundry room and I'm happy to ship for a fee. (Plus, my underwear's big so I feel the creeps would be getting the most yes for their yen.)

I'm dying to shop the flea markets in London after drooling over the Crown Jewels. I wonder, are there many pearl items as part of the Crown Jewel collection and if so, how securely do the Beefeaters guard them? (Asking for a friend.)

Provided I don't land in a UK prison, I'm beyond curious to see the indoor skiing place in Dubai featured on the Discovery Channel. Come on, a hundred and twenty degrees outside, but snow inside? How could anyone not want to witness this first-hand? How do they keep the place so chilly? I can't make the upstairs of my house cooler than eighty degrees in the summer.

Speaking of cold, I'd love to spend the night at the Ice Hotel, draped in pelts and drinking shots of vodka to keep warm, although I do have vague concerns about exactly how frigid the toilet seats might be there. I'm not in love with the idea of a bunch of Swedish firemen peeling me off the mug *Christmas Story* style, yet I'd be willing to take that chance.

I've always wanted to take a swim wherever it is they snap those screensaver photos—Fiji? Bora Bora? The Maldives?—and sleep in a hotel room that's more of a hut built on a dock over the water. After reading *The No. 1 Ladies' Detective Agency*, I'm dying to see the sun set in Botswana. I want to visit Indian temples and volunteer at an elephant sanctuary. I want to sample Serrano ham in Spain. I want to pay tribute at Anne Frank's house in Amsterdam and then stroll through a tulip field. And if I went to Paris, I'd like to find out if the French still mock me for my accent.

(My guess is *oui*.)

Joanna and I always talk about auditioning for *The Amazing Race* as a way to see the world, but (a) I don't actually want to run a Siberian obstacle course or eat crickets—unless they're stuffed in a date—and (b) I'm sure with our navigation skills, we'd be eliminated before we even left Los Angeles.

If we got there at all.

And, because I'm me and in terms of full disclosure, if I could experience any of the above *and* **fly international business class**?

Well, that wouldn't suck either.

But for now, I'd be ecstatic to get a single stamp in my passport, which reminds me:

Get a passport.

The last one I had expired twenty-five years ago, so it's probably time. What's funny is last year, I was gathered with the girls for lunch and we were discussing passports.

"How do you not have a passport?" Tracey asked.

"Why would I need one?" I replied.

"What if you want to leave the country for the weekend?" Gina asked.

I said, "Why would I want to leave the country? I don't even like to leave the house. Frankly, I'm surprised I made it down here for lunch."

"So, you've never thought, 'We should go to Montreal for the weekend'?" Stacey asks.

"Thus far, in my forty-five years on this earth, no," I replied. "Hasn't been an issue."

Although, once, in the nineties, I had a job interview for an amazing position with a streaming media company headquartered in Canada. I was all set to fly up on their dime to claim my dream job, but the day before I was supposed to go, it occurred to me that I not only didn't have a passport, but I had no idea where my birth certificate was. I made some calls and found out I wouldn't have much trouble getting into Canada, but returning to the US might be a problem, so I bailed. But it's not like streaming media ever became a *thing*, so I'm sure I wouldn't have even wanted to exercise all those stock options and . . .

Damn it.

"You'll change your mind," Stacey said.

Naturally, she was right. Don't tell her though. She'll just gloat about it.

Of course, I realize that nothing on my list matters if I don't take better care of myself, so I'd like to:

Lose twenty pounds.

I know I've tried this before, actually basing a whole book on the subject. What's different now is I finally realize that weight loss entails more than just limiting calories and maximizing movement. Before, I chipped away at the symptoms and never at the disease itself. What I need to do is figure out *why* I make bad choices and what leads me to self-sabotage. If I approach weight loss in wellness terms, considering not just physical factors, but also emotional, spiritual, intellectual, and social, I'll see some success. I don't need to fit into my high school jeans, but considering I'll likely fly coach to Italy, I'd like to fit comfortably in the cheap seats.

However, I can't discount physical activity as part of the process, so I'd like to:

Run a 5K.

See? I don't need to go nuts and pledge to complete a marathon because I'm sure I'd cause more damage to myself than I'd prevent. A 5K seems like a tangible goal that I can work toward without absolutely being miserable.

I also want to:

Learn self-defense.

I don't want to carry a weapon. I want to be a weapon, largely because if shit ever goes down, I'll likely be too slow to run away terribly far or fast, no matter how many 5Ks for which I might train. Also, I just watched *Point of No Return* for the millionth time and I'm inspired anew by how much ass Bridget Fonda could kick.

(Sidebar: Where the hell is she now? I loved her and then, poof! Totally gone.)

And while I'm on the subject of the physical, I want to:

Learn to ride a bike.

I know, I *know.*

The fact that I've not been on a bike since I was about twelve is super lame. They say you can't forget, but I'm pretty sure I've forgotten. Plus, the whole thing makes me anxious. It's not that I'm afraid of riding a bike so much as it is I'm afraid of falling off of one and ruining my dental work. Also, I'm worried—and I hate that I worry—that everyone will hear Queen lyrics when they see this fat-bottomed girl on the bike path.

I have to get past this.

Ultimately, my goal in life is to arrive at the finish line without having regrets. I don't want to reflect on my time on this earth and beat myself up for not having made an effort, for not pushing myself, for allowing small obstacles or personal pride to stand in my way. I don't want to be there on my deathbed wondering what was so damn hard about riding a bike in the first place.

As I draft these ideas, I realize that most of what I want to try requires some planning, which totally makes sense. I believe a bucket list item should entail effort, practice, or execution because if anything on the list were easy, I wouldn't feel like I'd earned the check mark.

My theory is that success will help rebuild the kind of confidence that I've allowed assholes on social media to chip away over the past few years.

Remind me, was everyone happier back in the days before anyone with a broadband connection and a keyboard could absolutely crucify complete strangers with their words? I suspect that yes, we were. Jesus, I'm still reeling from the anonymous *Chicago Tribune* commenter who suggested that I "go back to [my] job behind the perfume counter" rather than continue to try to write a column.

That stung. Big-time.

On a more positive note, I'll wager that the *pursuit* of achievement in each case will be just as important as checking the item off my list. Sure, I'll go to Italy, but all the planning, the research, and the preparation that goes into getting me there will make me appreciate the journey even more.

In terms of striving for success and personal development, I'd also like to:

Start a new line of business.

I'm very happy writing books and I can't imagine I'd ever willingly retire. Work fulfills me too much and I'm at the point where I've developed a better work-life balance. I'm more conscientious about scheduling time to vacuum, even when I'm on deadline. And our diets are far less cupcake-based now than when previous manuscripts were due. So, that's a bonus.

I'd love to write forever, but there are a couple of inherent problems here. First, my whole industry's been flipped on its ear due to changes in not only how books are published, but who publishes them. Five years ago, the notion of self-publishing was a joke, but now it's a viable option and suddenly the market's flooded with new material. With the advent of the iPad, if I'm any indication, people are reading less. Honestly, I'm much more likely to watch a movie on a plane than I am to read a book. Doesn't mean I love books less, but I don't have as much time for them now. Because of the above, bookstores are struggling, so they're carrying less inventory, which means fewer choices for the consumer. And who knows how long my style will be in style.

Anyway, writing enhances my life in so many ways that I'll never give it up, but I'm practical enough to not disregard the stack of bills that arrives every month. If I could find an additional way to generate revenue in some form, I'd feel less anxious about the future.

Everything listed thus far requires effort and commitment. The only item I have that will require more luck than effort is:

Have a conversation with an icon.

Is it shallow to say I want to meet someone I've idolized for years? Because I do. But I don't want to just have a picture taken

with them, like I did when I met Alec Baldwin a few years ago. Sure, that was cool, and that snapshot's definitely on my mantel, but we didn't really converse or connect.

There was no spark of recognition or mutual understanding. There was no feeling, even for a second, of being colleagues, even though we were at an event for authors and I'd written more books than he had. He was a movie star and I was some asshole in a cheap dress with an iPhone. Maybe it's a weird thing to want, but it's a goal, nonetheless. I have no idea how to pursue it, but I'm putting it out there *Secret*-style anyway.

Finally, the last item on my list is simple but necessary:
Remove this damn tattoo.

(No explanation required.)

This list is a jumping-off point and my intention isn't to check out as soon as I'm done. Rather, I want to begin to undertake a series of challenges in this second chapter of life to keep from stagnating, to keep moving forward.

I wonder, how will this list change my life in the short term? What about the long term? Will I find Italy so dirty and frustrating that I never want to visit Europe again? Or will I love it so much that I make plans to eventually go all ex-pat? What will pursuing a new line of business bring? How will my self-defense classes shake out? Will I eventually see myself on the news as one of those innocuous old ladies who literally beats the dog shit out of her teenage attacker? Will I become my own Internet meme in my housedress and support stockings, all, "I took that boy to SCHOOL." Will I love training for a 5K so much that there will be marathons in my future?

I'm excited to find out, so let's light this candle.

Because, really?

I'm not getting any younger here.

5.

She's the Man

"Whoa, check out that awesome bike!"

We're taking a spin in our own personal midlife crisis–mobile (read: a used convertible) through the lakefront Fort Sheridan neighborhood, which formerly housed officers from the local army base. When the base closed in the 1990s, the Department of Defense sold the land to local developers and now the area's been reborn by way of attractive housing units. Every house, apartment, and townhome was gutted and refurbished, but developers saved the exteriors, so all the homes are still made of the original yellow brick. This makes for a neighborhood that's either beautifully cohesive or super-Stepford, based on your point of view.

(Sidebar: Why is a reference to *The Stepford Wives* now the benchmark for that which is evil and off? I mean, sure, there are some inherently feminist problems with turning women into man-pleasing robots, but, my God! The landscaping! The lemonade stands! As a relatively new homeowner, I have a profound appreciation for anything that ups neighborhood property values.)

(Additional sidebar: I'm sorry, Ms. Steinem.)

We've driven by this development a hundred times since moving to the suburbs but never actually explored the area until today. After running our errands earlier, we bought beverages at the drive-through Starbucks across from the entrance. I used to gripe about Fletch's constant coffee consumption until I finally realized that it's a small way to make him happy. Also, it's easier than arguing for twenty minutes on why we don't need to stop. Sometimes compromise tastes like caramel macchiato.

We've always been interested as to what is behind the iron gates, and, as it's warm and sunny, this seems like the perfect time to reconnoiter. Convertible season is pathetically abbreviated in Illinois, so we take advantage of it whenever we can.

By the way, never tell the Trader Joe's cashier that you "spent the day with the top down" because he will wrongly believe you're talking about your shirt and not your retractable canvas roof. He'll assume you're hitting on him, despite the fact that (a) you're married to your best friend, (b) you're tubby, (c) you're twenty-five years his senior, and (d) you're vehemently opposed to ever making out with someone who voluntarily wears a Hawaiian shirt. Plus, he'll notice all the two-buck Chuck and mini peanut butter cups in your cart and give you that bless-your-heart look and you'll want to smack the pity off of his annoyingly sympathetic young face.

Speaking of going to Cougar Town, a while ago, Fletch and I were at the dinner table when we saw an ad for some super-explode-y, CGI-filled, possibly alien-invading movie. Now, the only thing I love more than body-swapping flicks are those where action heroes spout a few quips while battling creatures from another planet, à la "I could have been at a barbecue!"

"Hey," I said. "Rewind that." If you aren't one to watch television during dinner, then please congratulate yourself on not slogging along in the cultural morass that is my life. "I believe I'd like to see that film."

Fletch rolled his eyes. "Of course you would." He took a bite, chewed thoughtfully and then added, "I think Channing Tatum might be in the movie," which caused me to make what can only be described as an unholy noise coupled with a massive intake of breath.

He shook his head with a mixture of pity and disgust. "I don't get it—how come you're allowed to ogle Channing Tatum with impunity?"

I replied, "Because my interest in him is innocent. I don't want to marry him. I want to be married to you. I don't visit Cougar Town, if for no reason other than a twentysomething wouldn't understand my cultural references. Remember last summer when we were playing Catchphrase with Julia and Finch and the word was 'champion.' And I sang, '*We are the mm-mm-mms, we are the mm-mm-mms . . . of the world!*' and Julia had zero clue because she's ten years younger? I can totally be friends with that, but I could never marry that."

"Well, that's a relief," he replied.

"Seriously," I said, "I don't even want to *make out* with Channing Tatum. Pretty much my plans would include gawping and giggling. Maybe I'd put him in a bow tie and shirtless vest and have him serve drinks poolside, but that's it. I'd keep my hands to myself."

Saying nothing in response, Fletch loaded his fork with a large hunk of osso buco and a small piece of red potato.

I pointed at his plate. "I couldn't be with Channing because I'm sure he doesn't touch carbs or red meat. Total deal breaker. You can't love me for my spaghetti Bolognese if your trainer doesn't let you near pasta, right? And then, if we were to somehow have a meal together and he were to take a monster bite of something, he'd never get the reference when I'd say, 'Bart! Sensible bites!' You know, from the episode when Lisa went vegetarian on *The Simpsons*."

"Probably because he was about twelve when it aired the first time."

"Exactly my point."

Fletch speared another bite. "Let me ask you this—what would you do if I went all Pavlovian like you do every time you hear his name? What would you think if I was apeshit over—give me a name of some big female star today."

"Um, Miley Cyrus?"

He grimaced. "Ugh, no. How about . . . Scarlett Johansson? What if I carried on like you do? What would happen? Listen, I know what would happen. You'd punch me."

I nodded. Sounded pretty likely.

"And that doesn't strike you as bullshit? Like a massive double standard?"

I sneaked the marrowbone off my plate so that Libby could lick it under the table. "It's totally a double standard."

"How is that acceptable?"

Huh. That really was a puzzler.

I quietly reflected while I worked it all out; then I snapped my fingers. "Got it! It's because for every dollar a man makes, a woman typically makes seventy-seven cents. Those twenty-three disparate cents are our justification."

He didn't look convinced. "So what you're telling me is that because of pay inequality, you're allowed to ogle Channing Tatum like you're some Teamster on a construction site?"

I replied, "Yes. Those twenty-three cents allow us to say whatever we want. That disparity is what I call The Channing Tatum Tax."

My statement left him speechless, as he was clearly awed by my feminine logic. As well he should be.

Anyway, I eventually saw the movie and it was kind of terrible. First, there were no aliens *at all*, and second, "Get your hands off my Jordans!" isn't nearly as quotable as "You know what the difference is between you and me? I make this look GOOD."

As for today, Fletch and I are on the same page, oohing and aahing at the matchy-matchy residences with their wide porches and curved windows. We idly wonder what life might have been like had we bought a home here instead of a few miles west. We slowly cruise around the neighborhood, admiring the old-growth oaks, with the radio at a respectful volume, speculating about which ranking officers lived in which units. We figure the higher the rank, the closer they'd be to the waterfront.

As we loop down Whistler Road, I spot an old woman pedaling by on a three-wheeled bicycle. I wave and she nods crisply in return. I admire her shiny rims and slow, steady path. I love how, despite her age, she moves with steely determination, which is when I notice the best part.

"Check out the basket on that thing!" I say. "I bet she could hold three bags of groceries up there!"

Suddenly I notice that Fletch has completely changed our own trajectory and we're no longer headed toward the heart of the development.

"Are you actually turning around so we don't see that old gal on the bike?" I ask.

"Yes." He nods. "I don't want you getting ideas."

For as long as I've yearned for a three-wheeled bicycle, Fletch has loathed them. He was traumatized during his childhood, back when he outgrew his old tricycle and his batshit mother opted to purchase him a bigger trike instead of a regular bike like the other kids, which led to a fight of epic proportions between his parents. Fletch says the old man almost never stuck up for him, but in this one case, he actually did.

At top volume—as was his way—Daddy Fletcher explained how he did not fight the Commies in WWII and come home to work in a coal mine only to have his only son ride around on a three-wheeler "like a goddamned Frenchman." His boy would get a proper two-wheeled bike like every other young man in the neighborhood, save for the kid across the street who was always badgering Fletch to play "Dolly Parton" with him.

(Sidebar: Fletch eventually found his old neighbor on social media. He's currently living in his grandmother's basement, making his living as . . . a Dolly Parton impersonator! His page is covered in photos of him in his padded, bewigged gear, and there's a whole section of shots taken with Dolly herself. Fletch thought this was hilarious until I pointed out that this guy's living his childhood dream, and isn't that kind of nice? Fletch had no choice but to agree.)

Point?

Three-wheeled bikes are Fletch's Kryptonite. Throughout the twenty years of our relationship, we've had two unbreakable rules: One, I don't buy a three-wheeled bike until he's dead, and, two, he doesn't hide a severed head in my toilet.

Now, I realize that in a world full of danger, where a single spider bite can kill on contact, where brutal despots annex neighboring countries without a second thought, where tainted lettuce can bring an entire cruise ship to its knees, and where constant vigilance is as necessary as oxygen, the odds of my opening the lid to the toilet, finding a severed head, and dropping dead from shock are fairly low. And yet that remains my single greatest fear, so here we are.

I'm not sure when I decided that I'd be better off rolling on three wheels, as I grew up tearing around the neighborhood on a regular ten-speed Huffy. (RIP, old banana-seated, Stingray Schwinn that I outgrew before we moved to Indiana.) I had no problem with balance or speed and I loved the freedom my bike afforded me. I lived in a subdivision about ten miles outside of town, surrounded by countryside, so I was always out exploring. To this day, I could probably plot out all the best places to ride in my old town. Head due west to hit the Civil War–era cemetery, surrounded by the most lush, dense willow trees I've ever seen, which are surely now even more verdant with thirty extra years of growth. Go south to see the abandoned Girl Scout camp on the creek and relax at one of the many splintered picnic tables that I assume are still there. Travel north and I'd likely still smell the hog farm long before I ever saw it. Even now, the scent of manure and the sound of wheels crunching over gravel give me an odd feeling of comfort.

The only reason I ever stopped riding is that my juvenile delinquent neighbor decided to play chicken with me and my bike was subsequently ruined. That's right, Across the Street Kent. I mean you. You plowed right into me because you thought it was funny and you bent my front tire in such a way that my bike became inoperable. Despite my insistence you pay for the damages or at the very least apologize, you did neither and I was never allowed to get a new bike after that because I didn't, and I quote, "take care of the one [I] had."

It's been over thirty years and I'm as angry today—despite possessing a shiny pre-owned convertible—as I was back then. Possibly more so. Across the Street Kent would be wise to avoid me still, if you know what I mean.

(What I mean is, never mess with the little girl who will eventually develop an entire career due to the depth and breadth of her bitterness.)

As it turns out, a quick Google search tells me that Kent fixes driveways for a living. As I'm pretty sure that a career pouring tar wasn't *his* childhood dream—I vaguely recall his yen to drive in a demolition derby—I feel a level of schadenfreude at this news. Is it wrong that I hope he wallows in collective misery with the bitch who used to torment me on the bus in junior high? Last I heard, she was giving manicures in a shop across from the jail and I bet that he and she . . .

Ahem.

It's possible that holding on to resentments from 1982 is actually keeping me stuck in many ways, in which case, I shall move on.

Begrudgingly.

Returning to the topic at hand—there's something about a three-wheeled bike that thrills me even more than Magic Mike. I didn't even know these existed until the mid-nineties, but I loved the notion of them long before I ever set eyes on one. Back then, Fletch had graduated from college but he was still living with me at school until he found a professional job in Chicago. In the interim, he worked security at a local Isuzu manufacturer. He'd come home from the job, often complaining about having to ride this "ridiculous three-wheeled death machine" around the massive plant.

"When I'm not assigned to the front gate to check in trucks, I spend the night covering ten interior acres, chugging from vending machine to vending machine," he said, unpacking his work bag. I was sitting on the bamboo Double Papasan couch in the living area of our dismal studio apartment. Once I graduated, this piece was the first item I junked, as it would not allow the user to sit up straight, instead turning me into what I used to call a Cup o' Jen.

"Hold on a damn minute," I interrupted, attempting to right myself in the chair, which caused it to go only more bowl-shaped. The cats who'd been sitting with me flew off in all directions, as though vacating a sinking ship. "There are *three-wheeled bikes* for *adults?* This is really a thing? Like with a big basket?"

"Yes, and they're as fucked-up as a soup-sandwich," he replied. He took off his polyester shirt and unclipped his awful fake tie, gingerly placing both items on a hanger. "I hope to God no one ever breaks into the plant because if they spot me on one, wearing this outfit with my pretend badge—"

I failed to understand his issue. "Whoa, hold it there—so you could just be tooling around all no-handed, holding a Mountain Dew in one paw and a bag of Fritos in the other, cruising up and down the empty production lines as fast as you want without any fear of tipping over? How fun is that?!"

My whole life I've harbored a resentment toward those who could ride no-handed. To this day, I can't even sit on an exercise bike without clinging to the handlebars with a serious G.I.-Joe-kung-fu grip. Every time I see someone on the road, all smug and well-balanced, using their cell phone and gesturing while they talk and ride, I secretly want to bash them with my car door. It's not fair that they can be so cavalier when some of us are so scared of getting back on a bike that we're ignoring what is likely the easiest check on our bucket lists.

"Yeah, but less the fun. I don't think you're picturing how ludicrous they are—imagine a big yellow behemoth with a gigantic metal basket and white wheels and huge fenders and—"

I shifted in my tub-couch. "How many cats could you fit in the basket, would you say? Like, on average?" I immediately envisioned myself wheeling around campus, the sun at my face, the wind at my back, and my two black cats sitting up front, enjoying the breeze. Fletch's dad was right—the whole notion seemed so very . . . European, which was a tremendous selling point in my opinion. In fact, just that day we'd been discussing *la bicicletta* in my college Italian 101 class and I felt there could be a synergy here.

The three-wheeled bike was my destiny; I was sure of it.

I immediately became enamored with the idea of using a cool bike to run the errands I'd normally do in my stupid un-air-conditioned Toyota Tercel. Hell, if I was going to ride around in a vehicle without a radio, at least I could get some exercise while doing it. This notion came on the heels of the brief period in which I believed I could accomplish the same on roller blades, like a real urban achiever. One ineffectual set of toe-brakes plus one hill plus many tubes of bacitracin and a newfound fear of motion later, I let go of that dream. But a basket and three wheels? I'd never lose all the damn skin on my knees again!

At the time, I was still very careful to incorporate cardio into my daily life, so I was one hundred percent on board with the idea. Fun *and* fitness? Sign me up!

As I played out the scenario, I could see how the idea of transporting my cats could be an issue, but I'd been training Mr. Bones to walk on a leash and he rose to the occasion. I believed he'd be game for the bike, as would Mr. Tucker. Clearly these were more formal times in pet ownership, hence the proper names.

(Sidebar: I'd just seen *Reservoir Dogs*, so I thought I was cool by association.)

(Additional sidebar: I was mistaken.)

I envisioned us all together, zipping to the market for baguettes and wine, with me in my ballet flats and Audrey Hepburn pedal pushers and a striped boatneck shirt. I'm not sure why those items were on my fantasy shopping list, considering I was far more likely to purchase the thick, soft Wonder Bread-y goodness of Texas Toast and I drank Miller Lite almost exclusively. (I bet Mr. Tatum wouldn't even dream about touching white bread.) Plus, I'd probably encounter some difficulty finding tiny berets for the cats to complete the look, but I was up for the challenge.

Fletch narrowed his eyes at me as he pulled off his work shoes. "That's a . . . really specific question. Are you getting ideas? Don't get ideas."

"What? I'm just asking you about your day," I mildly replied. If I wanted to visualize Messrs. Tucker and Bones hanging out in a basket up front, well, that was none of his concern. "Also, is there a place to attach a tall safety flag on the back? Like one of those fluorescent orange ones? I ask for no particular reason."

He crossed the room to stand over me in my massive cushioned teacup. "This is a deal breaker, you understand. I love you, but I can't be with you if you buy a three-wheeled bike."

"I'm not going to buy one!" I replied truthfully. Not because I didn't want one, mind you. Largely it's because I needed to save my money to purchase a couch that couldn't double as a martini glass.

Fletch finally got a job in the city and moved north. I followed him later that spring when I graduated. With a new life in (the crappy suburbs of) Chicago, I had other priorities, such as carrying a better couch upstairs from where we'd found it by the Dumpster, so I put three-wheeled bikes out of my head. However, I never quite forgot about their exotic allure, especially now as I view this ideal specimen growing smaller and smaller in my rearview mirror.

Fletch observes me watching the old lady pedal away. "No. Not happening. Not now, not ever, not while I'm alive," he says definitively as we pull out of Fort Sheridan and head for home. He takes a long pull of his iced coffee as though to punctuate his point. "A three-wheeled bike will be your reward for when I pass."

Now, I would never have the kind of midlife crisis that would in any way disrespect my husband. I'd die before violating our most sacred marriage vows, no matter how many times Channing Tatum texted me, even if he promised to try my spaghetti.

But the bike thing?

Well, that's just silly.

And now I have to have one.

6.

DIVORCE IMMINENT

A week later, Fletch and I are driving home from Milwaukee. I've been invited to join hosts Molly and Tiffany for the opening segment of *Morning Blend*, a local television talk show. I've been up there a few times promoting various books and previously clicked with the hosts and their producer. As I live only an hour south, it's often easier for me to get to Milwaukee than it is to drive down to Chicago, so I'm psyched when they allow me to fill in.

As a natural-born ham, I relish being on live television, although the old adage about the camera adding ten pounds is a lie. Pretty sure it's more like fifty. I've done TV interviews all over the country and each time I watch a recording, I don't appreciate my own snappy repartee and pithy answers. Instead, I end up Zaprudering the whole appearance, wondering what I could have worn that would be more flattering and less likely to emphasize stomach rolls, angrily composing letters in my head to the manufacturers of my clearly faulty Spanx.

Also, didn't I used to have a neck?

And when did my head become so potato-shaped?

A few years ago, I cohosted an entire afternoon talk show in Oregon, even sitting in on the editorial portion beforehand. I was party to the opening rap and the cooking segment, and I helped interview comedian Dov Davidoff (who I secretly believe found me enchanting). Everything was going spectacularly well . . . until the final segment. The hosts were talking about some new kind of frozen yogurt and they suggested I be the one who added the toppings and I couldn't help but quip, "Oh, yeah, have the fat girl work the dessert."

The crew laughed, which is always my goal, but the other hosts stayed frozen for the five longest seconds of my life, their eyes huge and their mouths forming perfectly shaped Os. Apparently they didn't realize that I knew I was overweight and the whole thing became too awkward for words.

To be clear, I'm not faulting the hosts for having a genuinely uncomfortable reaction. I can't place the blame anywhere but on myself, even though I figured I was simply verbalizing what they were thinking.

I don't know why I insist on pulling stunts like this, but I wish I could stop myself.

Seems like the more exposure I receive, the more open I've made myself to criticism. I hate how there's no barrier to strangers informing me about how terrible I am on my own pages. With the mere click of a mouse, I can be put in my place but good via Facebook, Twitter, Instagram, Tumblr, Pinterest, or Google+, just to name a few. (But not MySpace, which has been a ghost town since 2008. I hope Tom's okay.)

The thing is, I get it. I do. I understand why people are vicious on The Internets. We live in a time when more than ninety-five million Americans are currently unemployed. Sure, these numbers include kids in school, the retired, and those who've simply opted out of the workforce, but a whole bunch of them are fine people who would absolutely love a job, but they've hit a run of bad luck.

They're scared.

They're angry.

They're bitter.

And because of social media, they're constantly bombarded by the images/messages of those who they perceive are doing better than they are, even though studies show that what people post on Facebook isn't an accurate depiction of their lives. But in a pictures-or-it-didn't-happen world, the images ring true.

Trust me, I understand that viewing someone else's plummier reality—even if it's not accurate—is a recipe for unhappiness.

So, my assumption is that when someone's having a bad day and they see me, the original poster child for bad choices, no longer scared, angry, and decidedly less bitter, it's really freaking annoying. Some people definitely preferred it when my life was miserable. When your own life is grim, it's comforting to hear stories about someone else having her car repossessed. A drowning man doesn't want to see shots of his old boss's swimming pool. A starving woman would rather not witness her ex–college BFF live-blogging her hundred-dollar dinner. And thanks to social media, there are few consequences for the venting of spleens. I don't like it, but I get it.

But how come no one says anything to my face? I do dozens of events per year and I've met thousands of readers, and every single person I've ever encountered has been lovely. Why is that, I wonder? Am I more charming in person, or is it that face-to-face blunt-force-trauma honesty requires a modicum of courage?

You don't have to be a writer, though, to know that making fun of yourself is a good way to deflect being made fun of. Like many people, I am hypercritical about myself so that I beat the haters to the punch. When I acknowledge my foibles first, no one else can use them against me. I've taken away everyone else's power to make me feel less about myself by doing it first.

The thing is?

Sometimes people aren't actually trying to make me feel less about myself so much as they are following a teleprompter to inform Greater Portland about a new place to buy fro-yo.

Also? I've not yet been invited back to that show. Am sure that's not an oversight.

Clearly there's a lot to think about here when I get to the weight loss portion of my bucket list. I realize I can't change what people feel about me, but until I'm good and invisible, there has to be a way to alter how I process my reactions for my own sanity.

For now, I'll concentrate on checking off the tangible. Maybe if I have some bucket list success, the other issues will somehow feel less pressing.

Fortunately, today's show passed without incident and I'm happy and confident, particularly since Fletch is with me. He decided to join me on the drive because I've not shut up about this spectacular honey latte I had at a local coffee shop up there weeks earlier.

(Sidebar: The Stone Creek Roasters Boston Latte is worth the drive.)

As we meander home along the lakefront, I can't help but notice how many people are out riding their bicycles.

"What's up with the billions of bikes? It's like Holland or something up here," I remark. "You notice they're not dressed like all the Lance-Armstrong-try-hards around us? It's strange." We live very close to a bike trail and every day I see dozens of spandex-clad, logo-covered, Tour de France wannabes whizzing past my house on four-thousand-dollar road bikes at thirty miles an hour, which makes for an unexpected thrill when trying to pull out of our semiblind driveway. However, these people up here in Milwaukee? Folks are out riding around in their regular street clothes, midday.

"It's weird, right?" he replies. "How come they're not in sweats or Under Armour? We just passed a guy in a sports coat and two girls in dresses."

"Maybe everyone has DUIs?" I muse. "We are in a town built by breweries."

As we proceed, I lose track of how many Milwaukeeans I see on bikes because there are too many to count. They're all ages and ethnicities and sizes, too. The only common denominator is a demonstrable lack of proper cycling gear and a distaste for helmets. Are folks' heads harder up here? Is this some form of Wisconsin Tough I've not previously encountered? We keep passing bikers smoking while they ride, too. What's up with that? Do they keep Miller Genuine Draft in their water bottles, as well? I guess this really *is* a party city.

A number of overweight people are tooling past us just as breezily as their thin counterparts and that makes my heart smile. *Good for you!* I cheer in my head. *You ride that bike* like a boss! The cyclists appear cool and carefree, and not a massive bundle of nerves like I'd be, all worried and self-conscious that my weight might throw off my center of gravity.

Each of the bigger bikers seems as serene as Buddha as we pass, which makes me seriously ponder my own history with bikes. I loved my bike and I feel like our relationship ended far too soon and that's why learning to ride again is on my list. When I used to go to the gym, I'd often hit the stationary machines, but they didn't offer the same thrill as pedaling along a lake path, the warm summer breeze to my back. The road to nowhere on the treadmill never bothered me, nor did the elliptical, but there was always something intrinsically wrong with staying in the same place on a device designed for locomotion.

We continue to work our way toward home and at one point, the entire car is surrounded by bikers. When did Milwaukee become China? What's the deal? I start Googling to see if I can get to the bottom of Milwaukee's clearly rich and diverse bike culture and discover that it's ranked in the top twenty-five of Best Biking Cities. Hey, good on you, Milwaukee!

The bikers' enthusiasm is contagious and I begin to get excited, yet I wonder if riding a bicycle is like . . . well, riding a bicycle? Is it truly impossible to have forgotten how?

While I'm digging around for more info on what a newbie might ride, I run across a photo of a three-wheeled bike for adults.

Oh. My. God.

Each of its wheels is a triumph of thick tread and grippy black rubber, with white walls for that extra touch of class. I bet this bike is steady as a mountain goat in a meadow pass. Imagine the stability of a *whole extra wheel*! Like, no one would build a two-legged table, right? But a three-legger? Yes, please!

I bet a person could be as pudgy as she wanted and she couldn't fall off of a bike like this even if she tried. She'd never be in danger of taking a tumble in front of some weekend warrior in padded Rapha gear. I bet if she rode it for a while, she might be less pudgy, too.

I continue to tab. Aha, what's this? The three-wheeled bike has just one speed, so there'd be none of that confusing shifting that can be so vexing if you're twelve and don't read instructions. As I never could quite figure out what gear to use when going up and down hills, it seems like one gear would take away a lot of the guesswork. Like opting for an automatic instead of a stick shift. Sure, you give up some performance on the road, but it's way easier to eat a Filet-O-Fish in traffic; ergo, it's a fine trade-off.

The color is to die for, too—it's a cherry-cola-red, so it's not too bright as to be showy. The bits of iridescence in the paint give it just the right amount of shimmer, and the wire basket on the back? Sweet baby Jesus, this could hold every cat I own or possibly a couple of pugs whom I would name Sid and Nancy and dress in tiny leather motorcycle jackets with matching wind goggles!

I'm pretty sure I already love the *me* who rides a three-wheeled bike.

I tab through the buyers' comments and see that this particular three-wheeled bike has been well reviewed for use by the elderly, the infirm, *and* the developmentally disabled.

I can imagine a no more ringing endorsement than that.

And if I click now, this spectacular bit of engineering could be delivered to my door by Friday!

Without another moment's hesitation, I click to process my order and when I receive confirmation, I can't help but clap and squeal with glee.

This is real!

This is happening!

This is the best idea I've ever had!

The joy I feel over this purchase is almost incalculable. Why did I ever wait so long to bring this degree of magic into my life? How could I have let a measly two hundred and twenty-four dollars stand between me and a decades-long dream? I congratulate myself again and again because this is *going to change everything!*

Fletch glances over at me and smiles. "What's going on?"

Oh, shit.

I broke his cardinal rule, the one thing he felt so strongly about that he wanted to work that promise into our marriage vows, except the minister in the casino was working off a set script and we couldn't exactly freestyle.

I've violated his trust and I'm about to get divorced. Or, I'm about to find a severed head in my toilet.

What will the Internet have to say about that?

7.

I DON'T BELIEVE IN PETER PAN, FRANKENSTEIN, OR SUPERMAN

How do I tell Fletch I bought a three-wheeled bike? Seriously, I'm worried here. Is there a Wikipedia entry on how to break terrible news?

Fortunately, the Internet isn't just a public burn-book. With a quick search, I find an entry about how to explain to your spouse that you have venereal disease. This is perfect for my purposes, except I'll substitute the words "three-wheeled bike" for "genital herpes."

From WebMD: *"Before you tell, learn all you can about ~~genital herpes~~ three-wheeled bikes so you can be prepared to answer any questions your partner may have. Stress that ~~it's~~ they are very common. Hearing the one-in-five statistic could be a relief. Also explain what it means to have ~~it~~ a three-wheeled bike."*

Okay, I can work with this.

Farther down, the article explains *where* to tell your partner: *"In addition to language, the setting can affect the outcome, too. Don't interrupt what your partner is doing to break the news. That is, don't call*

him or her at work, or barge into a room and say, 'Hey, we have to talk.'
That's how you might deliver news of a death in the family or start an
argument."

Good to know. I do tend to barge.

"The right setting is a relaxing one, just the two of you, where there
won't be any distractions. A conversation over a quiet dinner or a walk in
the park is preferable to a bowling alley or the supermarket."

So, no bowling alleys or Whole Foods. Got it.

"It would be best to let the topic come up naturally in conversation.
That way, it would seem less like a bombshell and more like any other
development in your life. For example, you could say, "Just so you know,
~~my doctor~~ amazon.com called me yesterday with some ~~test results~~ shipping*
updates, and said I have ~~the virus that causes genital herpes~~ a three-wheeled
bike on the way."

Hmm.

This may not proceed as planned, because I'm not sure Amazon calls anyone. They seem strictly Net-based. What are my other options?

I Google "How to tell your partner you've cheated." That might be better, as this is sort of a gross violation of trust.

AllWomenStalk.com suggests I stick to the parameters of being honest, apologizing, and understanding that he might need time to process the news. Their advice feels less useful because (a) I don't think I stalk anyone—much, and, (b) all I've really done is purchase a piece of exercise equipment that will, in theory, make me healthier, add to my longevity, and complete a bucket list item.

Besides, his is an unreasonable prejudice. I could understand if he didn't want me to attempt something profoundly risky, like buying a motorcycle or heli-skiing in a mountain inhabited by Afghan warlords. What's the worst thing that could happen to either of us here? Maybe he'll have some secondhand shame over my tooling around on three wheels, but he doesn't have to accompany me when I ride. (Even though he'd likely fit in the basket if he scrunched up and was willing to hold a cat on his lap.)

Also, I have to stress that *I'm not sorry* for buying the bike.

You know what? I'm being silly about all of this. I'm just going to tell him straight up and that will be that. Our marriage is built on a solid foundation of love, respect, understanding, and forgiveness and it's not like I'm engaging in anything illegal/immoral/fattening.

I'm going to barge into his office and tell him right now.

Or, definitely later today.

Or Tuesday.

You know what? My calendar is wiiiiide open on Wednesday.

Shit, my bike is being delivered *tomorrow*. I'm out of time. I have to fess up before UPS wheels it down the driveway.

(Sidebar: I wonder if they'll put a big bow on it for me like in those Lexus December to Remember ads? I didn't see where I could select a huge ribbon as an option, but maybe it's an assumed with Amazon Prime? They are really service-oriented, so it's totes possible.)

I'm on the computer frantically checking the tracking number to see how many hours I have left before the truth becomes evident when Fletch calls to me.

"Hey, Jen, can you come into my office?"

My stomach drops down to my feet, my thoughts race, and I think, *OHMIGOD, I'M GETTING FIRED.*

How is it possible I'm getting fired? What did I do badly this time?

I quickly scan my mental Rolodex of potential transgressions. I did nothing wrong, that's what! Oh, I will fight this. I'll get a lawyer. A good one, too, not one of those bus bench bozos, and we will have our day in court.

Fired?

Bite me.

I'm not standing for this. Let me tell you something—*he* can't fire *me* because *I* quit!

Wait, what am I quitting, exactly?

I wonder if this flash of insanity is going to be my knee-jerk reaction to being summoned to anyone's office for the rest of my life? The last—and first and only—time I was laid off was in 2001, but somehow that worry still surfaces every time I'm asked to enter anyone's office.

Fletch pokes his head into my office. "Jen? It's two o'clock. We have a call with Scott."

Oh. I forgot we scheduled a chat with my agent. That makes more sense than being fired from a job I don't actually hold.

I follow Fletch to the spare bedroom that he's appropriated as his workspace, with three dogs in tow. I'm not sure what useful information Libby, Hammy, and Loki can offer to our conversation about contract terms and manuscript due dates, but I love that they insist on being a part anyway. Fletch closes the door behind us—who, exactly, is he keeping out, as all the cats are in here as well?—and he dials my agent's number.

The call connects and Fletch and Scott share pleasantries while I have a total lightbulb moment. I've got it! I should break the news to Fletch while we're *on the phone;* that way he can't be mad at me or else he'll look like some sort of unreasonable jerk, hulking out over nonsense.

The guys are going over the calendar of when I get paid so we can plan our spending accordingly. The upside of being an author is that I get to pursue what I love for a living. The downside, other than opening myself up to unsolicited insults, is I receive only a handful of checks a year, so we must carefully manage our outlays.

"We're on the honor system," Fletch explains to Scott. "We don't buy anything over a hundred dollars without telling the other person first, in case those funds are earmarked for something else."

"Sounds like it's working for you," Scott replies.

"For the most part, it does," Fletch responds. "Except once in a while something unexpected comes up, like we have a repair that requires something specialized, say, a wet/dry vac or a drill press or—"

I'm not going to get a better opening than this.

I brace myself and swallow hard before blurting, "Or a three-wheeled bike."

At the same time, both Fletch and Scott say, "A what?"

"Well," I explain, my words rushing out in a pique of panic, "ever notice how sometimes you're in the car coming back from Wisconsin and you find yourself thinking, *Sure are a lot of happy fat people on bikes up here,* and then you're all, *'Hey, I could be a happy fat person on a bike'* and you wonder if Amazon sells them because if they do then that's a sign from God, especially if there's a Buy with One Click button and somehow there's a cellular data connection even though you're driving past a field so it's definitely meant to be and that's kind of what I did and it's significant because Fletch is afraid of three-wheeled bikes but in my head, I'm all, *'If not now then when, especially because the meat in my knees isn't going to last forever and if I wait until I'm an actual senior citizen, that ship may have sailed?'* which is kind of the whole point of pursuing a bucket list, so I'm mentioning this to you both now to make sure Fletch doesn't go apoplectic and fire me from our marriage."

The ensuing silence is deafening. Hammy and Loki begin to slink toward the door, while Libby tenderly places a paw on my knee as if to say, "You deserve any heads you might find in your toilet."

In measured tones, Fletch asks, "Did you buy one?" His expression registers the trifecta of shock, revulsion, and confusion.

"Maybe?" I reply, baring my teeth in my best approximation of a smile.

"Is it maybe or is it definitely?" Scott clarifies.

I say, "Definitely?" which causes Fletch to close his eyes and shake his head.

"And this is problematic?" Scott probes.

"Do you consider divorce problematic?" I say. "Not buying a three-wheeler is one of the unbreakable rules in our marriage, which is *weird*, if you ask me. Like, who's afraid of an awesome bike? I'm not afraid of buying coffee every twenty-six minutes because I believe marriage is all about compromise."

Fletch is unmoved. "You *did* buy one?"

"Yes, and it'll be here tomorrow, which means we can ride together over the weekend! Won't it be fun for us to have a healthy outdoor activity we can do as a couple like all those folks in the Cialis commercials? Also, FYI, I would not be opposed to getting two big cast-iron claw-foot tubs and soaking side by side watching the sunset." He says nothing, so I continue to try to sell him. "And my new three-wheeled bike is the kind of cherry-cola-red color that will totally enhance my tan."

There's a long moment of silence until Fletch says, "No, no, two wheels is a bicycle. Three wheels is a tricycle. You bought a tricycle. An adult *tricycle*."

"It's a one-speed!"

Fletch purses his lips so hard that they disappear. "Not a selling point."

"And I bought a separate wicker basket to put on the front so I'll have double the carrying capacity."

"Also not a selling point."

"There's a superwide gel-filled seat so it's extra squishy."

Fletch responds by exhaling loudly.

"I could fit three pugs in the back of it."

"Do you guys have pugs? I thought you had pit bulls," Scott says.

"No, but we could totally get some," I reply. "I've been looking into handlebar streamers, as well as a flag for the back. For visibility. And style."

"Do you need attention? Is that what this is about?" Fletch asks.

"Here's what you do," Scott suggests, fully embracing his agent-fixes-everything role. "The bike will be a bucket list item—"

I jump in. "Already the plan."

"Perfect," Scott replies. "Write off the cost since it's for a book and when you're done with it, you have a contest to give it away."

Best. Agent. Ever.

Except I'm never giving this bike away, but I feel now's not the optimal time to mention this.

Resigned, Fletch sighs and leans back into his seat. "So we have a tricycle now. Do I have to assemble it, too?"

Feeling a huge weight off my shoulders, I finally allow myself to be excited about the purchase. "No, I'm pretty sure UPS will wheel it down the driveway all birthday-present-style."

Fletch has bike parts scattered from one end of the garage to the other. "This is not birthday-present-style."

Apparently I was way off on how UPS delivers bikes.

"I luff you," I reply and I mean it. For all his bluster and protest, he's still out here in the trillion-degree garage, assembling the enormous box of tricycle. The sweat pours off of him, so I duck inside to bring him a bottle of water and a glass of iced tea. He downs them both in about fifteen seconds flat.

I sit on the cement garage step. "You want me to keep you company?"

He declines, mumbling something about not wanting to make any marriage-limiting remarks, so I go check on the dogs in the back. They're all wandering around, chewing grass, which is a massive relief. A couple of days ago—and I still can't figure out how—the girls got out of the fence. Their escape nearly ended me, even though they never left the wood line in the front yard and we found them five minutes later. If how I am with these dogs is any indication, I would be the world's worst helicopter parent, equipping them all with helmets and never once letting them cut their own pork chops.

Fletch and I both inspected every inch of the fence and we'll be damned if we can figure how they slipped away. When we first moved in, we noticed an opening about a foot high, under where part of the bathroom juts out and the fence doesn't overlap. Spotting the potential for trouble, Fletch immediately pounded in stakes to prevent exit and I planted a bush, so the gap was never an issue. If these girls have learned to scale a five-foot fence, then we're all in big trouble. There must be something we're missing, because surely they haven't grown wings.

Surely.

About an hour later, Fletch comes inside, soaked in sweat, but satisfied at having completed the job. "It's all done." I head to the garage to inspect.

As one prone to exaggeration and with a tendency to turn even the smallest victory into something both epic and heroic, it's with all seriousness that I say THIS IS THE GREATEST THING TO EVER HAPPEN TO ME IN MY ENTIRE LIFE AND I HOPE I GET REINCARNATED AS MYSELF SO I CAN COME BACK AND RELIVE THE MOMENT WHEN I SEE MY AWESOME NEW THREE-WHEELED BIKE FOR THE FIRST TIME AGAIN.

"Aiiiiiiiiiiiieeeeeeeeeeeee!"
There is giggling and there is
clapping and there are lumbering
leaps of joy as I dance around the
sweltering garage, while yips of
glee squirt out of me, forming nonsensical utterances.

"If I'd known you'd have
this reaction, I'd have given in
sooner," Fletch admits. "Now, why don't you take her for a spin?"

I pull Big Red out of the garage and onto the blacktop. (Naturally a craft this fine deserves a name.) Like an Alaskan pilot inspecting a seaplane for her maiden voyage across the Bering Strait,
I scrutinize every inch and seam, running my hands over her spar-
kly paint job and squeezing the handbrakes until I'm satisfied that
she is, indeed, ready for flight.

I swing my right leg through the opening and place my foot
on the pedal and then pull myself up onto the seat, which is cush-
iony as a cloud and generously proportioned even for those of us
with the most ample posteriors.

Then I have a mental picture of how I must look.

"Do you suddenly have Queen lyrics in your head?" I ask
Fletch.

"I'm not dignifying that with a response," he replies, even
though I'm fairly sure Internet trolls would be sure to comment on
how I make this rockin' world go 'round.

As I get my bearings, I note that I'm able to sit up straight, so
I can focus on what's in front of me, rather than staring at the
ground beneath me. And I love how the whole thing is balanced,
even as I sit completely still. Big Red feels solid and sturdy, ready
to stand up against anything Across the Street Kent could throw
at me.

"Are you just going to sit there?" Fletch asks.

"No, sir," I say. "I'm going to ride."

(Sidebar: As I type the above sentence, my iMac changes my word choice to "I'm going to die." And *that* is what you call foreshadowing.)

8.

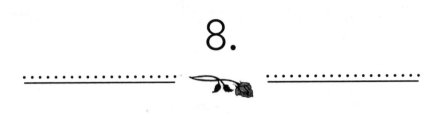

WE BE ROLLIN'

You know that old adage about how you never forget how to ride a bike?

Lies.

Damn lies.

Somehow I thought the three wheels would make for a smooth ride, and I'm sure to an extent they do, but the last time I owned a bike, I weighed eighty-five pounds, which was a lot easier to balance and control. Plus, back then I wasn't desperately afraid of falling off and splatting on the ground like a cartoon coyote after an unfortunate incident with an anvil.

I pedal down the driveway with great hesitation and I'm deeply dismayed by how placing even a tiny bit of inconsistent pressure on the handlebars makes this thing veer all over the place. If I were on the road, I'd be pulled over for suspicion of operating under the influence. On my way back up the drive, I careen off the pavement twice and once into a small oak tree that never stood a chance.

I take another spin toward the mailbox and this time I actually fall off, scraping the bejesus out of my knee. How did this happen? How can this be? This is like falling off a golf cart or small tram. My God, what if I biff and chip my stupid veneers? I don't even want to imagine that.

I figure I'll improve with practice, so I take a third trip down the driveway, followed by a fourth, fifth, and sixth. Down seems to be the operative word. I can't seem to master the turns and each time I try, I begin to list dangerously to the side.

Now that I've fallen off, I'm spooked, so I'm riding even more tentatively and each trip is an exercise in dread. If this driveway is any indication, I fear I'm going to seriously injure myself when I ride on the road. Would it be weird to not only wear a helmet, but also a mouth guard, elbow protectors, and kneepads? Maybe some soccer shin-guards for good measure?

I try and try for the next thirty minutes, assuming at some point my instincts will kick in and I can relax, but they don't so I can't. Why is this so challenging? Bike riding is a basic skill that can be mastered by your average elementary school student. Aren't I smarter than a fifth grader?

So far, no, not in this instance.

After my third major fall and my sixth slaughtered sapling without ever actually having left the driveway, I call it quits and I slowly wheel Big Red back into the garage.

In my life, I have a tendency to pursue only that which I might have a talent for doing. So, sometimes it may look like I'm unfairly successful (aka the Facebook effect) but it's only because I've already eliminated ninety-nine percent of the activities at which I'd fail. I feel deep-seated terror over being embarrassed by poor performance, which is why there are so many things I've never even tried. Couple that with the Things I Don't Want to Do Until I'm Thinner (come on, you know you have them too) like taking horseback riding lessons or learning to tap-dance, and suddenly the options that are open to me in my universe can feel limited.

I thought this bike thing would be a fine, tangible way to push my boundaries, but right now, I'm defeated. And how is it that in pursuing this bucket list item, which is all about thumbing my nose at my impending mortality, I actually feel older and more useless?

Fletch is in the kitchen making a sandwich when I enter the house.

"How'd it go, Lance Armstrong?" he asks.

Do I tell him that I'm an abject failure at bike riding and that purchasing a three-wheeled bike—I mean, *tricycle*—was a huge mistake? Do I admit that he's been right all these years and that buying this thing was a terrible idea? Do I say we need to disassemble and return this thing in order to take advantage of Amazon's generous return policy?

"Ready for the Tour de France, bro," I reply with all sorts of false bravado.

I'm going to keep my internal struggle quiet.

For now.

"Hey, Jen, feel like going for a ride later?"

"Can't. Conference call."

"I'm thinking about taking my bike out—want to come?"

"Wish I could, but I'm in the middle of this chapter and I can't walk away right now."

"Want to pedal over to Starbucks for an iced coffee?"

"Oh, no, I just made myself a latte."

"Are you ever going to ride your new bike?"

"Of course!"

Eventually.

I'm outside watering the plants when I sense that something is amiss in the force. "Ham? Libby? Come here, girls." We've been keeping an extra close watch on them when we're outside, but I got distract-ed slaying the Japanese beetles eating my Peace roses (how's that for ironic, Alanis?) and took my eyes off them for a minute.

I call them again, waiting for them to dash up to me, but the yard is eerily silent.

"Guys? Come here. Hammy, Libby, come to your mumma."

They don't materialize, so I call a little louder, dropping the hose and heading over to the side of the house. They're nowhere to be seen. I hurry inside.

"Fletch, did you let the girls in?"

"No, I thought they were outside with you."

"They're gone again! Damn it!"

We live on a busy street, not far from the highway, and I can't help imagining the Ding-a-ling Sisters blithely chasing each other into traffic. I grab my phone, instructing Fletch to head east while I search west. I chug along maybe fifty feet before I realize that I'm ill-equipped for running for a variety of shame-inducing reasons, hampered even more by my flip-flops and bathing suit. (I did have the foresight to pull on some cutoff sweatpants, but, still.)

I need to cover ground quickly because Hambone's the fastest dog I've ever seen and she's still such a baby that she'll really panic if she somehow loses her Libby. But I can't take the car because I won't be able to hear their collars jingling. And we've already de-termined that running is not an option.

Without even thinking about it, I dash back to the garage and hop on my bike. I tear down the driveway, completely forgetting that I'm old and unstable and that my bike scares the pants off of me.

I just ride.

Fueled by adrenaline, I'm steady and quick, decades of muscle memory finally kicking in, because I'm more focused on the dogs' safety than my own. I've always heard stories about moms lifting cars off their babies, so perhaps this is my equivalent.

As I speed down the street on the way to the forest preserve, it barely registers that all it took to succeed was to stop listening to my internal critic and to just start doing.

Perhaps I can apply this concept to the rest of my life, as well, after I find the girls, of course.

I speed along, calling out their names, but there's no sign of them.

I'm about a mile away from the house when my phone rings. It's Fletch telling me that the dogs have emerged from the woods, panting and grinning their massive pit bull smiles, so pleased to have taken themselves on yet another adventure.

So I turn around and head for home, now conscious of being on the bike. I can feel myself growing anxious again, but I fight it, instead concentrating on how exhilarating it was to be unafraid of the consequences of letting go.

I can't stress this enough: I have to learn to apply this concept.

I pull into the driveway, where Fletch is luring the girls into the house. He seems surprised to see me on my bike.

He closes the door behind the bullies and then follows me into the garage. "You finally rode your tricycle."

Indeed, I finally did.

I put away my bike and head inside. Then I clip the girls to their leashes and take them out to the backyard, while Fletch circles around to the front. I watch as they make a beeline for the space under the house that's blocked with stakes and a forsythia bush. The stakes came unanchored over the winter, so the girls must have recently discovered they could nudge them aside and barrel through the branches to go straight to Narnia. They don't expect Fletch to be standing there, waiting to grab their leashes on the other side, but, really, they view seeing him as rather serendipitous and thump their tails. He immediately finds supplies to enclose the whole area, much to their profound disappointment.

After that day, Fletch and I begin to regularly ride our bikes on the trails by our house. Every time we take a spin, I notice how much slower I am than him, even though I'm working my hardest. I have to pedal three full revolutions to travel as far as he can on one.

"Is it possible this bike is malfunctioning? Do I need air in my tires? I can't seem to really 'cruise,'" I say, when we're putting them away after a frustrating ride to Lake Bluff.

"That's because your tricycle weighs a thousand pounds. Have you not noticed how heavy it is? Here, lift this." He motions to his bike and I pick it up. Although it appears really solid, it's amazingly lightweight. "Now try yours."

I can't even get the damned thing off the ground.

"The weight creates drag. If you had a two-wheeled bike, you'd be faster."

I choose not to entertain this possibility. "What if I got a sheepskin cover for my bike seat? It's relatively comfortable now, but I still can't go more than seven or eight miles without wanting to cry because my booty hurts."

"That's why you get padded bicycle shorts," he replies.

"You're suggesting I wear skintight Lycra with extra cushion built in around the buttocks? In public? Not in this lifetime."

We make a plan to swing by the bike shop to look at squashy covers, although Fletch insists they don't carry them, while I argue that I'm sure they do.

We have brunch with our friends Gina and Lee and on our way home—after hitting Starbucks, of course—we stop into a high-tech bike store one town over. A short white kid greets us while we peruse the accessories section. Fletch and I immediately confer, agreeing he looks almost exactly like Spike Lee's character in those awesome old Michael Jordan Nike commercials. It's all I can do to not say, "Money, it's gotta be the shoes," back to him. However, I decide to err on the side of not sounding like a jackass, especially with a reference that so dates me.

We scan the aisles, but I don't really see what I'm looking for. Everything here seems more geared toward performance biking. I don't need Pearl Izumi sun sleeves or Shimano road pedals or packets of GU energy gel supplements. Really, I could probably get by with a folded towel.

We find Not Spike Lee again. "Hi, I'm looking for a sheep-skin cover for my bike seat," I say.

"I'm sorry, you want a what?" he asks, squinting at us as though deeply confused.

"Something to make my bike seat squishier," I explain. "I see a few pads, but none of them will fit."

"She essentially has a tractor seat," Fletch explains.

"A tractor seat?" he asks.

"It's a three-wheeled bike so the seat is bigger," I explain.

"No, it's an adult tricycle," Fletch says.

"Honey, you're gonna have to let that go eventually," I reply.

Not Spike Lee gawps at me from behind his massive horn-rim glasses and states the obvious. "You have an adult tricycle."

He's looking at me as though I'm speaking gibberish. "Um, yes? That's not weird, right? I'm sure you sell a bunch of them."

Not Spike Lee is vehement, his eyes swimmy behind his huge lenses. "No, not one, not ever. We don't carry them. I didn't even know they existed."

Fletch smirks. "Trust me, they're real."

I add, "You can buy anything on Amazon."

He's trying to process what I'm saying but it all seems to be too overwhelming. "You have a bike with three wheels."

I nod. "Yep."

"Why?"

"Why?" I repeat.

"Why?"

"Um, for balance, I guess."

"Can you not ride a regular bike?"

"I don't know. I haven't been on one for thirty-plus years."

"You haven't been on a bike for thirty-plus years? How have you not been on a bike in thirty-plus years?"

Although this seems like a point where I'd normally ball my fists, ready to punch out some lights, the kid isn't trying to mock me. Instead, he's genuinely flummoxed and dismayed. Couple that with the fact that he works in a place where every single customer lives to ride and I can understand his attitude; thus I remain calm.

"Because I'm forty-six. I started driving thirty years ago and I didn't need a bike."

"Wow, forty-six."

"Wow, forty-six indeed."

Now I might be ready to punch him.

Fletch chimes in, "I keep telling her that she'd be happier on two wheels."

"I doubt that I could stay upright," I say, imagining myself looking like a Russian circus bear on a moped. But truth be told, I'm getting a wee bit tired of lugging all those pounds of steel around, even if they are painted a snappy cherry-cola-red. And a couple of times on the bike trail when I've run into the semipro riders, I sort of felt like a little kid pushing his bubble mower behind his daddy with the real Lawn-Boy.

Is it possible that riding an actual bike should be my ultimate goal?

"Have you even tried?" Not Spike Lee asks.

"Have I even tried?" I reply. "No, when would I try?"

"I dunno," he offers. "Now?"

Somehow over the course of the next five minutes, I am badgered, bullied, and browbeaten into test-driving a two-wheeled bike. And by badgered, bullied, and browbeaten, I mean I can't come up with anything to counter Not Spike Lee's rather pointed question, "Why not?"

The easiest thing here would just be to get on a stupid two-wheel bike, give it a half-assed attempt, pick myself up off the pavement, explaining why it won't work using terms like "circus bear" and "moped," and find an old towel in the laundry room. Problem solved.

Except . . . the problem really isn't solved.

Because apparently . . . *I can actually ride a two-wheeled bike!!*

Did not see that coming.

When we went outside, Not Spike Lee ran along beside me like a doting parent, keeping me propped up on my full-sized cruiser bike until I could make it down the sidewalk by myself. I closed my eyes and braced for an impact that never came. Instead, I was flying and I couldn't believe how well the bike handled. How unencumbered I was without a third wheel! I made swooping figure eights in the alley behind the store, each time amazed at my ability to stay upright.

I felt fast and free, finally.

Not Spike Lee doubled back to grab a banana-seated kid's model to ride behind me.

He pulled up, asking me what I thought.

I stopped in my tracks. "Whoa, is the one with a banana seat an option?" I asked, admiring the lines of his Stingray-type model while we pause by the Dumpsters in back of the store.

"No. You're forty-six. You can't ride kids' bikes."

"Did my husband tell you to say that?"

"Yes." He adjusted his glasses. "But I would have said it anyway."

So, now we're a family who rolls exclusively on two wheels. You've never seen a man whip out a credit card faster than Fletch did when I admitted that I didn't hate the bicycle.

I guess you could say I decided to Do the Right Thing.

When Fletch heard that our friend's special-needs daughter had learned to ride an adult tricycle, he dropped everything to disassemble Big Red and put her in the car so that we could give her away.

I haven't named the new bike yet because this one doesn't inspire the same kind of passion that my three-wheeled bike did. But having an appropriate name isn't nearly as important as actually succeeding at something I assumed I was destined to fail.

Because I can now ride a bike, my world is a wee bit larger and that's an incredible feeling. Conversely, my backseat is a wee bit smaller. That's nice, too.

Since I've been biking, I've discovered all kinds of pretty paths by my house, and I'm awed by the lovely things I've witnessed. One day, I got thisclose to a herd of deer hanging out next to the trail and later I had to brake for a family of ducks waddling across my path. I do take my phone with me when I ride, but not to monitor Facebook responses. Instead, I use it to track my mileage.

I'm really delighted to legitimately be able to cross off **learn to ride a bike** because it speaks to an accomplishment, minor though it may be. But, it's mine and I earned it and that is enough.

I'm still not buying bike shorts, though.

9.

LIVING LA VIDA MARTHA

The year 2011 blew goats.

Yes, I just made a *Wayne's World* reference because I'm all about the classics.

To keep 2012 from following suit, I came up with a yearlong project in which I decided to live my life via Martha Stewart's dictates, spanning the domestic spectrum from cooking to crafting to cleaning. From apple cider vinegar to zucchini fritters, I quickly discovered that there's nothing Martha hasn't mastered, at least under the roof of one's house. My theory was that if I could whip my home life into shape, I would be a happier person.

Spoiler alert: Despite an almost pathological need to derail myself, my plan worked, but that's a whole different memoir.

In April of 2012, I'd barely scratched the surface of the Martha Universe, having tackled only some minor closet organization and one disastrous Easter party at that point, which had culminated in a couple of visits to the emergency room.

(Sidebar: Sometimes my learning curve looks more like a learning roller coaster.)

One of the reasons I was so damn crabby in 2011 was my frustration over not having had any traction in Hollywood. (What's my favorite wine? "But aaaaaaaall my friends have moooooovie deals.") In the very beginning of my writing career, I spent an entire day at my temp job fielding calls from film studios.

That was surreal.

There I was in a corporate real estate office, making twelve dollars an hour, sitting at a desk that wasn't even officially mine. I was just assigned there until the real assistant who was out having knee surgery could come back. I spent my days looking at framed pictures of her family, using her stapler, and trying not to eat all the M&M'S in her jar. (Failed, FYI.) Yet for a very brief period, I also was using that full-time employee's phone (having been too broke for my own cell phone) to talk with producers who asked me questions such as whether I preferred to work with Reese or Jennifer.

Um, wait, which Jennifer? Aniston or Garner?

Guess what?

NOT PICKY.

Another spoiler alert? Nothing ever happened.

In terms of bucket list items, selling a book to Hollywood would have been at the very top of mine for many years, because I assumed that was my segue into wealth and power, or at least out of taking the bus to work. Yes, I liked the idea of cashing a Tinseltown check and finally bringing all my past-dues current, plus who wouldn't want to sit in a dark theater and see their name on the screen.

(Sidebar: If so doing happened to get back to everyone who went to my high school and called me a drama nerd? In your face, A-list. In your face.)

Every morning back then, I'd wake up with the lines to The The's song "This Is The Day" in my head while I showered. I would hope against hope that this really would be the day that my life would truly change, and that this would be the last time I'd have to answer phones and schedule meetings for anyone other than myself.

I quickly learned that Hollywood operates on the basis of whatever is new is best, so I was the flavor not of the month but of the minute. I spent two more years fetching coffee and making copies as I built my writing career to the point I could quit taking temp gigs and write full-time.

I kept writing while waiting for Hollywood to call.

They never did.

So, when my film agent Tiffany called me out of the blue in April 2012, shortly into my *Tao of Martha* experiment, I never expected to hear her ask, "How do you feel about doing a show with Martha Stewart? Is that something you'd want?"

What kind of question is that?

She may as well have asked, "Would you like to have your high school waistline back?" or "Is it okay if Channing Tatum gives you a foot massage?"

Yes, yes, and hell, yes.

Tiffany had me write up a summary of the whole project, which began with what Fletch dubbed The Drawer of Shame, given that it was filled to capacity with free-range antacids, old dental floss, and broken hair bands. I also catalogued each and every Easter disaster, from the science behind what happens to a Reese's Cup left to incubate for three hours in a plastic egg in eighty-degree sunshine to my best tips for cleaning exploded yolks off the ceiling.

Over the next few months, Tiffany tried to entice Martha's team to come on board, and meanwhile she hooked me up with a talented screenwriter named Austin. Austin took the concept of the *Tao of Martha* and turned it into a sitcom, using portions of my life for inspiration.

He showed his first draft to his production team and they loved the idea of someone trying to improve her life by living via Martha's rules. Unfortunately, they *hated* everything about the condescending, egomaniacal, self-centered, smart-ass protagonist, so he had to change the "Jen" character into a single mother who was younger, thinner, and nicer than me, with bonus bigger boobs, and who was not named Jen.

Again, in theory this was fantastic, but I had other things on my mind.

In September, two significant events occurred. First, we lost Maisy, and such was my love for this dog, I thought my heart would never mend. I'll always look to Martha as being a sort of salvation at that time. Not only did throwing myself into Martha-type projects help me manage my grief, but in the second stunning turn of events, Martha herself agreed to *costar* in the sitcom.

(Sidebar: We also adopted Hambone in September. This is significant in that her arrival marks the last day of my ever having clean carpeting.)

What happened next was so surreal that to this day it feels like a dream. Within a couple of days of Martha agreeing to be part of the show, meetings were scheduled with the heads of all the networks. And on the day Tiffany, Austin, Brian Grazer of Imagine Entertainment, and Martha herself were going from ABC to NBC to CBS to FOX to pitch the *Tao*, I was . . . picking up Hambone's poop in the dining room.

That night, I learned both NBC and FOX wanted to buy the show.

If there was a better word for surreal, I'd use it here.

I celebrated by having dinner with my lunch girls, and then going home to pick up the fresh deposits that puppy Hammy had left in the living room.

For all the years I'd fantasized about how a Hollywood deal would revolutionize my life, I was surprised at how nothing had actually changed, particularly the part where my dogs shat with abandon.

Ultimately, the show didn't even get a pilot. The networks buy dozens of scripts each year and film only a handful of them. Even fewer of those ever make it to the air. So, though I was disappointed to not see my name on the screen, what really bummed me out was that America would never hear Martha Stewart say the line, "Glitter is the STD of the crafting world."

A moment of silence for this loss, if you will.

Ironically, the Hollywood option process doesn't pay off unless the product is made, so in the end, I came out with less than one mortgage payment. This would neatly explain why all my contemporaries who do have "moooooovie deals" are still doing their own grocery shopping.

But hey, I was now on Martha Stewart's radar, and that was a very good thing. Right before Christmas, my publicist Craig told me that the *Today* show wanted to feature Martha and me on the day the book came out!

"What do you mean?" I asked, clearly confused. "Like, she'd be there?"

"Yes, indeed," he said. "Isn't that great news?"

"And I'd be there?"

"Yes."

"In person, right there, with me next to her on the couch? Spitting distance."

"Please don't spit on Martha Stewart."

"I would never!!" I cried. "Well, not intentionally. I think I might get spitty when I'm really excited. Anyway, she'd be close enough to me that I could reach over and touch her. Like, if I were wearing terrible perfume, it would offend her. Or if I forgot my deodorant, she'd know. Real live-in-person BO," I clarified.

"Correct," he replied.

"If I showed up in a chambray shirt and khakis and cut my

bangs so they'd be side-swept, she'd see all of that because we'd be on the couch together?"

"That's generally how *Today* show interviews work."

"Oh, my freaking GOD!" I exclaimed, the magnitude of his news finally sinking in. "I'm gonna tell EVERYONE."

Craig said, "Except that you can't tell anyone because the producers don't like information to get out before the fact. You'll have to keep this quiet until it happens."

"I have to sit on the secret of the greatest thing to ever happen to me for six months?"

"Yes. You up for it?"

"I guess we'll find out," I replied, truthfully.

Here's the thing about me and secrets: We are matter and antimatter. There's virtually no secret that I've ever been told that I didn't inadvertently blab within twenty-four hours of having heard it. I don't know what's wrong with my brain when I hear, "You can't tell anyone," because I interpret that as, "You must tell EVERYONE." I'm a plastic liter bottle and secrets are sixteen ounces of fresh soda having been given a vigorous shaking.

I can't stress this enough: I am not to be trusted.

Not only are confidences bound to come out, but they'll actually burst out of me with great velocity, spraying everything within fifteen feet. I never mean to be a gossip and I want to be honorable, but I'm profoundly terrible at keeping my yap shut. When people ask me, "Can you keep a secret?" my answer is always an overwhelming NO. I beg others not to share their clandestine news because I am truly the worst.

With the kind of willpower I never thought possible, I manage to keep my fat mouth closed until May when *Today* comes to my house to film a Cinco de Mayo party. The five months I stayed quiet were the longest of my life and I've never been happier than the day I'm able to spill each and every bean via Evite.

The one wrinkle in prepping for the party is the discussion about moving the sectional in the living room.

"We should vacuum under it," Fletch says.

"Are you high? Have you started taking The Drugs?" I ask. "We have ten thousand more items on the To-Do list and you want to dismantle heavy-ass furniture?"

"What if the producer wants us to move the couch to set up a shot?"

"Then we'll explain that it weighs eight tons and if they want it moved, then they should send some guys."

In the end, Fletch wins the debate, pulling out an "I insist." Having been together almost twenty years, some of them during very stressful times, we've learned a few tricks to keep problems at bay. One of them is the measured use of the "I insist." In the midst of an argument on whether or not to do something, a partner can end the discussion by saying "I insist" and the other has to comply. The theory behind the "I insist" is that the invoker is saying it because he/she believes it's for the greater good, which means no one can argue once this card has been played. We each get a couple of them a year, so we're quite judicious in doling them out.

The other great trick is to ask the question, "Do you want me to problem-solve or do you want me to sympathize?" when the other is upset about something. This question is the equivalent of a marital air bag; it cushions any impact. Master this step and I promise it will prevent a large portion of the misunderstandings that cause fights. For example, you might be mad that your co-worker Judy is always trying to take credit for your ideas. And you know it, and you're handling it, but you're still pissed about it. What your spouse/s.o. won't realize is that in offering you a solution, he's made you feel like he doesn't value your ability to deal with the sitch on your own, even though he's actually trying to be helpful. Because that's how guys operate. They see a problem; they come up with a fix. Really, all you want from him is to say, "Boy, that Judy sure is a thundercunt. And she looked hella old at the Christmas party." Train each other to clarify what you each need and you can get back to the important business of being a happy couple.

In regard to the "I insist"—Fletch is indeed right, because when we dismantle the couch for the first time since moving in, we find three years' worth of pet fur, an entire constellation of peanut M&M'S, six tennis balls, twelve half-chewed rawhides, ninety-four cents in nickels and pennies, and one Chinese food container, with the sweet and sour cup fused to the bottom of it.

How do we not have ants?

A couple of hours later when the film crew shows up, the first thing they do is pull apart the couch. If we were keeping score, it would read Fletch: 1, Jen: 0. (But don't keep score, because you can be happy together, or you can win. Pick one.)

I head to New York in June to kick off the tour for the *Tao of Martha*. Joanna comes with me to have fun for a few days in the city and hold my jangly bracelets during interviews.

(Sidebar: Mindy Kaling describes "best friend" as being a friendship tier and not a singular person. Mindy Kaling is wise beyond her years.)

When we arrive at the hotel, I discover that the air-conditioning doesn't work in my room, so there's a big scramble to repack and move rooms before I have a phone interview with *USA Today*. I'm winded and frazzled as I chat with the reporter, and I'm so off my game that I begin each sentence with, "Oh, God, um . . ." as I catch my breath and collect my thoughts. (Later, my answers show up word for "Oh, God, um" word in print. Shameful.)

None of my stammering matters when I get to tell the reporter that I'm going to be on *Today* tomorrow with Martha herself! I figure I can officially blab because when I set my TiVo this morning, I clearly saw both our names on the show's listing. I gush on and on about how much I love Martha and how I'm probably going to make a damn fool out of myself tomorrow, sobbing happy tears the moment I spot that familiar chambray shirt.

I can't believe my "meet an icon" is about to happen! I could not be more excited. In my career, I've gotten to say hello to a couple of famous people, but that's not the same as meeting Martha freaking Stewart. What I've always wanted has been an actual conversation where we look each other in the eye and exchange ideas.

Knowing I'm so close to the finish line, I can't help but obsess. I wonder what Martha thinks of me? I hear she has a wicked sense of humor. I wonder how she feels about the finished product? We sent her some copies about a month ago and I'm on pins and needles about her response. I wonder if she'll even read the book. I heard through the grapevine that she liked the concept and that she was amused that she was kind of acting as a god for me. But because I didn't witness this directly, I have no way of discerning her opinion.

But I guess I'll find out tomorrow.

Joanna and I are primping for an early dinner when the phone rings.

"Hey, Jen, it's Craig." Craig's always so positive and upbeat that I'm immediately concerned when I hear the hesitation in his voice.

"What's up?" I ask, my stomach clenching.

"There's been a scheduling change. Martha can't make it tomorrow, so they're moving your segment."

"To when?"

"Wednesday or Thursday. They're doing some rearranging right now."

"Oh," I say, blood returning to my cheeks. "That's no big deal. I'll just see Martha then." I've had a lot of time to think about our meeting and what I could say. I'm planning to speak with her about her pets. She's as much of a fanatic as I am when it comes to cats and dogs, so I'm curious if she has any idea how to better housebreak Hammy.

He sighs. "I'm actually not sure. The producers weren't able to confirm or deny."

"But we *have* to be on together. I've told, like, *everyone* now. I just went on and on to *USA Today* on how I was going to meet her. I thought because it was on the TiVo guide that I was able to finally tell people."

"Maybe you should stop mentioning it. You'll definitely be on, but her portion may not yet be nailed down."

Oh.

OH.

Hold the damn phone—I see what's going on here! They're pulling the ol' takeaway. All of the footage they've filmed is essentially me geeking out over the idea of finally getting to shake her hand and tell her I luff her, so to not have us meet would be cruel and unusual punishment and they wouldn't do that to me.

This is a classic *Ellen* show ruse. You know how she'll have a segment about a really lovable kid in a wheelchair who wrote to her saying how much he wants to visit Disneyland but he couldn't go because his church's minibus isn't handicapped-equipped, so he did his second favorite thing that day, which was to watch her show? And Ellen is so touched by the story that she brings the kid on to give him a set of mouse ears personally? And the kid's so ecstatic that he has tears in his eyes? And Ellen's like, oh, wait, forgot something, and then she enlists Luke Perry's help to pull back the curtains to reveal a handicapped-equipped bus that she's gifting to his church and says that he'd better hurry up and hug Luke Perry because he and his church friends are about to take their new bus to the happiest place on Earth? And then *everybody* has tears in their eyes?

They're doing this for me. I'm sure of it. Granted, I've done nothing to merit an awesome Ellen-like surprise, but maybe the fact that I will freak the hell out over having Martha show up when she's not supposed to will make for excellent television, so that's their plan.

(Minus the Luke Perry, even though I'd have definitely chosen him over Jason Priestley back in the day.)

Except *Today* didn't realize that I'm clever and that I'd be on to them. They're going to expect the big, ugly, baby-with-an-oatmeal-bowl-on-his-head cry, but I'm not about to end up on *The Soup* with my over-the-top reaction. I mean, yes, I want to demonstrate my excitement, but in a way that's cute and not horrific, especially for those watching in HD.

What I'll do is practice. I have a day or so to nail this, so over the course of dinner with Joanna, I demonstrate my surprised-but-attractive expressions for her. We determine that I have limited range of motion around the eye area due to the Botox, so I have to supplement with opening my mouth in shock. Ha! I *told* Fletch that replacing all my metal fillings with porcelain was an investment that would eventually pay off!

We decide the open mouth isn't enough and add a move where I clutch my hands to my heart. I feel like the jangly bracelets will make the chest-clasp more dramatic, so I plan to wear them instead of having Joanna hold them. Joanna raises the question of what if Martha's actually not coming, but surely that can't happen, so I don't even entertain the notion.

I'm ready as can be on Wednesday morning. I verify with the TV listings that I'll be on with Martha and I'm ready to go. This isn't my first trip to *Today*, so it's not officially on my bucket list. A few years ago, I did a segment where I drank wine with Hoda and Kathie Lee and it was everything I ever imagined it could be. (One would have been tempted to not bother starting a list after that, because what could be better?)

I'm not even nervous because I'm too full of joy. I continue to play it off that I don't know what's about to happen next, while I'm downstairs in the green room having my makeup done. Regular-people guests like me wait it out in the upstairs green room, whereas the celebrities get their own little mini-dressing-rooms behind the makeup area. I see that all the doors are closed and I'm convinced that Martha and Co. are behind one of them.

Although I don't run into her downstairs having my makeup touched up, I do bump into Paula Deen on my way up to the Loser Lounge and we have a lovely con-versation with lots of quality eye contact. I make her laugh, so auto-matically I find her taste to be impeccable.

This is approximately three weeks before everything goes side-ways for Paula. When the story breaks, I don't know how to re-act—I have trouble reconciling her terrible, hurtful words with the lovely woman in the green room who calls me a "hoot," so, looking back, I can't consider counting her as having met an icon.

Plus, *that's* about to happen in fifteen minutes.

I'm on set with Savannah Guthrie, who weighs as much as a lacrosse stick and I try not to envision our looking like the number 10 while we talk. The pretaped portion rolls before our live inter-view and I can barely pay attention. I'm sitting to Savannah's left, so the whole time, I'm keeping my right eye on her with my left eye toward the back of the studio. Halfway through our conversa-tion, I see a statuesque, seasoned blonde enter the back of the room. I can't make out her face, but her general outline is very, very familiar.

YES!

THIS IS IT!

THIS IS HAPPENING!

We continue our interview, and I keep waiting for Savannah's flash of recognition or sly nod to the camera, indicating that now is the time, but it never actually comes.

The segment ends, she thanks me, and that's it.

That's it? How is that it?

And how come the statuesque, seasoned blonde is . . . not Martha? Martha, *where are you??*

Okay, I'm devastated that I didn't get to meet her. But she's still indirectly responsible for helping me turn one of the worst years of my life into one of the best. She was my guiding force, even if it was the idea of her and not her herself. That has more value than any brief interaction we might ever have.

If I've learned anything in my forty-six years, it's to keep pressing past a disappointment, because there's always something better on the horizon.

I decide to keep the goal to meet an icon, as this can still totally happen. I don't know who it will be, but I'll try to look surprised when it does. (That practice was not for nothing!)

I consider adding **fully housebreak Hambone** to the list, but I don't.

Because nobody can perform that kind of miracle.

10.

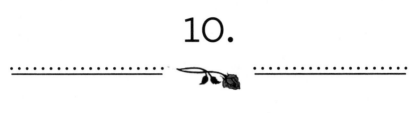

NOT THE BULLSHIT, JUST THE GOOD SHIT

The fact that I'm butt-hurt over Martha doesn't stop me from listening to her show on Sirius radio. In fact, I suspect the one who's truly butt-hurt is Martha herself, as she's recently lost her dedicated station and instead now has only a couple of hours on the Starz channel.

Cough *karma* cough.

I have no specific proof of Martha's said butt-hurtedness here, yet the fact that she eats her lunch while on the air is a heavy clue. I'm not kidding; she doesn't even try to hide the fact that she's chewing. I'm sure there's a legitimate explanation, like she's broadcasting from her test kitchen and is so busy that she must sample items between commercial breaks. Still, it's disconcerting to hear her through a mouthful of what sounds like a pecan chicken salad croissant.

I'm listening to Martha while I'm out picking up supplies for our annual Fourth of July party. Hopefully this will be an improvement over last year's redneck, white-trash, hee-haw showdown, considering it's not a hundred and five degrees, I'm not allowing Fletch to serve Dew Drivers (Mountain Dew and vodka), and most important, I'm not completely panicked over having a dog in the specialty clinic's intensive care unit.

Between jaunts to the grocery store and Costco, I get a real piroshki vibe from the sound of her chewing. I think I hear chives.

A person by the name of Thomas calls in to the show, but when Martha takes the call, the voice belongs to that of a woman. Across the satellite waves, I can actually feel the thousand-yard stare she's inevitably pointing at her call screener.

So fired.

However, the screener got it right—the feminine-sounding Thomas is indeed a young man, and he's calling in to ask Martha about fun Fourth of July games he might play with his family. Giggling, he explains that he has a high voice and that people often confuse him for a girl.

I certainly can't discern someone's sexuality over the radio, and even if I could, it's not only none of my business, but also no big deal, so I won't speculate on Thomas's preferences. Say what you will about all the sharks that the program *Glee* has since jumped, but that show has done so much to demonstrate the beauty of different and I'm glad. For all that annoys me about kids today, I love that they're growing up in a world that won't tolerate intolerance.

As for Martha?

Well, she's not letting this voice-thing go. She spends what feels like half the time on the phone arguing with this sweet kid over whether or not he's actually a girl. In my head, I imagine her suggesting he play "pin the tail on the faggot" because I doubt she's read the time-to-stop-using-hate-speech memo.

Maybe that's how I'm dealing with my disappointment—imagining the worst of her.

Regardless, I decide I need to run more errands because when Martha's on a roll, I don't get out of the car.

Her next call is even more astounding. A college girl's moving into her first off-campus apartment and she wants to make it cute, so she asks Martha about inexpensive ways to decorate because she doesn't want it to be all futons and bookcases made of stolen milk crates. Now *that's* a massive climate shift since I went to college. If you and your roommate had coordinating comforters, you two were basically Tom Ford for Gucci. My contribution to being fancy back then was to keep my posters in their original plastic wrap.

I suspect this new emphasis on design for everyone is due to HGTV. Mind you, I adore HGTV and had it on twenty-four hours a day before we bought our house, which is why we didn't run into too many snafus along the way. We knew to look past some highly unfortunate wallpaper to see our home's fine bones and true potential.

Fletch and I recently started watching *Love It or List It* during dinner because O'Reilly makes me too shout-y. Except this may not have been the best idea because now we *both* end up yelling at the television. Personally, I always thought of Canada as a fine place, all toques and Timbits, really a kinder, smarter, more polite version

of America, but now? Now I'm not so sure. How is every single home owner surprised that their crappy hundred-year-old row house has foundation damage? How did they not have that place inspected before they closed escrow? And designer Hilary is trying to help you, you ingrates, so maybe you shouldn't holler at her when she discovers the kind of wiring that will incinerate everything you ever loved while you sleep, even if that means you can't have a second-floor laundry room. You're still close to transit, so you'll live.

Literally.

Not long ago, there was one episode where the house had essentially given the home owner cancer because of long-term exposure to asbestos, but after they updated their kitchen, they were all, "It's okay now, eh?" and decided to love it.

What?

YOUR HOUSE TRIED TO KILL YOU! MOVE, YOU STUPID CANUCK.

(In all fairness, I imagine the home owners on *Love It or List It* are to Canada what *Honey Boo Boo* is to America, but still.)

Anyway, the college girl pings Martha to see what she might suggest in terms of furniture and Martha comes back with one of the most myopic, out-of-touch, let-them-eat-cake answers I've ever heard.

Martha says, and I swear I'm not making this up, "Why don't you shop at Pottery Barn?"

Pottery Barn.

Bitch, I'm not only a grown-ass adult, but I've written eight *New York Times* bestselling books and that's *still* where my very nicest stuff comes from.

I'm in my car, flabbergasted, when Martha remembers her sponsors. Almost by default, she throws in, "You could also buy your furniture at Macy's."

I'm sorry; has Martha never heard of IKEA? Or Craigslist? Or Etsy? Or outlet stores? Or consignment shops and yard sales? What kind of terrible advice is this? Is she suggesting that this girl fork over her parents' hard-earned USD so she can buy a couch that will be splattered in Jell-O shots and frat boy emesis the very first week? How is this a good idea?

Does Martha honestly expect the kid to use her student loan

money, so that she ends up paying monthly for her Charleston Roll-Arm for the next fifteen years? And if she were to somehow miracle a Pottery Barn sofa into her apartment now, what's left for her to strive for? Desiring better seating was my driving force for *years* after college. All I wanted was the *Fight Club* epiphany that I'd finally taken care of that whole seating issue. I understand the student may not want to live with a Dumpster couch, but surely there's a happy medium between the sublime and the ridiculous.

I spent all of the *Tao of Martha* trying to find a way to out-Martha Martha and I came up completely empty-handed. Granted, I definitely improved my quality of life, but I never came close to achieving the Pinterest-perfect lifestyle to which Martha subscribes.

Yet I sense an opening here, a flaw in The Martha's grand plan, if you will. Is there a way to maybe show Martha up? To prove her advice wrong? How hard could it be to decorate a college apartment on a shoestring while still providing visual appeal?

A while back, my friend Angie told me about this chalk paint that allows the user to transform furniture without benefit of sanding or priming. I guess it has grout in it? After we'd discussed the product, I looked to see if I could find it on Amazon, but they didn't carry it. As I trend lazy when it comes to nonessentials, I gave up the notion of repainting a couple of my ugly end tables before I even began. But now there's a potential quest involved, so I put a pin in this idea, deciding to circle back as soon as I finish preparing for an extraordinarily classy Fourth of July party.

Or not.

And P.S., I hope Thomas and his loved ones have the best holiday ever.

This stupid chalk paint is harder to procure than I thought and it seems really expensive—thirty-five dollars for what looks to be about a pint! Strike one. However, according to the Annie Sloan

Web site, this is enough paint to cover one hundred and fifty square feet, which, according to my stellar math abilities, I estimate will coat my entire house. What's annoying is I'd have to go down to the city to buy it, since products are sold exclusively in interior design shops. Strike two.

The only reason I'm even considering heading to Chicago is that I'm trying something new. Instead of ordering whatever I need on Amazon Prime and having UPS bring it to me like so many monkey butlers, I've decided that it's better for me to actually leave the house to procure items. I've been trying to make small changes to my lifestyle in terms of diet and fitness, so I figure anything that forces me to park and walk is a good move.

Earlier this week, I went to the Habitat for Humanity ReStore after reading about it on a design blog. I heard that they stocked a variety of items that people chuck when remodeling their homes, so I wanted to see for myself. My goal was to find an inexpensive piece of furniture I wouldn't mind ruining before I slopped paint on what I already own. I found a hideously stained coffee table, but it had decent lines and was made of solid wood. And at twenty-five bucks, the price was right. I was willing to take the loss, but I figured on the off chance that this worked, I could use this table instead of waiting for Pottery Barn to finally, finally restock the Carolina Blue one I'd been saving for/lusting after.

With Martha on the radio, I travel to buy the paint, double-checking that the lid is on tightly before I drive home. As anal as Fletch is about not eating in the car, I can't imagine his reaction if I accidentally dumped a hundred and fifty square feet of paint all over it.

I bring my supplies down to the basement, which, to this point, has been entirely Fletch's domain. He's nice enough to set me up with my own workbench, yet not so benevolent that he doesn't immediately begin to second-guess the process.

"Why aren't you sanding?" he asks, hovering behind me like he's my boss and I'm a ditzy teenager on my first day behind the register at Dairy Queen.

"Because I don't have to, according to the label."

"That doesn't sound right. You're not priming, either? The paint's never going to stick."

"No, I'm pretty sure it will. The paint's supposed to be miraculous. Look, it says right here, 'It's paint for girls but boys can use it, too.' I realize that sounds sexist, but I don't care if it means I can avoid the boring, labor-intensive parts." After a vigorous shaking, I pry open the lid. The color is that perfect bluish-purple of the sky on a cloudless July day. I brush on a section and step back, already delighted with the results.

"You should really try to paint with the grain," he says.

"The instructions say it's fine to go in all directions," I reply. "If you had your way, you'd spend six incredibly exacting weeks to do what Annie Sloan promises will take an afternoon."

"I prefer to do a job right."

"Uh-huh." Ignoring him, I continue to cover the awful table with quick dabs while Fletch continues to supervise.

"You realize this violates every single rule I ever learned in high school shop."

I finally set down my brush and face him. "Hey, Hank Hill, are you going to let me do this myself or not?"

He makes a low, flat humming sound, which I assume is an affirmation. As he walks away, I opt to play some music to muffle his almost palpable wariness. I'm about to pull up my usual eighties pop/new wave gym mix, but reconsider, deciding I want to try something different. After all, I've been meaning to cultivate a new playlist, so I begin to thumb through the stations on Sirius. I see that Kool Moe Dee's "Wild Wild West" is playing on Back-Spin, an old-school hip-hop station. I've never been much of a rap fan, save for Fletch's NWA and Public Enemy downloads that somehow got mixed into my playlist. However, this particular tune comes with so many fun memories attached. The second I hear the opening notes, I'm immediately taken back to when I waitressed in a college bar and didn't even have to report for my shift until eleven thirty p.m. When I close my eyes, I can practically smell the intoxicating combination of Aqua Net, Budweiser, and Polo. I can't remember how I felt about the song back then, but it's definitely hitting the spot right now.

I paint in time with the music, pleased at how energized I feel.

Next up is Rob Base and DJ E-Z Rock with "It Takes Two." Again, not something I'd have normally picked, but I'd forgotten how this was a Breakfast Club anthem, which was when the Purdue bars would open at six a.m. on home football game days.

Worst Idea Ever or Best Idea Ever?

As I recall, it was both.

Memories of swilling fuzzy navels out of a giant pitcher while dancing on a table in my bathrobe rush back as the song hits the chorus. I wonder what College Jen would think of me now, opting to paint in the basement in lieu of chugging margaritas poolside?

LL Cool J goes back to Cali next, and he's followed by a

Run–DMC song called "Down with the King," which I've never heard but I instantly love.

At this point, Fletch wanders over. "Since when do you have decent taste in music?"

I bob my head in time. "This is good, right?"

"Yes," he confirms. "Turn it up."

We spend the rest of the afternoon working on our projects and listening to BackSpin, which is only made a thousand times better at four p.m. when I discover the Ed Lover Show on this channel! Party music makes the time fly by and before I know it, I've not only painted the whole table, but also aged and distressed it with wax and sandpaper.

I can't get over the results.

I call Fletch over to inspect my handiwork.

"Am I biased, or does this look professional?"

He walks around my whole workbench, turning the table this way and that way, running a fingertip over the glossy finish.

He finally says, "This shouldn't have worked. This is all wrong. This goes against every principle of woodcraft."

I'll take that as a yes.

At some point over the next month, inexpensively rehabbing furniture becomes less about proving Martha wrong and more about hanging out in my basement, spinning the kind of old-school tunes that are entirely new to me. How did I exist in the decade this music helped define and never pay attention to any of it?

Every time I find myself inadvertently tuning in to my usual playlist, I realize I can't "Melt with You" or "Take on Me" one more time and switch back to BackSpin. Much as I adore the whole channel, Ed Lover's Show is my favorite. I adore him. I do. I thought he was great on MTV, but I have so much more respect for him now. He hit hard times after he peaked with *Yo! MTV Raps Today* and he's honest about them. Now he's working as a DJ again and he's both happy and humble, so listening to his show is a true pleasure.

When we were in Savannah, Trenna complained about my choice of the eighties channel in the car. She said, "I did the eighties once. I have no desire to do 'em again." At the time, Joanna, Kathleen, and I were all, "Blasphemy!" but now I finally grasp what she was saying. Loving something during my formative years doesn't obligate me to keep carrying that same torch my whole life. I'm not disavowing my own past by moving on.

The day I realize I recognize a very young Lil Wayne's voice performing with Hot Boys is the day I cross the **discover new music** entry off my list.

Because I'm not currently on deadline, I have a break in my schedule for the first time in a couple of years. I write a television pilot called *This Is Why We Don't Have Kids*. In retrospect, I should have called it *This Is Why You Won't Sell a Screenplay*. But I believe you're not a "real writer" until you have a failure stuffed in your desk drawer, so . . . congratulations to me?

However, my reward for meeting my day's page count has been to spend the evening in the basement, working on new pieces. Or should I say *old* pieces, because I'm bringing home some

real junk. I'm talking water stains, chips, scratches, and flat-out break-age.

Here's the thing, though—even trashed, a lot of what I run across in thrift stores is a thou-

sand times better made than what's brand-new and mass-produced at places like Pottery Barn. With some digging, I can find solid cherry or mahogany furnishing with dovetail joints, fine lines, and brilliant details like antique toe caps. Plus, I hate the idea of these pieces end-ing up in a landfill. So, with time, elbow grease, and creativity, I've been able to create the kind of furniture I bet that college kid would kill to have in her apartment.

As no one loves a makeover more than I do, I'm having the time of my life with the hunt for inexpensive items. Wisconsin is my new favorite place on Earth because they practically give you a rickety dresser for free the moment you cross the state line. Not kidding.

Painting furniture definitely counts as my new hobby. Although I'm pleased to check this off my list, what's so much fun is breathing new life into what had been garbage. As it turns out, my author friend Beth Harbison is equally enamored with chalk painting. Her theory is that as creative people with a very long production schedule, writers naturally love being able to take a project from start to finish in a matter of days.

Fletch is so pleased about my new hobby that he's ceded half the basement to me and built me a tiered set of shelves for my cans of paint. Of course, both our work areas are getting squished due to all my finished pieces because I don't actually have anywhere to put them upstairs. But I'll figure out something to do with them.

For now, I've completed two items on my list, I own more end tables than I'll ever need, I have music that keeps me stimulated and a hobby that keeps me moving, plus I've discovered the smug sense of satisfaction of having finally, finally gotten one up on Martha.

And that's a *great* thing.

11.

······················· ⟶🌹 ······················

ITALIAN FOR DOUCHE BAGS

"How goes the list?" Stacey asks.

Fletch and I are out to dinner with Stacey and her doting husband, Bill. Bill's a real Southern gentleman, always opening doors and pulling out chairs for her. He's exactly the kind of man you hope your friend will marry, even if you're more of an "I can open the damn door myself, thanks" kind of gal. Stacey quickly got used to being spoiled and once in a while when we ride somewhere together, I have to poke my head back in the car to say, "Let yourself out, princess."

Stacey and Bill spend most weekends at her family's home up north, which isn't that far from us, so we've met up at a nice restaurant in Libertyville, a town that's halfway between the two places.

I reply, "Considering we're always talking about having dinner here, but this is the first time in almost three years that we've actually done so, I'd say pretty good."

I recently added **say yes to friend face-to-face time** to my bucket list when it dawned on me that I was allowing social media to take the place of a social life. All of the tweets/Facebook/Instagram/Tumblr/etc. can make it feel like I'm among pals, and the give-and-take can be amusing and engaging, but I've come to realize this isn't "real" and there's no substitute for actual interaction. The difference between social media and a social life is the difference between eating a marshmallow Peep and dining on a tomahawk-cut rib eye: one is substantial and nutritious; the other is just a momentarily satisfying puff of sweetened air, offering no long-term benefits. I can enjoy the fluff, but I can't subsist on it.

Back in Chicago, Stacey and I lived within walking distance for four years. Our long-standing joke was that we never *actually* walked to each other's house, but we appreciated having the option. I used to see her all the time, like if one of us was running to the grocery store, we'd call the other to tag along. Plus, we had weekly luncheons with the girls and our usual Wednesday night Bravo date, where we'd get together to watch housewives or hairdressers or chefs yell at one another, depending on which show was on. The best part was, she was always up for an adventure. Sometimes our adventures entailed going to the cobbler to have a pair of boots reheeled or dropping off dry cleaning, but still.

Stacey and I grew so close because we were in each other's house almost every day, whether she was bringing over an extra piece of banana cake or I was stopping by to return her meat thermometer. Couple proximity with zero children and a million shared interests and, bam!

Best friends forever.

It's not that I don't equally adore all my friends who have kids, but it's a challenge to book time with them because they're so busy. Spontaneity flies out the window the minute one buys their first car seat.

Now my home is twenty-five miles north of Stacey, which means sometimes I can be at her house in half an hour, unless there's traffic, in which case it takes an hour and a half. I've gone from seeing her almost every day to once a month if I'm lucky.

I miss Stacey, and sitting here across from her, I can't imagine why I'd ever have taken a pass on getting together.

"Well, then, cheers to your yesses!" She raises her glass of wine and we all toast.

"Cheers to this not being Irish dancing," I say.

A few weeks ago, right when I began to Say Yes, Joanna mentioned that she was heading up to Milwaukee for her daughter's Irish dancing competition. She was sure I'd decline, but figured since she had to drive past my house anyway, she'd extend the invite.

When I told her I wasn't allowed to say no, she was delighted. Did I *want* to spend my Saturday surrounded by little girls with oddly curled wigs and way too much red lipstick? No, but neither did Joanna. The most important part of friendship is being there during the times that are boring, annoying, or hard.

"Oy, how'd that go?" Stacey asks.

"The morning was kind of cool because all the girls were in these little slippers and they just hopped around to the sound of lutes. Like, light and lithe and kind of magical. But then, after lunch, those five hundred little girls all donned their tap shoes at the same time. They were banging away so hard that the walls began to shake. How does seventy-six pounds of nine-year-old make that much racket? I told Joanna, 'I bet this is what Afghanistan sounds like.'"

Fletch interjects, "You didn't tweet that, right?"

"Not on your life," I responded. This is another reason I'm trying to wean myself off of social media; there's too much room for misinterpretation. For example, I have oceans of respect for the armed forces and years ago when I made my checklist about my ideal man (are you sensing a checklist theme here?) "ex-military" was in my "would really like to have" column. When we met, I was thrilled to learn Fletch was former active-duty army. Because military service is so important to me, I donate generously to veterans' charities, have sent many care packages to those serving overseas, and always mark Memorial and Veterans' Day by hanging our flag at half-mast. And I vote for politicians who are like-minded in terms of armed services, so there's no question on how much I respect each and every branch.

Joanna appreciated my little quip, but that's because she understands my intentions. Even though I thought my remark was clever as it juxtaposed the agonizing ballet of battle versus little girls in embroidered dresses banging around on a stage by an ice rink, I didn't dare share this thought because I didn't want to spend the rest of the afternoon trying to explain how no, really, I swear I support the military.

How does an innocuous observation like, say, "There sure are a lot of Subarus up here in Seattle," so quickly devolve into an angry mob demanding to know why I hate lesbians? What? How did—where did—*what??* This bizarre telephone-game interpretation social media engenders has become flat-out insanity. When did everyone begin to take everything so seriously on these sites? Personally, wouldn't the fact that my home page boasts a photo of my cat wearing a tiny sombrero be a small clue as to my irreverent nature?

Overreactions to what should be completely inoffensive make me so crazy. And at what point did "clicktavisim" take over for actually trying to do good? I mean, people can retweet about hunger awareness until their thumbnails fall off, but if they really wanted to do something that would help feed people right this damn minute, they'd go to the grocery store and load up their cart with shelf staples like peanut butter and pasta, dropping everything off at their local food bank.

(Sidebar: If you try this—and I hope you do because you'll feel AWESOME afterward—be sure to grab a few items that kids like. According to the man at the Northern Illinois Food Bank, most of those who've lost their SNAP benefits are families with small children. As much as they appreciate the stewed tomatoes and canned pinto beans, I'm sure they'd love a bag of Goldfish crackers or a few Hershey bars so they can feel like the other kids in their class, even for a minute.)

(Additional sidebar: Was that soapbox-y? If so, I apologize, but I'm sick of others who equate *posting* about doing good with actually having done it. Also, if a supermarket sweep isn't in line with your budget, giving your time is equally important.)

At this point, our server swings by to tell us about the specials. She's not a terribly skilled waitress because she keeps trying to give us every other table's drinks and on her last stop, she spilled the better part of Table Twelve's martini down Fletch's back. But considering that I myself was a terrible waitress, I'm sympathetic.

After she rattles off the list, I'm torn between the pork loin with caramelized onions and the swordfish, so I ask how the swordfish is prepared.

She responds, "I like fishes."

"Um, okay," I say. "I'll have the swordfish then."

She takes the rest of our order, which includes salads and appetizers, and then wanders off without collecting our menus. On her way to the kitchen, she plows into a busboy.

"Was that weird?" Bill asks. "It's not me—that was weird, right?"

"I wonder if she's delayed somehow," Stacey speculates.

"Yeah," I say. "I got that vibe, too. '*I like fishes.*' Really? Then bless your heart, sweetie. Well done."

Fletch's eyes twinkle as he smiles at us over the rim of his craft brew. "Uh-huh. Delayed. That's what she is."

"Anyway," Stacey says. "What's next on your list?"

"Well, I start Italian lessons next week," I say.

"Ah, *molto bene!*" Bill cheers.

"I know, I'm really excited. All summer long I've been using an Italian workbook to get familiar again and I just bought Rosetta Stone. I had the budget to buy either that or a home laser hair removal kit. So, I figured I was going to embrace my Italian heritage and leave my mustache alone. Oh, stop rolling your eyes, Fletcher. I still wax."

Our waitress materializes at our table again with a big tray full of frozen drinks and drafts.

"I definitely didn't order anything blue," Stacey says, waving the frothy concoction away.

"Wait, was blue an option?" I ask. I'm charmed by any blue cocktail. Fact.

"None of these drinks are ours," Bill says, gesturing toward all the full glasses on the table. "We're all fine with what we have, thank you."

The waitress cocks her head like a German shepherd trying desperately to understand if he heard the words "doggie park" correctly. She looks at all of us for a solid thirty seconds and then, without saying a thing, tries to give the six drinks to the two-top behind us.

Bill says, "Wow. She's not good at this."

"That poor thing," Stacey says.

I chime in, "I know, right? I just read this book about traumatic brain injuries and—"

Fletch puts down his glass and shakes his head at all of us. "She's shit-housed."

"What?" We all look at Fletch.

Our mouths agape, Fletch continues. "Oh, yeah. Hammered.

Blotto. Cockeyed. Crapulous. Sauced. Wrecked. Tanked. Pixelated. Three sheets to the wind. All sloppy and no joe. Do you not see it? The slurring? The giggling? The stumbling? And she smells like a gin mill."

"Oh," I say. "I assumed that was the martini all over your back."

"I have a *martini* all over my *back*. Was that not a big hint?" Fletch is far more amused than he is aggravated. "The three of you are the worst detectives ever."

"That's so funny," I say. "I was a drunken waitress in college—you'd think I'd be better at spotting it now."

"Yes, but that was at Purdue," Stacey replies. "The context is off. You don't actually expect to see this in a non-college-town restaurant with cloth napkins and a selection of artisanal cheeses."

"What do we do?" I ask.

Bill puts down his napkin and stands up. "I'll handle this. Let me say something to the manager. Excuse me."

We return to our regularly scheduled conversation. "So, are you doing private lessons or classes at Lake Forest College?"

"Neither. I definitely didn't want to be with a bunch of eighteen-year-olds and private lessons were expensive. I found a group and it works out to about ten bucks an hour for twelve lessons."

She fist-bumps me. "Nice!"

Bill returns with an odd look on his face. "Well, I spoke with the manager." He sits back down and places his napkin in his lap.

"And?" Stacey asks.

Bill nods slowly, like he's trying to come to terms with something. "He's drunk, too."

When our entrées arrive before the salads or appetizers, Bill then has a word with the hostess. She appears to be about eight months pregnant and is absolutely mortified by our experience. She instructs a busboy to drive both the manager and the waitress home and has the bartender take over our table. Everything works out and the rest of the night is a happy blur of old friends, laughter, and conversation.

The swordfish, by the way, is delicious.

When we say our good-byes, we make definitive plans to do this again very soon. Not here, but definitely somewhere.

Saying yes has already proven to be a fine idea.

The rest of the summer passes by in a flash because I'm so tied up with working on furniture and saying yes to garden walks and lunches and farmers' markets. My friend Becca tries to trick me into babysitting but I explain that *she's* my friend, not her kids, so I'm able to skate out of it.

Not only has saying yes been a lot fun. I believe that upping the social portion of my life is actually helping my goal of **losing twenty pounds**.

In the scheme of things, twenty pounds will make a difference for me only psychologically, as I doubt I'll even be able to see the results. Yet I can't not be satisfied as the numbers on the scale finally, finally trend downward, no matter how slightly.

I love when a plan comes together!

For the past couple of weeks, I've been telling Fletch that my class feels too good to be true.

But I should have realized that when something seems too good to be true, it generally is.

I've spent each week in excited anticipation of Monday night because I'm so eager to learn. I spend tons of time practicing on my own, whether it's using my computer discs or playing the Italian language version of MindSnacks on the iPad. (BTW, I just learned that "the shin" is *"lo stinco"* in Italian and that word makes me giggle every time.) Also, my circumstances are far different from when I studied Italian in college as I no longer have to make the choice between attending class or working a lunch shift to pay my rent.

I'm learning for my own pleasure and it's so gratifying.

I adore my instructor, too, which adds to the whole experience. *La mia professoressa* Donatella doesn't just grill us on vocabulary and grammar. As a native Italian she's able to offer us an understanding of the country as a whole. She figures what good is speaking a language without a concept of the culture, too? She says we're not trying to stuff in as much vocab as possible to pass a standardized test. Rather, we're all here because we eventually want to go to Italy, so we're picking up the lingo and the skills that will help us best navigate. Donatella explains that context is so necessary when teaching adults, so that's a good piece of her focus.

For example, a few weeks ago we spent the final fifteen minutes of class honoring Giuseppe Verdi's two hundredth birthday. We discussed the great composer and his impact not just on Italy, but the music world in general. I love Verdi's operas because he wasn't afraid to go dark, like when (SPOILER ALERT) everyone dies in the pyramid at the end of *Aida*.

Donatella gave us the Italian lyrics to the aria we were listening to, along with the English translation, and we followed along. I left class that night really feeling as though I'd learned something significant. Then, because Joanna's a fan, too, we had something entirely new to discuss over lunch.

In fact, I enjoy my class so much, I've taken to arriving a few minutes early to chat with the other participants. Years ago, I saw the foreign film *Italian for Beginners* and although I wasn't looking to find love, I did hope to make some new local friends like in the movie, and thus far, this feels really possible.

I'm happy that the movie was, in a small way, prophetic, because everyone in class seems so engaged and interesting. Like the woman who sits across from me—she mentioned how her baby was born at two and a half pounds when that same baby had just come home from college to celebrate her twenty-first birthday!

I also quite like the gal who sits on my side of the conference table. She has to miss class in a few weeks because her son is getting married—on 11/12/13. Or how about the adorable young Moroccan couple who already speak so many languages that sometimes they forget their Italian and answer in Spanish or French? Their collective cuteness slays me.

I can't believe how fast time goes by in class, either. I remember practically growing old and dying in some of my college courses, but here the hour passes in a wink and I wish I had so much more time.

Of course, I should have known there'd be *una mela marcia* (a bad apple) in our midst.

There's an older couple who sits at the end of the table, clad in weird sweatshirts and elaborately framed glasses. The husband's attendance has been sporadic for the past few weeks, first due to work schedules and then to this being cold and flu season. (It's not an accident that I sit as far away from these two as possible, FYI.)

We begin every class by going around in a circle and greeting one another. As most of us are super-geeked to be there, our responses are basically Italian variations on "I AM FRIGGING SPECTACULAR, THANK YOU FOR ASKING!!!!" But I've noticed that the wife of this couple has been saying she's *cosi cosi*, which means so-so. Except she can't seem to just say *cosi cosi*; for four weeks running, she's insisted on asking what the word for so-so is before she can give her response.

Um, number one, write that shit down so you don't have to ask every week; number two, we don't actually care *how* you are because that's not the purpose of the exercise—just say you're *molto bene* so we can get on with the class; and number three, stop giving us the big sigh before you ask what so-so means, all right? It's abundantly clear you'd like to discuss your troubles at length and *that is not okay*. This is

Italian class, not therapy, so if you're compelled to talk about all your feels, please consult an appropriate professional. I paid for a full sixty minutes of this class and every minute you waste being cagey about your emotional health is a minute I'm not learning.

In other words?

Chiudi il culo! (STFU.)

Also, this lady wears a bowling hand brace to compensate for her carpal tunnel and that bugs me.

When Fletch asked how I was sure it was a bowling brace, I replied, "Because it says *Brunswick* on it."

After our instructor tacitly ignores Brunswick's weekly cry for attention, we begin to discuss numbers. Our homework was to study numbers one through twenty, so naturally, I learned up to number one hundred. (Again, it's with deep regret that I wasn't hip to the pleasures of being the teacher's pet back in the day.)

So, Donatella says we're going to count to twenty and asks us to repeat after her. We get to number three before Brunswick throws us completely off course. Here's the thing—when you're learning a language, it's imperative to hear the word BEFORE you can pronounce it, hence the listen-*then*-repeat command. But like every single other time, we get a couple of words in of listening and repeating before Brunswick loses the pace and begins to say the words *with* the instructor, ergo, no repeating. Dollars to doughnuts, this woman could throw an entire stadium off by clapping on the wrong beat.

Accidenti! (Damn it!)

When we finally manage to count to twenty, Brunswick makes an important discovery.

"I thought *venti* meant coffee," she begins. "At Starbucks, venti means coffee."

"Actually, it's a size," says the nice 11/12/13 woman next to me. "It means twenty ounces."

(Fine, maybe I don't know everyone's names yet, but I figure

I have only so much brain capacity, so I'm better off filling it with verb conjugations.)

"But I thought everything was in French, because of the *grande*," Hand Brace argues. "Does *grande* mean sixteen ounces in French?"

"*Non,*" reply the Moroccan students in unison.

Donatella tries to move us along to the numbers after twenty, but Brunswick is having none of it. "Then why would Starbucks do that? That makes no sense. They should do Italian OR French because it's confusing. In fact, that's why I don't even like their coffee. *I'm* a Dunkin' Donuts person. Why would anyone pay four dollars for a cuppa joe when Dunk's is so much better?"

It now occurs to me that Brunswick spends a lot of class time asking why about questions that have no answer except, "Because that's how it's done." Why do the Italians use the indefinite article? Why are there masculine and feminine words? Why are flowers masculine when very clearly it's ladies who like them? How come the h is silent? How come our teacher pronounces *h* like "hache"? Why are some verbs irregular?

What matters is not the why of these rules, but that they exist at all. We need to *learn* the specifics, not *debate* them. This is Rudimentary Italian, taking place in the basement of a far-flung suburban insurance office, not a seminar on Advanced Linguistics at Oxford University.

Brunswick continues her diatribe. "What about tall, then? Is that Italian? How come tall is actually small at Starbucks?"

That's when it hits me that Brunswick is a *time burglar.*

Specifically, she's stealing *my* time with her inane questions and now she is my nemesis. It's one thing to have legitimate questions—I mean, this is a classroom and we're here to be taught. We're all beginners and it's expected that we'll make mistakes. Being able to ask questions without feeling like a dipshit is one of the biggest benefits of having become middle-aged. I can think of dozens of instances in my college classes where I didn't seek clarification because I was too embarrassed to raise my hand. What might have been illuminated had I not been afraid to ask?

Yet what this woman fails to realize is that she's ignoring the social cues that her questions are not appropriate, as they do nothing to edify any of us. What's even worse is she's now thrown the entire class off course and everyone's busy trying to explain beverage sizes to her in regard to a coffee shop she *actively avoids*.

Nothing about our conversation matters, so it's up to me to get us back on track.

I snap, "It's a marketing term, okay? Can we please move on?"

Donatella shoots me what I swear is a grateful look and we proceed to thirty, which is *trenta*.

"Hey, trenta is the newest Starbucks size and . . ."

Accidenti!

Donatella wrests control of the class away from Brunswick and we continue with our lessons. Once we complete the numbers section, we begin to discuss geography. She explains how Italy is a very diverse country, and each region has distinct characteristics. Before she can describe any of said characteristics, Brunswick feels compelled to chime in. "Do the north and the south still hate one another?"

Donatella takes a moment to consider the least stupid question Brunswick has ever posed. "Well, the relationship is a little more complicated than that," she begins. "You see, the south does not have the economic opportunities found in the north, so—"

Brunswick says, "When I was a kid, we lived in Highland Park, a block away from the Highwood border, and Highwood used to be full of Italians."

The fact that she doesn't actually say Eye-talian is a pleasant surprise.

She continues. "Why was it full of Italians, I wonder? Anyway, we had northern Italians on one side and southern Italians on the other and they HATED one another. They fought about everything—the hedges, the trees, who was supposed to shovel. We never did understand why they hated each other so much. My dad said he never saw anything like it."

I glance around the room and notice half a dozen students mid-eye-roll.

Donatella takes a breath, smiles tightly, and continues. "So, Italy is made up of twenty regions."

I want to cheer her ability to ignore the intrusion, but I'm too interested in what she has to say. Turns out, she's just finished the itinerary for the annual trip she hosts in the spring—a cooking tour of the Amalfi Coast! The trip is all-inclusive, with luxury accommodations and tons of side trips.

(Sidebar: Apparently Brunswick is a huge fan of gnocchi, but she doesn't understand why we don't pronounce the *g* the same way we do in the USA.)

This tour might be just the thing for me. I'm in this class because I plan to go to Italy, but maybe I'd be better off going with a group and a set itinerary? I fear that on my own, I would eat my own weight in gelato while sitting in my hotel room watching Italian soap operas. (If my history is any indication, my *Eat, Pray, Love* goal will morph into *Eat, Eat, Lounge*.) Maybe I need the social interaction of a group tour? Unless Brunswick is going, in which case, I will look at my globe to determine the farthest point away from her I could get.

Classmates begin to ask questions about the tour, as we're all quite interested. 11/12/13, who's traveled with our instructor before, wants to know if some of the same guides will be used because they were great last time. The mother of the preemie is curious if she could book her own flight. Instead of Lufthansa, she'd prefer to use her miles on American.

(Sidebar: Did you know you can get a ticket to Rome off-peak for twenty-five thousand miles?! How was I not informed?)

I ask if I could upgrade, not because I'm so goddamned special, but more because I'm fairly claustrophobic and dread wedging my large ass in a tiny seat for eight hours. Also? Snacks!

"Upgrading costs money," Brunswick informs me.

Really? *That's* a news flash. I thought I could just work my way to the good seats on the merits of my charm alone, or perhaps trade some shiny beads. Does Lufthansa accept repainted dressers as payment? I seem to have them in spades.

She continues. "Why would you want to upgrade? It's not like Business Class is so much better. Why can't you sit with the rest of the tour? What if your upgrade puts you on a different flight? If I go, *I'd* definitely sit in Coach."

Upgrade it is.

Our session ends promptly at seven o'clock every week as Donatella has another class directly after this one. We're all too courteous to linger because our time is up, so we quickly gather up our *quaderni* (notebooks) and, in my case, empty venti-sized Starbucks cup.

Except, of course, for Brunswick.

"Hey, can you check my homework from two weeks ago?" she asks, wedging in front of where I'm currently donning my coat. She thrusts the sheet toward Donatella's kind face, because, of course she does.

"You understand I have a class waiting, yes?" Donatella asks.

"It won't take you long," Brunswick replies, flopping down in a chair next her.

I exit, making a mental note to look up the Italian word for *douche bag.*

As annoyed as I am, I still find myself smiling as I climb into my car. How am I concurrently so annoyed and yet still feel so happy?

As I drive home, I realize that the only thing I enjoy more than saying yes, checking items off my list, or learning Italian is having found a new nemesis.

Game on, *doccia borsa.*

Game on.

12.

THE RECORD SHOWS I TOOK THE BLOWS

Partway through the semester, Brunswick quits the class. Our teacher relays she was too busy to make it on Monday nights. Doubt it. I bet with all the other hypermotivated students, she felt like she'd fallen behind and she couldn't catch up because it's impossible to learn something new when you never, ever once shut your word hole and open your ears.

She shan't be missed.

(Sidebar: I may miss her a little. I kind of loved actively hating her for sixty minutes every Monday. Now I need to find a new nemesis. I may go back to despising our mailman, as he's taken to leaving our mailbox open, but only when it's snowing or raining. I am thisclose to renting a PO box so I can up my battle properly with this assclown.)

On our last night of class, we discuss how Italians do Christmas. Apparently it's not nearly as commercial over there and the celebration is far more about food than presents, with loaves of raisin-studded panettone everywhere. Instead of beef tenderloin or roast turkey, the big holiday meal is all about the Feast of the

Seven Fishes. Entire villages come out to rejoice together. They begin their partying on the day of the Immaculate Conception on December eighth, ending with the Epiphany on January sixth, and there are nativity scenes *everywhere*. I wonder if teenage boys are always stealing the baby Jesus in Italy, too. Or is it no fun because there are so many that it's all like shooting (seven) fish in a barrel?

Babbo Natale is the Italian version of Santa Claus but there's a character named La Befana who's also important. She's a good witch who rides around on her broom and fills Christmas stockings, usually on January sixth. In La Befana lore, she was mixed up with the Wise Men somehow, but I'm unclear on the hows and whys. I guess she's as plausible as a space-time continuum–bending rabbit bringing chocolate eggs to kids in multiple time zones at Easter or a rich, nocturnal fairy with a tooth fetish. In practical terms, it sounds like La Befana isn't a witch so much as she is a savvy shopper who waits till after the holiday to buy marked-down candy. Personally, I always snap up all the Christmas ornaments on December twenty-sixth because they go half off at Target that day. (If you wait until the twenty-seventh, all the best items are gone. I'm serious—set your alarm.)

Donatella brings homemade tiramisu and we lose our minds over how she's made it both dense and velvety, but also so very airy, the whole concoction infused with the promise of espresso and liqueur. Then, fueled by sugar, Kahlua, and a competitive spirit, we play Tombola, which is basically Italian-style bingo. Instead of daubing our cards like we would in a VFW hall or church basement, we cover the spaces with large dried beans. I love how we use the same deck that Donatella's been playing with ever since her childhood. She's definitely connecting us with her personal history in a way I never experienced in a college classroom. Again, this is the difference between voluntarily learning as an adult and taking a required class for a grade in pursuit of a degree. Both have merits, but this way feels more meaningful.

Oh, and, I don't mean to brag, but I *do* win seventy-five cents over the course of the game, so . . . coffees are on me tonight.

The merriment of the year's last class nicely kicks off the whole holiday season and I really want to celebrate. Every year, it's depressing to go from the full-court holiday press of glitter-spackled, mistletoe-hung, beribboned first floor to what looks like any other day upstairs in the family room, so I purchase a small artificial tree, adorning it with all the extra ornaments from last year's day-after-Christmas sale.

I figure I must truly be middle-aged now, having previously fought to the death over having a "fake tree." Yet I quickly adapt to not vacuuming up shed needles every fourteen minutes and not worrying the whole thing will spontaneously combust when I make a spark dragging my slipper-clad feet across the carpet. Plus, manufacturers have come a long way with the design and technology and these trees are so realistic! Gone are the days of green pipe cleaners stuck in a metal pole. I still have a live Frasier fir downstairs (and two fire extinguishers within grabbing distance) but I can imagine a time when I fully convert to artificial. When I do cross over, I suspect I'll also finally understand the allure of the decorative holiday sweater and earrings made out of jingle bells.

Feeling extra-festive, I decide to start baking early in the season. Thanks to Martha, I'm fully confident in my newfound culinary abilities, and inspired by Joanna's Twenty-Four Days of Christmas Cookies, I take to my kitchen with a metric shit-ton of supplies, ready to craft cookies for everyone I've ever met. (Except my mailman.)

This is the first year I've listened to BackSpin while baking—did you know there are actual holiday rap songs outside of Run–D.M.C.'s "Christmas in Hollis," such as Snoop Dogg's "Santa

Claus Goes Straight to the Ghetto," or Eazy-E's "Merry Mutha-fucking X-Mas"? Believe it. Ensconced in a funky backbeat, I be-gin to make some elfin magic.

(Sidebar: Was the Keebler reference above too esoteric?)

I'm vaguely disappointed when my first variety of cookies turns out badly, but sometimes that happens. My oven confuses me because there's a convection feature and I've been known to hit the wrong button, usually when wine is involved or if I'm pan-icked before a dinner party. (Redundant?) But today, I'm having hot chocolate, so I chalk it up to bad luck.

Of course, when my entirely different second batch ends up crumbling and dry to the point of Saharan, I'm aggravated. It's possible I'm grooving too much to pay attention, but come on—it's hard to focus when MC Shan's rapping about Santa trading in his sleigh for a Lamborghini with a spoiler kit. Best visual ever!

I turn down the music and proceed with another recipe. I'm shocked and dismayed when I ruin the stupid spritz cookies. These are supposed to be idiot-proof, but apparently not. And when my fourth bunch, this time sugar cookies assembled from a tried-and-true recipe, look less like "snowmen" and more like "testicular cancer," I'm livid, especially because there's no one to blame here except myself.

I'm not sure if I got a bad container of baking powder or if perhaps I'm experiencing some kind of divine retribution because Christmas carols are no place for profanity (regardless of hilarity factor), but absolutely nothing works.

As everything I touch is a disaster, I decide to quit.

Here's the thing—I still could plow through my supplies, confident that eventually I'd come up with a cookie that's both attractive and tasty. But after four failures in a row, baking stopped being a treat and started to feel like a chore. I don't have customers waiting for this product and I have lots of other desserts planned for my annual party. Fletch won't lack for anything sugary during the holiday season. And every year when I stock the freezer with Fourth of July supplies, I end up tossing bags and bags of leftover holiday peanut butter kiss cookies and Mexican wedding cakes to make room.

What a waste of time, effort, and ingredients.

I don't *need* to make cookies.

I don't *want* to make cookies at this point.

So I have to ask myself, why continue to press on? Why push blithely forward toward that which is frustrating and fruitless? It's not like holiday baking was on my bucket list, and even if it was, the whole notion of having a bucket list isn't about crossing off various items, as much as I do love me some checkmarks.

The point of this project, and really, my overarching goal for the year, is to minimize that which I regret. When I review my teens and twenties, I'm mortified by so much of what I did. My more callous and cavalier actions haunt me. In my thirties, the regrets were less about bad behavior and more about terrible choices, some of which I'm still paying for. (Hello, FICO score.)

But in my forties, my greatest regrets have been less about the content of my character and more about my caloric intake. Otherwise, I've actively worked to get my shit together, whether it's been adding culture to my life, or putting my house in order, or coming to terms with being an adult. I'm proud of my career and

I love the people with whom I've surrounded myself. I've striven to make the right decisions, no matter how difficult, and agonized over cutting ties with those who are toxic. I feel like I'm far better for the effort. So every time I do something counterintuitive to that which keeps regrets at bay, I'm mad at myself.

Generation X turns fifty this year, as we're defined by a 1964 start date. Although I can't speak for my whole peer group, I can say for myself that by the time I hit my fifties, I hope to have my life figured out. When I'm fifty, I want my default mode to be doing the right thing, making the right choices, and behaving in a way that never makes me cringe upon further reflection.

My friend Laurie tells me that she used to knock herself out to provide the full Martha Stewart Christmas for her family, slaving away all day in the kitchen over the elaborate meal. When it came time to eat, she was not only exhausted, but she'd missed out on all the magical moments with her boys and her husband. When she hit fifty, she decided she was through—not with the family, but with the nonsense and the noise and the unrealistic expectations.

Now her ritual is to buy a bunch of HomeMade Pizza Co. unbaked pizzas and Three Tarts Bakery pies on Christmas Eve, so anything anyone has to do on the day itself is toss in the oven whatever type of pie they desire. Friends and extended family come over to play games and watch holiday movies, happy as can be in their ability to connect without all the pressure of what they "should" be doing. Laurie said that nothing's been more freeing than letting go of the picture-perfect magazine holiday fantasy, instead forging a path that's ultimately more satisfying.

I believe the pursuit of a Pinterest-perfect, ultimate-Martha Stewart-lifestyle can be dangerous. Online, I see these women in their thirties exhausting themselves to make sure everything they do is Instagram-worthy. Instead of, say, simply playing with their kids at the park, they have their spouses shooting virtual lifestyle magazine spreads, where each shot is staged for maximum impact.

"No, Trevor, wrong! You have to come down the slide *smiling*, not *screaming!*"

"Salinger, throw the maple leaves in the air again, but this time, with *attitude!*"

"Maya, step out of the sandbox right now! You're going to get your Hanna Andersson play clothes dirty!"

For God's sake, childhood doesn't need to be art directed.

(Sidebar: As a friend, I'd humbly suggest that anyone who values their children's privacy and safety might reconsider splashing the kids' names, ranks, serial numbers, and difficulties with potty training all over the Internet.)

To me, the above is why so much of social media can ring false. Our lives are meant to be our lives, and not a facade presented for the consumption of others; or, WE ARE NOT A MAGAZINE.

I worry that younger women are striving so hard to present a compelling story via images that they're ignoring the substance that makes the story true. Ultimately, they're going to end up really bitter later in life (and not the good kind of bitter that sells books).

My message to these women is this—if you want to avoid regrets later, give yourselves a break now and just be real. Enjoy the mess. Revel in the imperfection.

So, if I'm being real, then I can definitely say I won't be sad about not baking because I'm neither a mini-Martha-magazine-mogul nor a tree-dwelling, cookie-making elf.

(Sidebar: I feel like I just gave the previous Keebler joke more context. Yay for me!)

I immediately scrap the rest of my baking plans, instead opting to donate the massive amount of supplies I've amassed. I supplement my unopened ingredients with additional items at the grocery store. I'm not sure if the food bank sees a lot of donated chocolate chips, colored sprinkles, or powdered sugar, but just because a family's hit a rough patch doesn't mean they won't appreciate being able to bake with their kids. If someone's in a circumstance where they're using a food bank, it's likely not by choice. I'm sure regrets are involved and I empathize. Having once been close to the edge myself, I understand and I want to do what I can to make it better for others. And if providing the materials to make cookies gives a family a chance to feel normal and step outside of their regrets, even for one day, then I'm glad I could help.

After I swing by the grocery store and the food bank, I buy some pretty sugar cookies at Three Tarts, and then I come home to settle in with *Holiday Inn*, basking in the warm glow of my little artificial tree. Over subsequent free weekends, I spend my time decorating instead of baking, not because I'm determined to garner the most "pins," but because I hope to make the house as welcoming as possible for those I love.

I feel I made the right choice.

By the end of the holiday season, I realize I've put back on every ounce of weight I lost riding my bike, which is currently trapped in the garage behind three feet of snow. I won't be able to ride again for months, considering the hellacious winter we're having. Even the most hard-core road warriors are currently in hibernation due to the bike paths being layered with six full inches of ice.

As it's a shiny new year, I decide that it's finally time to take care of some long-standing health concerns. I'm due for a well-woman exam and I'm worried that something may be amiss Down There. I'm not having any problems, per se, but with three contemporaries having had hysterectomies in the last year, I'm concerned it may be my turn, especially since I keep dodging bullets on my diagnostic mammograms. And at this age, it's generally one

or the other. I wonder if the husbands who opted for vasectomies in their thirties are all, "Man, I shoulda held out a little longer!" because this seems to be a thing now that Generation X is hitting our second act.

I'm definitely Team Take It All Out, I'm Not Using It if there's any kind of problem with my reproductive system. I'm at peace with my decision to not procreate. Fortunately, I've finally arrived at an age when people have stopped bugging me about when I'm going to become a mommy. I haven't heard a smug, "You'll change your mind," in at least three years. I don't miss the invasive questions; on the other hand, the fact that I must look like the factory's closed is a bit of a bummer.

(Sidebar: This feeling is similar to how every time I get carded, I wonder if it's my last.)

Anyway, it's my understanding that if you don't eventually use your baby-brewing parts, all the pieces become an attractive nuisance, kind of like an abandoned building. Without the possibility of a paying tenant, the wrong element comes a-callin'. Squatters are imminent. Personally, I'd rather tear the whole thing down, you know? In this case, I couldn't plant a public park in its place, but you get the idea.

And while we're down here, a word, if I may, about perimenopause? Or, three words, actually—WHY, GOD, WHY? This hot flash business is utter and complete bullshit. I mean, I'm a fat girl; I sweat enough on my own without Mother Nature turning up the thermostat. According to my medical education (meaning, using WebMD, which in my head translates to having an honorary medical degree) this foolishness can last two to eight years. *What?* A president could serve two full terms in eight years. Whatever crooked governor Illinois elects next could complete a prison sentence for money laundering and be out in eight years. You could build a federal highway or take a rocket to Jupiter in eight years.

This is so wrong.

And after I'm done with the potential eight damn years of the sweating and the irritability and the weird estrogen surges, apparently I can look forward to bone loss, changes in my skin's texture—I'm sure not for the better—and problems with my gums. You mean, I could have a beard *and* require dentures? Perfect. Sign me up.

I haven't been hit with the night sweats yet, so I guess that's a blessing. A while ago, Fletch and I were hanging out with another couple (whom I choose to not incriminate) and my friend was telling us how she'd had all kinds of tests run to determine why she was getting so hot in her sleep.

"Hate to break it to you, but those are night sweats," I said, giving her the full benefit of my WebMD degree.

"How can I have night sweats? I'm only thirty," Friend replied, to which I laughed. This particular pal has been lying about her age for so long that she's actually begun to believe herself.

I fully support her pretense, but at the same time, facts are facts. We *are* middle-aged. This is what happens. All the same nonsense that comes with puberty occurs again during perimenopause—the hormone surges, the moodiness, and the hair appearing where there wasn't hair before. Except instead of filling in under the arms and on nether regions, these coarse follicles of hate are showing up *on our freaking faces.*

Every night before bed, I spend quality time over the bathroom sink with a handheld flashlight and some tweezers. I thought I'd been doing a fine job of Jenscaping until the last time I stayed in a hotel with a super-magnifying mirror. My God, I wanted to hurl myself out the window, except it was hermetically sealed, likely for this very reason. I suspect this is why we all lose our close-up vision by the time we're in our forties. If women could actually *see* what was happening on their faces, there'd be nothing to stop us all from going on a twelve-state killing spree.

(Sidebar: I'm fighting the need for reading glasses with every ounce of my being. I have my computer display jacked up two hundred percent and I've transitioned almost solely to my e-reader because I can make the font massive. What really makes me mad, outside of the general indignity of beginning to deteriorate, even if ever so slightly, is that the print on every antiaging product is so damn small. Listen, skin-care manufacturers, do you have any idea who actually buys your products? Hint—it's not the dewy twenty-year-olds with perfect skin who still pass out face-first wearing full makeup.)

(Additional sidebar: I sorely regret having washed my face before bed only a handful of times in my twenties.)

Ignoring me, Friend said, "It's not my thyroid, and it's not hyperhidrosis or hypoglycemia. There's no sign of infection and I'm not on any meds that might cause this reaction."

"It's perimenopause," I insisted.

"Impossible."

"Not impossible. Just because you say you're thirty doesn't mean you're thirty."

"Of course it does."

Ah, denial's deep in this one, I thought.

As she kept coming up with possible causes, I kept replying with my same diagnosis. I'm an imaginary doctor, damn it! Listen to me!

Finally, Friend's Husband began to chuckle, saying, "I've been telling her for a month that she has night sweats because the bedroom is seventy-five degrees and she sleeps under three down comforters."

Then we both ganged up on him, because, sisterhood.

Anyway, I go to my well-woman exam and my new GYN suggests I have an ultrasound to make sure all is well. (I didn't like the gal I saw last year. Cold hands.)

"Have you ever had a full ultrasound?" she asks.

"Um, sort of?" I reply. "Once I had one scheduled, but somehow I didn't drink enough water beforehand and they couldn't see anything."

She makes a note on my chart. "And how long ago was that?"

"1988."

My doctor is incredulous. "You've needed an ultrasound for *twenty-five years?*"

I shrug. "I've been busy."

This new doctor isn't playing around, no matter how many pretend medical credentials I may hold, so she schedules me for a full workup tomorrow.

Because I don't want to regret not tending to what's deemed medically necessary, I comply. Actually, as much as I loathe having to take off my pants, I'm a little bit, dare I say, excited to find what might be lurking up there. I definitely don't want to be sick and I'm terrified of surgery, having never been under general anesthesia, but what if they discover a really big fibroid? Like, super weighty. That happened to an acquaintance—her doctors removed something the size of a football.

A football!!

How much thinner would I be if I had a football-sized mass extracted from my midsection? What if I'm not fat because of cake and it's all due to squatters? Granted, fibroids wouldn't explain the ham on my upper arms, but still. This could resolve everything, so I gladly come back the next morning.

I drink an entire gallon of water before my appointment and I feel like I'm carrying a football's worth of fluid when I sit on the tech's exam table.

She asks, "Have you emptied your bladder?"

"No!" I gleefully reply. "It's so full!"

"Then I need to have you use the restroom first."

"Really? I thought I was supposed to drink a ton of fluids before," I reply.

"No, we haven't done it that way for years."

Probably twenty-five.

I take care of business and then we begin. The tech squirts the jelly on me and I'm delighted that it's not freezing. "We use a warmer," she explains.

"Well done," I reply. Five Yelp stars go to the office that understands that there are places you never want to be chilly.

She first surveys the external parts and then uses the trans-I-can't-even-use-the-word-without-spelling-it-wand. "Hmm."

"Hmm?" I ask. Hmm is never positive . . . unless she's discovering something the size of a sporting good, which I can have removed and then finally wear a bikini again! "Do you see any footballs?"

"Footballs? No, no footballs, but I have a couple of areas I'd like the doctor to see. I'm going to go grab her." She exits, leaving me to contemplate buying pants that don't have elastic waists.

In the exam room next to me, I detect an odd sound. It's like a mechanical whump-*whump*, whump-*whump*. The sound continues for a couple of seconds, followed by a quick murmur, then a cheer and then sobbing. I realize I'm witnessing a pregnant couple hearing their unborn child's first heartbeat.

Whoa.

This is a rite of passage I never imagined experiencing, even secondhand. As the couple celebrates next door, I assess how I'm feeling. I always say I'm at peace with being childfree by choice, but am I?

Am I really?

Or, in this completely unexpected moment, am I finding myself suddenly devastated to have completely avoided this track in life? Do I yearn, even for a second, to be on the opposite side of the wall? Do I want to Instagram the hell out of a mini-me? Am I sorry that the miracle of life isn't occurring in the portion of my body specifically designed for the propagation of our species?

I look deeply within to gauge my feelings, and . . .

No.

I'm not.

While I'm elated for the couple next door, as their joy is profound and contagious, more than anything, I feel a comprehensive swell of relief that *it's not me*.

Motherhood was not a path I ever wanted to follow. Of course, it's wonderful for others, and I grieve for those who've tried and failed. It's heartbreaking and it's not fair. And yet sometimes, things work themselves out, like when we received the call out of the blue on Christmas night that after six failed rounds of IVF, four full years on an adoption waiting list they were rapidly aging out of, and a million false starts, Kathleen and her husband Chris had just brought their new baby boy home from the hospital.

(Sidebar: While we were in Savannah, Trenna prayed for a profoundly frustrated Kathleen. With great confidence, she assured Kathleen she'd have her baby soon. The more cynical members of Team Butter may or may not have rolled their eyes at this moment. Yet, who could have guessed that Trenna was right and a brave young woman was already carrying Kathleen's baby? Trenna kept telling us that miracles exist and now? Now I believe her.)

In terms of being a mother myself, I'm actually really proud for never having buckled, for never giving in and doing what was expected, for having the strength of character to understand that as a woman, my world can be complete and my life can have meaning without children of my own.

That doesn't mean I won't spoil the hell out of Kathleen's baby, though.

Now, if my doctor's about to come in, examine my ultrasound, and tell me I need to have a hysterectomy, that my time is up and I'm about to lose the option of ever reproducing?

Then I'm good.

For I have no regrets.

13.

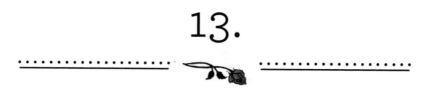

What's My Rule?

"They want to put a camera where?" Fletch asks, glancing up from his workbench. He removes his respirator and protective eyewear to better see and hear me. Not surprised at the overkill with the safety equipment here—this is a man who insists on donning a fully loaded tool belt and leather gloves to hammer a single nail in the wall. When I'm in my workshop area, it's a bonus if I remember to wear shoes.

(Sidebar: One would imagine I'd have learned about the importance of footwear after the time Fletch needed pliers to remove a carpet tack from the ball of my foot, but one would be wrong.)

Fletch is all hazmatted-up here in the basement, in the throes of stripping a magnificent oak dresser I found at a secondhand shop. The grain is so beautiful that I don't want to obscure it with paint, but the stain is that awful honey-colored nonsense from the eighties, so, good-bye.

Once the dresser's down to bare wood, I plan to lime the piece, meaning I'll rub in a little bit of white paint, just enough to bring out the grain before wiping off the excess. The look should be that of a very subtle whitewash. If my process proves successful, I'll have a Restoration Hardware–type item on hand, only truly antique and at one-tenth the price. I inspect his handiwork and, as usual, it's impeccable.

I reply, "I know, right? I've lived forty-six years without ever being the subject of a single compromising shot, not a nip-slip or an upskirt. I'm talking no tongue kisses, no inappropriate hugs, and not a single image that could in any way keep me from being elected to public office. But now? Now they want to photograph my holiest of holies. It's like going straight from *Highlights* to *Hustler.*"

(Sidebar: My gynecologist found evidence of squatters and she requires a closer look inside, which can be accomplished only by running a camera up my . . . blowhole.)

"Yikes."

I lean across the workbench, resting my head in my hands. "The great irony here is that when I was young and firm, I kind of wish I'd taken a few risqué shots. Never nude, because, Congress, but scantily clad would have been acceptable. I wish I knew what I looked like in my underwear circa 1987. I suspect I was hot."

Fletch nods, saying nothing as he scrapes residue off the top of the dresser with hands ensconced in thick rubber gloves, so I continue. "If I had old sexy pictures, I could pin those to the fridge and see them every time I want a piece of cake. Magazine models represent an unrealistic standard of beauty, but what's more representative than seeing the shape I actually had? Plus I could add a note saying, 'Why did you believe you were fat back then?' Youth is wasted on the clueless." I start feeling around my posterior, trying to gauge position. "Seriously, how much higher would you estimate my ass was then as opposed to now? Venice is sinking two millimeters a year—I bet I'm way ahead of that. A lady on my Facebook page said she remembered when watermelons used to be oblong and her butt was round and now it's the opposite. When did watermelons become round? And why?"

He shrugs, staying silent while he removes smooth swaths of bubbled finish.

I glance down at my legs, two thick trunks swathed in yoga pants. "Did I have a standing thigh gap when we met? Apparently that's a *thing* now. The healthy-living bloggers are always taking selfies of their standing thigh gaps. Your legs aren't supposed to touch. I wish I had underpants pictures from back then to know for sure if mine did. Stupid digital cameras—you were invented far too late! Hey . . . do you really have nothing to add here?"

He replies, "I find when you lose your mind, it's best not to get in your way. What's my rule?"

Grudgingly, I parrot his oft-repeated adage. "'*Don't engage The Crazy.*' Fair enough."

But I can't help mulling over how this whole horrible operating room photo shoot might go down, so I press on. "Wait, the doctor's going to use a fiber-optic camera and not, like, a Canon DSLR, right?"

He scrapes the last strip of goo from the dresser top and begins to tidy his workspace, wiping up the jellied bits of old finish and stripper. "Relax, I guarantee no one will foist one of those big paparazzi lenses on you."

"Well, good. Otherwise, everything sounds routine, so I'm not too worried."

(Sidebar: Do I come across plucky and courageous with my cavalier attitude? Because I'm not brave so much as I am compartmentalizing. I guarantee I'll be a basket case before the procedure, envisioning every single worst-case scenario, but for today, as I stand here with many comforting layers of fabric between me and infamy, I'm fine.)

"When does this all happen?" he asks.

"The procedure's not scheduled until mid-March. Apparently this is more preventative than anything else, which is why I can wait until after my upcoming trips."

"That mean they didn't find a boccie ball up there?"

My disappointment is profound. "Football, and no, unfortunately not."

On the bright side, at least I'm going to Seattle tomorrow for a conference. I'm beyond excited to get away from this winter that's destined to kill us all. Sure, I live in the Chicago region, so a Chicago winter comes as no surprise, yet I've never seen anything like this year. I've experienced plenty of early winters, bitter cold, and intense snowfall. But this is the first I've ever seen it all happen at the same time. We have at least two feet of snow in the backyard and it's frozen solid. A few weeks ago, we hit forty-five degrees below zero. Even though I'm on deadline for my next novel, I spend the whole frigid day tossing cups of boiling water into the air so I can watch it instantly freeze.

Worth it.

I feel for the poor dogs. As much as they love running around outside, they can bear it for only about thirty seconds. They do their business poised on two paws at a time. (No, they won't wear booties, and yes, we've tried.) I bought the girls nerdy matching sweaters and every time I see them, I threaten to steal their lunch money.

When I realize I'm sweating under all my layers, I ask, "Why is it so warm down here? Must be close to eighty degrees, which is odd because it's more like sixty upstairs."

"I have no idea," he replies. "I'd planned to spend the day in my office, but it's too cold. I could see my breath. Heat's supposed to rise, but apparently not in this house. We're skirting the laws of thermonuclear dynamics down here. I'm not complaining, but I am curious about the physics."

While he places his brushes in a turpentine bath, I check the weather on my phone. "Holy crap, it's fifty-five degrees and sunny in Seattle right now!"

"That's basically summer."

"Should I pack shorts?"

"Might be overkill."

"Okay, but I'm definitely not wearing my puffy coat to Seattle because I look like a silverback gorilla in it. Or does it give me more of a Michelin Man vibe? I'd also say the Stay Puft Marshmallow dude but the down's sewn in in baffle-channels, so I feel I trend more Michelin. Agree?"

He levels my gaze. "What's my rule?"

"All right, all right." But it's totally Michelin. "Hey, it's not too late if you want to come. I'm only scheduled for a couple of events and I have a lot of downtime. You'd have a free place to stay and we could do touristy stuff. I hear there's a Nirvana exhibit at one of the museums."

"I would, but I don't know what to do with the dogs," he replies. To this point, neither Hammy nor Libby has ever been boarded at a facility. Despite being wonderful little girls, we're uncertain any of the kennels in the snotty North Shore would be thrilled to host a couple of pit bulls. "Plus, I'm not at the best stopping point."

He's referring to the half dozen damaged pieces of furniture we've scavenged in the past few months currently being rebonded with clamps and industrial wood glue. We've found so much on the cheap because most people don't have the tools or inclination to fix their furniture properly. C'mon, folks—hot-glue guns are for crafts, not mending table legs. We unearthed one cute little piecrust table that had been stuck back together with *chewing gum*. Dentyne, I think.

We've assembled quite the production line down here—Fletch makes each piece functional again and then I paint 'em pretty. We've completed a number of pieces so far. In terms of hobbies, rehabbing furniture is way less expensive than if I were to, say, shoot competitively or ride horses or build radio-controlled airplanes. And yet the basement looks like a terribly elegant garage sale, so I should probably find some use for it all.

"Okay. But at least consider Florida." Next month I'm touring for my new novel and I'm hitting four Floridian cities in a row. Since I'll be traveling by car, we'd have to pay for only a single round-trip ticket. Fletch has never accompanied me on tour before, largely because he was always home with Maisy. But now that she's not a consideration, he could finally join me.

"Maybe," he replies. Sometimes Fletch experiences the same type of home-based inertia that I have. I'd simply book the trip for him, but I believe if he really wants to get away, he'll figure out a way to do it himself.

"Not being a nudge, I just don't want you to regret it if you don't come. I'm going to go pack now." As an afterthought, I add, "And I'm bringing my bathing suit."

Because at this point?

Fifty-five degrees = SPRING BREAK!

Though the weather outside is frightful, it has nothing on the shitstorm currently raging on my Facebook page.

Before I wrote professionally, I assumed authors had the sweetest gigs ever. I pictured long, leisurely days where the writers were free to ponder the perfect word choice, sitting in front of a roaring fire with a pen and paper perched on their knees, cups of tea at their side, and faithful companions curled at their feet. They'd have sophisticated lunches with their publishers and they'd be the toast of the town at their book launch parties. Life would be words and accolades and adoring fans.

And in this fantasy world, no reader would ever leave them a Facebook comment saying, "You deserve to die in a fire."

Yet here we are.

To backtrack, almost no part of my fantasy is actually reality. For a professional author, the words are the gift—writing is the fun we have between all the other balls we juggle.

Make no mistake, we're incredibly grateful for the chance to be published in such a competitive arena. The fact that I can afford to live indoors because of what I'd otherwise do for free is the greatest blessing imaginable. However, for any working author, most of our time's spent outside of the creative process. This is neither good nor bad—it's just part of the job. What authors have to accomplish aside from writing is no different from, say, a professional musician or a police officer—their passion is performing for an audience or chasing down bad guys, but most of their time will be spent on that which supports the passion, like riding on the tour bus or writing arrest reports.

In addition to the creative, we also have to network, strategize, build our readership, and court media contacts. We're tasked with finding ways to differentiate ourselves/our words from all the other talented writers out there doing the exact same thing.

(Sidebar: Sometimes these duties can be a lot of fun, like traveling to Seattle for a conference to hang out with booksellers.)

(Additional sidebar: People were actually outside in the pool! In January! I'm convinced everyone in Seattle lies about their weather so I don't move there and crap up the place with my pit bulls and gas-guzzling SUV.)

More important than almost any other task, we have to promote ourselves and this can be tricky. Writers must walk a fine line between building awareness and being the pain in the ass who gets unfollowed after a barrage of pushy buy-my-books tweets.

It's imperative I let readers know *Twisted Sisters* is about to come out, but I'm loath to be in-your-face about it. I generally err on the side of caution because no one likes being sold to, especially me. But publishing *is* a business and other people's careers *are* impacted by my sales, so I can't pretend I don't have a product to promote.

I decide to marry necessity and entertainment by posting some kind of "twisted" picture every day. I start with the shot of my nerdy be-sweatered dogs sitting next to my book.

I proceed for a couple of days with various other photos and the feedback's positive.

Okay, I think, *this seems to be working.* I make a mental note to continue in the same vein.

Meanwhile, during this raging winter, Julia sends lots of group updates about how much better the weather in Atlanta is because she's always lobbying for Team Butter to move down there. (I love Atlanta, but I'm not sure my liver could handle living in close proximity to the fun that is Julia and Finch.) So, I wake up and brew some coffee, checking my e-mail before I hit my news feeds. I notice there's a note from Julia, probably telling us the tulips are blooming or they're on a picnic or something.

This morning's so cold that the windows in the kitchen actually have frost on the inside and it's snowing like *The Day After Tomorrow* out there. (Also a top ten favorite movie for the cheese factor. Would be top five if Will Smith/alien life-forms were involved.)

Surprisingly, Julia's e-mail is somewhat sheepish. *"I guess weather karma finally caught up with me. Yesterday it took me three hours to go five miles because we got half an inch of snow and no one down here knows how to drive."*

Fletch comes into the kitchen, swaddled in layers of flannel pajamas and a turtleneck, topped with a bathrobe so thick it could double as a coat. I relay her message and then I glance at one of the headlines on my news feed.

I say, "Whoa, check this out—says here that Atlanta got three inches of snow and everyone abandoned their cars."

Fletch looks from his polar garb to the frosty sliding glass door, shaking his head as he surveys the deluge of fresh flakes filling the canal we had to hack out between two frozen feet of snow in order for the dogs to do their business. We've been shoveling, salting, sanding, and deicing now for four months, as it snows three inches here approximately every five minutes. At this point, we don't know how to *not* navigate the Arctic clime.

"Huh," he says, rubbing the sleep out of his eyes. "With our fat coats and our snow tires and our superior shoveling skills, we'd be weather gods down there."

The imagery makes me laugh, so I'm inspired to write a quick "twisted" Facebook post about Julia's note and weather karma and include a shot of Fletch driving while wearing his Canadian-down-filled, coyote-fur-trimmed *Nanook of the North* coat.

By the way, why does he look cute in down, while I resemble wildlife/movie monsters?

At the end of the post, I make sure to say that I hope the storm wasn't too scary and that no one's been inconvenienced in my favorite town and I wish everyone smooth sailing across calm seas.

Somehow this post ranks up there with disasters such as running the Exxon Valdez aground, introducing New Coke, and casting Lindsay Lohan to play Liz Taylor in that Lifetime movie.

The outrage comes fast and furious.

As I hadn't read the newspaper and didn't know that some people had indeed had a very scary experience, and because I wasn't actually poking fun at anyone, I could not understand the vitriol. Like, why would I laugh at those who live in a place where they don't usually have inclement weather? I thought it was clear that I was actually *envious* of them.

Obviously, it was not.

On top of the general outrage at my blatant insensitivity, my comments section turns into a massive North versus South battleground as potshots fly back and forth across the Mason-Dixon line.

Apparently NO ONE is over the War Between the States.

Did not see that coming.

I apologize, I retract, I rescind, but apparently that's not enough and somehow over the course of the day, it becomes MY fault that the city of Atlanta doesn't have the infrastructure to deal with snow removal, and MY fault that their mayor didn't declare a state of emergency until far too late, and MY fault that families had to sleep on the floors of the Home Depot because traffic was at a standstill.

Have I actually turned into a capricious god who controls the weather and no one told me?

E-mails pour in telling me I'm vile and that they'll never read my books again. They wish my Yankee ass was dead. They wish Fletch's Yankee ass was dead. They don't say anything about the dogs' Yankee asses, but I suspect they're on the bubble.

How did this happen?

I guarantee that tonight people like Jon Stewart and Jimmy Kimmel will make plenty of jokes about the storm, far less good-spirited. Will folks raise their pitchforks to them as well?

After I put out a heartfelt apology, explaining everything within its context, and say I'm sorry again and again, I begin to hear from other readers who are deeply disappointed that I have given in to a vocal minority and thought I had more strength in my own convictions.

Every move I make is the wrong one.

I take to the basement and try to shake it all off while I sand and wax.

Over the course of three days, my posts go viral, reaching more than half a million people, *none of whom like me.*

I am the worst self-promoter ever.

How did something so innocuous and good-spirited turn so ugly so fast? It was almost as though people were sitting by their computers waiting to find a fight they could join.

Fortunately, the uproar's short-lived, because even though the Internet is forever, there's always something newer and more scandalous around the corner.

After this I resolve to limit my time online, especially in regard to social networking. If I'm truly to live a life without regrets, then I have to stop pursuing something that brings no tangible joy.

This should be easy because I've fallen out of love with Face-book. First, I want to be the kind of friend who hears about others' milestones in person. I hate learning about major life events buried in a timeline between photos of fresh pedicures and pictures of lunch. When someone close to me has a baby or goes through emergency surgery or suffers a loss, they deserve more than a "like." A click should never take the place of real interaction.

Plus, I almost never visit anyone else's page because I'm uncomfortable with all the fighting and the general mood of disrespect. There's an excellent reason someone came up with the expression to never talk about politics or religion in polite company because *it quickly ceases to be polite.*

I mean, I don't want to have to find a new plumber when I

see that my current guy "likes" the a-holes who are always protesting at soldiers' funerals. I've spent four years in search of a decent colorist in the suburbs; I don't want to have to start the process all over again when my present stylist reposts an anti-Semitic rant. And please don't give me a front-row seat to a family about to disintegrate as a couple of ex-high-school sweethearts rediscover each other online, flirtations growing more and more blatant over status updates.

While none of the above are true stories (to my knowledge), the fact that this does happen all day, every day, is what makes me want to run away in the first place.

And what of the Fear of Missing Out? And the exclusionary and incendiary nature of strategically timed unfollows, or of not accepting friend requests? Personally, I stopped following those who follow me on Twitter because the interface changed and now I don't know how to add the new people. And I feel bad that my not following back might possibly upset someone, even though it has nothing to do with them and everything to do with my not knowing how to find that screen.

As for privacy? I'll never fathom how so many hesitate so little to share even the most esoteric details of their lives online because almost every Web site out there makes it so damn easy.

"Do you want to tweet about your So-and-So Pizza Company order to your followers?"

NO. NO, I DO NOT.

Number one, why would I believe I'm so important that it's imperative the universe be informed in real time that I'm having extra pineapple on my So-and-So's Famous Blue Hawaiian 'Za, and number two, why would I invite others to have an opinion on what I've chosen for dinner?

It's not so much that I don't care if a follower doesn't like pineapple pizza, it's just that . . . wait, actually, I *don't* care if someone who isn't eating with me doesn't like pineapple because that has no bearing on my life. Will this knowledge make me a better person? Will I be edified? Informed? Inspired? Spurred into action? Overcome by beauty? No? Then there's no reason to offer this information. Unless I'm trying to figure out whether or not to take an upside-down cake to a couple's next dinner party, then their pineapple preferences are their own damn business.

If I don't ask, then no one is obligated to tell.

And what's the benefit of sharing data on who we're with and what we're doing, other than it makes it easier for companies to target us with their marketing? Is this about saving five percent on our next latte? Really? Personally, I believe my privacy is worth more than thirteen cents. Or does this desire to share speak to a yearning for connection? In my opinion, anyone who wants to connect should put down her damn phone and actually talk to the person sitting in front of her.

Going forward, I'll ask myself if my words or images enlighten, amuse, or entertain, and if it's none of the above, then I need not post. I decide I should maintain current accounts because lots of nice people do offer that which is enlightening, amusing, and entertaining (like the watermelon lady) and for that, I'm thankful. I figure I'll occasionally share my interests, such as book suggestions, but I'm no longer going to invest the time or the effort it takes to garner "likes."

I'm through stopping midconversation to post a funny quote because I feel like it's my job. I'm done creating "link-bait." I'm going to *be* in the moment rather than upload the moment, because the purpose of my life is not public consumption.

I don't want to measure my success in clicks.

I don't want my value as a person determined by retweets.

When I die, I guarantee I won't care how many Tumblr followers I've had.

And why is anyone following me in the first place, as I've yet to determine where I'm going?

Satisfied with my decision to take a giant step back, I pour my nervous energy into my newest find, a freshly glued fifteen-dollar rocking chair that I've made fabulous with mint green paint edged with golden gilding.

I want to learn from this situation and to figure out what's next. Yet I'm thrown by how quickly people turned on me.

With Ed Lover spinning the hits of 1992, I buff the rocker's spindles to a glossy sheen. I reflect on the clusterfuckery of the past couple of days, trying to reframe the experience into something positive.

All I can do is to take comfort in knowing that at least no one can post naked pictures of me.

Despite WEATHERGATE, my tour proceeds without a hitch, and I'm psyched to have Fletch join me for the Florida portion. He said the logistics seemed too complicated so he wouldn't come, but as he sat there alone in our freezing cold house, looking outside at the glacial monotony of gray and white, he wondered if he'd made the wrong call. And then Loki began to slowly and methodically lick a portion of the couch while staring directly at Fletch.

Lick, stare. Lick, stare.

That's when Fletch snapped . . . into action. In the hour I spent having a drink with a reporter in Jacksonville, he not only booked a flight, but arranged for a cat sitter, and found a local kennel where all the staff brought their pit bulls to work, so he knew our guys would be well cared for.

My Florida events are extra festive with him in tow, and we return from tour refreshed, relaxed, and ever so slightly tanned. Even the dogs are reinvigorated, ecstatic to have gone to the kind of happy-fun camp they didn't even know existed.

The only odd bit is what happens after we've been home for a few days. Fletch's contact information is listed on my Web site in case any 501(c) organizations have a charitable request. Once in a great while he'll receive an appeal that, um . . . stretches the boundaries of charity, like when a husband asked Fletch to have me call his wife. Apparently the man had cheated on her and he figured if the entreaty to forgive him came from me, she would comply.

Oh, honey.

No.

Fletch comes into my office with a sheet of paper. "You need to read this to believe it."

He hands me the printout of an e-mail. Someone's contacted him to say how *he's* really the star of the show and it's not fair that I'm always going around saying I'm his meal ticket.

Beg your pardon?

"He says I tell everyone I'm your 'meal ticket'? I mean, (a) horseshit, and (b) since when? Have I ever once said anything like that? Because I vaguely recall you working a lot of thankless jobs to support us while I tried to build a career," I reply. "If I'm your meal ticket, then it took you eight years of starving before I figured out a damn thing."

"Yeah, the meal ticket part's news to me," he says. "Keep going, it gets better."

I read how the man says he approached me in Florida, asking to have a book autographed for a friend with cancer. According to him, I snapped, "Signing's over, go home," which would never happen for myriad reasons. I'm thoroughly wigged out that some stranger would e-mail Fletch to lie about me as a way to curry favor. How bizarre is that?

The more I sit with this, the angrier I get. "This is so creepy. If he'd actually come to the event, he'd have seen that you were *there with me the entire time.* This is why I want to learn self-defense. Oh, I will karate chop a lying motherfucker. Ninja all over his deceitful ass. So, what are you going to do? Are you writing back to him? Will you tell him to pound sand?"

"Absolutely not. What's my policy?"

I sigh. *"'Don't engage The Crazy.'"*

"Bingo." He goes to sit down with the dogs on the bed across from my desk. The girls, who collectively can't weigh more than one hundred and fifteen pounds, are sprawled out to all four corners. Fletch manages to wedge his way in, so they both place their heads in his lap. "Honestly, I figured you'd get a kick out of this. I'm sorry, I didn't think you'd be mad."

"I'm not mad, just . . . bothered. I feel like everyone's ganging up on me lately. You don't believe him, right?"

Fletch laughs hard enough to disturb the dogs. "Please, I was there, I know you, and like you'd *ever* pass up the chance to give someone your autograph. Just thought it was funny, that's all."

I nod as I don't have anything else to say.

Fletch scans my face, noting how I'm gritting my teeth.

"So, sure you're okay?"

I exhale loudly. "Yeah, I'm Kool and the Gang," I say, even though my mind's still turning. This letter isn't of any more significance than that of a lonely person seeking Fletch's attention. And who wouldn't want to know him? He's funny, he's considerate, and he has exactly the right kind of glue for any task.

But when this letter's coupled with all the other events of the past month—the doctor's visit, the social media snafu, the surprising ease with which we were both able to leave the house—the message I receive is clear: I need to double down on my bucket list, lest I regret it. That which went wrong, and that which went right, would have been made easier if I were more focused on my goals.

And now I know exactly where to begin.

"All righty, I'm going to go reglue the new rolltop secretary. Gimme a shout if you need something." He rises to leave and comes over to give me a hug.

Right before he descends the stairs, I call after him.

"Hey, Fletch, what do you think of the name Yardapple Vintage?" I ask.

"For what?"

"For the furniture business I'm starting. I'm calling it Yardapple because remember last fall when I wanted to cut down those trees, but I discovered that the horrible, spotty, misshapen little apples were actually tart, juicy, and totally worm-free? Then I used them to make our Thanksgiving pies, and we were all amazed at how something that originally looked so ugly could be repurposed into utter perfection? I feel like 'Yardapple Vintage' tells the story about discovering the magnificent in that which seems like a lost cause."

"I like it." Smiling, he leans against my doorjamb, arms crossed against his flannel-clad chest. "So, you're finally turning pro."

I say, "Starting a new business has been on my list, and this furniture stuff happened so organically that it seems like a good fit."

As soon as I declare my intention, I'm overcome with self-doubt. I believe I have a decent skill set in regard to finding great pieces and giving them interesting finishes, but do I really?

Or am I just fooling myself?

As a kid, I remember bringing home a picture of a bird I'd colored because I was so proud of it. Mine was no typical second-grade scrawl, oh, no. I hated to throw around the word "prodigy" and yet, there I was. As I walked home on that windy day, I imagined the bidding wars the local Boston museums would wage over my masterpiece. Having my genius recognized was enough, of course, yet if a curator or a discerning collector chose to write me the kind of check that would buy Barbie a vacation Dreamhouse, well, that was okay, too.

While stopped on a gusty corner, I noticed a bunch of paper

on the ground. I saw the same bird drawing my class had been doing, but this one was terrible! The artist clearly had no concept of staying within the lines and his color choices were simply abysmal. Pedestrian. What kind of savage would choose Burnt Sienna for the beak? News flash—Burnt Orange is the new black. And what kind of lunatic would opt for Periwinkle over Cornflower for the sky? No one was going to put this rank amateur's work on the fridge, let alone in a museum.

Then I noticed that *my* name was on the upper right-hand corner of the page. These were my dropped papers, caught by the wind.

I realized I'd accidentally judged the drawings based on actual merit, rather than filtering the page through my eight-year-old, narcissistic haze. What a kick in the Toughskins.

What if I'm only talented with the furniture because I've decided I'm talented?

What if all those nice people on Facebook have given me an inflated sense of self? As treacherous as social networking can be with all the negativity, there's an equal danger of receiving undeserved head-pats.

"Is this the worst idea I ever had?" I ask.

"No, that was the day you tried to cut your own hair," Fletch replies.

(Sidebar: If you're not someone who revels in wearing hats for two straight months, don't trim your own bangs.)

"Then am I delusional for believing my stuff's good enough to sell?"

With great confidence, he replies, "Of course not."

"Are you humoring me? How can I tell this isn't The Bird Picture, Part II?"

He frowns at me. "The what?"

I wave him off. "Long story. But how can I be sure that I

won't humiliate myself trying to sell my work, and that people aren't going to post photos of my Charlie Brown dressers on snark sites with the caption, 'Oh, honey'?"

"Simple," he replies. "Because I say so. And you *know* I never engage The Crazy."

14.

Spring Fever

"I said, 'I'm sorry, I'm not giving up my underpants. I know that I'm supposed to, but I refuse and you can't make me.'"

"You fought with the nurse?"

"I wouldn't say I fought. It was more of . . . okay, yes, I fought."

Joanna and I are at a sushi joint together as there's been a small break in the weather and I'm finally comfortable driving thirty miles south to see her. (Am not nearly as much of a weather god as Fletch.) Although we don't normally meet up often enough, we've managed a few outings lately. Last month, we saw *The Barber of Seville* and a couple of weeks ago, we hit a concert with one of her daughters, which was a rare school night treat.

(Sidebar: Why am I so insane about staying home on school nights? I'm not in school, I don't have children in school, I have a DVR to not miss any Important Television, and I work for myself so I can sleep/rise any damn time I want. School nights *shouldn't* be an issue, and yet.)

(Additional sidebar: Sometimes I don't understand my own

stupid motivations and proclivities, like why I refuse to turn on the air conditioner before May first or the heat before November first. What do I win by freezing or sweltering completely by choice, save for not violating one of my long-standing, nonsensical rules? Fletch ignores these rubrics, of course, as we all know how he feels about The Crazy. He's completely bypassed my odd prejudices by installing a few Nest thermostats, which I haven't learned to operate.)

(Third and final sidebar: If in an impotent rage you try to smash a Nest thermostat with the heel of a loafer, you'll be unpleasantly surprised at how sturdy it is. Also, I find these thermostats overeager, always springing to attention whenever I pass by their sensors, like they're somehow looking to engage me. Recently, one of the sensors kept reminding me to change my furnace filters every time I walked into the dining room. Listen, when I want an appliance's advice, I will ask for it. Until then, STFU, Nest.)

I've been telling Joanna about my "photo session," which turned out to include minor surgery. After seeing my squatters up close and personal, the doctor excised them in order to have the pathology run. Thankfully, all came back clear. However, prior to the event, I was waiting in pre-op and I was told to change into a surgical gown long before they were supposed to wheel me away, meaning I'd be lying there for an hour without benefit of underwear, which, no.

Not happening.

I continue. "Turns out being a jerk was the right thing to do—they improvised with a pair of these stretchy hospital boy shorts and said they'd cut them off when I was under in the OR so I didn't have to be commando while I waited. I also kept my pearls on."

"Everything's okay? I'm so sorry. I feel like a bad friend that I didn't even know any of this was happening," Joanna apologizes.

"That's because I didn't announce it on social media. Privacy's still an option, even in the digital age." Here's yet another issue I have with social media: Vaguebooking, in which a poster alludes to something being amiss, but won't actually spill said beans. For example, posting a hospital selfie, and when everyone responds with, "OMG, are you okay? What's going on?" replying, "I'd rather not talk about it."

THEN WHY START THE CONVERSATION?

Or how about when a person publishes something along the lines of, "This has been the worst day EVAH," but then gets all closed-lipped about why it's been so bad. This is attention-seeking at its worst. At least with oversharing, followers have the satisfaction of learning what happened. Alluding to, and then not doling out, the gossip is simply annoying. No one wants to begin a book, only to have it snatched away right at the climax of the plot.

I explain, "When I saw you for the concert, I didn't want to mention it. I figured there was no reason to worry you over what was routine. See? All's well and no one had to stress."

"You could have told me," she insists.

"Yeah, but I'd have to use proper medical terminology and neither one of us likes to say those words."

"That is true." Joanna and I both graduated *summa cum modest* from Uptight University.

"Anyway, the worst part was when the anesthesiologist came in to say hello before it all happened, and I'm telling you, she was fifteen years old. She could have been in Anna's grade. No lie. I wanted to ask her if her mommy knew she was skipping Driver's Ed that day."

Joanna scoops up a bite of the tuna and avocado tartare appetizer. "Don't you hate that? When'd we get older than our doctors?"

"Seriously! But I kept my yap shut, thinking maybe I shouldn't inadvertently insult the person who's responsible for keeping me alive."

"Smart. Ever been under a general before?"

"No, that's why I was worried. You hear all these horror stories about simple stuff going awry, like when one of my favorite authors died during a routine chin tuck. I still feel terrible every time I think about poor Olivia Goldsmith—ever read *The First Wives Club*? There she was, looking forward to a new life with her twenty-year-old jawline, and within four minutes, that's it. Game over. She'd have never written such a tragic ending for one of her characters because no one would have believed it."

"I loved her books. What a heartbreak."

"Agreed. If only she held out a little longer, there'd have been a world of lower-impact cosmeceuticals she could have used instead of going under the knife. Awful, all the way around."

Personally, I'm fortunate to have handled the anesthesia well, even though I'd been cautioned it might take me hours to get my bearings. My only real experience with anesthesia was when sweet little Maisy had her surgeries and each time, it was a nightmare. The poor thing would pace around for hours in an agitated haze while I trailed behind her, making sure nothing happened to her stitches. But I guess my constitution differs from that of a pit bull because I woke up shortly after they'd finished with me and felt so good for the rest of the day that I wanted to finish painting the trim in my office.

(Sidebar: Big veto from Fletch on doing any work the rest of the day. He parked me on the couch, cued up *Frozen*, and demanded I rest. He also confiscated my paintbrushes.)

Right before the anesthesia was administered, Fletch and I had been watching CNN, which had the missing Malaysian plane story on a constant loop. To this day I'm absolutely obsessed with this mystery, because planes are not supposed to go missing. For years, Fletch had been promising me that airplanes don't just fall out of the sky or disappear, that there was no way my routine flight to New York would somehow divert to the Bermuda Triangle and vanish into thin air. (His business cards should read: *J. B. Fletcher, Not Engaging The Crazy Since 1994*.) But now that a massive 777 is gone without a trace? All bets are off, and suddenly, *Lost* seems so much more plausible.

Flight 370 must have been at the top of my mind during the surgery because the moment I came to, I asked the doctor if perhaps they'd located the plane *up there*. No one thought that was funny, save for me, who was braying like a jackass. Then the doctor explained how while I was under, she'd also removed the weird little cyst on my West Virginia that had formed after the World's Most Unfortunate Tick Bite two summers ago. She said I'd notice a few stitches and I'd likely have a scar. I replied, "Oh, no! That's going to ruin my porn career." Again, no one laughed.

So maybe I didn't handle the anesthesia *that* well.

(But I totally could have painted that trim.)

Joanna runs a hand through her never-once-colored hair. The parts that used to be pale blond have a few streaks of gray threaded in. With her fair coloring, she looks great au naturel. She's always been Team Minimal Processing. She didn't even own a hair dryer when we first met—unheard of in the Aqua Nettiest decade in history. I, on the other hand, can't even remember what my real hair color looks like. "That's why I plan to age gracefully. A face-lift can't go wrong if you don't have one. Your roots will never be a problem if you don't first bleach them."

In college, Joanna would occasionally let me turn her into a human Barbie styling head, but I haven't been allowed to lay a hand on her since the Great Crimping Calamity of 1990. "If you change your mind, I can help. You know the picture of us Anna took before the concert? I was playing with photo-editing software and I took twenty years off of both of us. I can PicMonkey you completely blond again, although I don't know how to give me back my standing thigh gap. Do you remember if I had a standing thigh gap?"

Joanna scrunches up her forehead in a way that's patently impossible for me. "A *what*?"

I swear standing thigh gaps are a thing, even though no one else in my orbit seems to have heard about them.

"Never mind. Did Anna enjoy the show?"

During the summer of 2011, Joanna and I took her daughter to see the *Glee* tour, and every single tween in the twenty-thousand-seat arena lost her shit when "Jessie's Girl" was performed. I was pleasantly surprised to realize this song meant something to an entirely new generation. I'd turned to Joanna and said, "How mad is Rick Springfield right about now?" The whole thing became a running joke, so when I saw that Rick Springfield was coming to an auditorium near me, I bought us tickets.

(Sidebar: Ticket prices for his shows have dramatically increased since I last saw him in South Bend, circa 1982. As have the size of the underwear I'd have chucked at the stage. I guess that's how inflation works.)

"She did! She kept marveling at all the crazy women, though. They were a trip."

We attended the concert out of a sense of nostalgia, but that wasn't the case with everyone else sitting around us. Because I bought tickets the day they went online, our seats were smack in the middle of the Serious Fan section. All around us, ladies were chattering about their most recent Rick Springfield fan cruise, outdoing one another with the depth and breadth of their Springfield-related trivia knowledge, and wearing homemade

shirts emblazoned with slogans that read THIS IS MY SEVEN-
TEENTH SHOW!

Which . . . really?

I couldn't mock anyone for being there because *I* was there.

But, *really?*

Seventeen shows?

I mean, (a) I didn't realize he'd been so prolific in the thirty-
two years since I'd seen him last and, (b) *really?*

Hell, I can't imagine doing *anything* seventeen times, let alone
seeing Rick Springfield that often. Sure, I worshipped him when
I was younger and his music made my prepubescent heart ache.
Who could be so coldhearted to that beautifully soulful man who's
done *every*thing for her, while she's done *nothin'* for him? But if
someone were to offer me the chance to not only solve the mess in
the Middle East, but also wear Cameron Diaz's body to my thirti-
eth high school reunion and the only stipulation was to see a show
seventeen times, I'd be all, "No, thanks. School night."

"Weren't you surprised at how charming he was?" I ask. I was
vaguely concerned that everyone around us would be up and
dancing because that seemed exhausting. I didn't want to *rock*; I
wanted to *sit*. But the format of his performance was a nice surprise, almost more of a spoken word show. He spent most of the
night on a stool, surrounded by various guitars, explaining the
backstory for each of his songs before singing them.

Well, there's nothing I love more than a compelling narra-
tive. A couple of years ago when his memoir came out, I was all
smug and "good for you, sweetie," but at the concert I realized
that someone who's written hundreds of songs is as much a writer
as he is a singer. He was both charismatic and witty—always a
winning combination.

At the end of the night, he held up an early copy of *Magnificent Vibrations,* his first novel, about a man who finds a book con-
taining God's cell phone number. I made a mental note to preorder

the book because if it was half as engaging as he'd been onstage, I was sure to love it.

I'd gone into the night all judgmental about women stuck thirty years ago, but what's more likely is these true fans had been evolving right along with him.

"We'll have to remember to buy his book," she agrees. "So, roomie, what else is up?"

"You're never going to believe this—I'm having an art show! Because I'm an artist. Remind me to shop for a beret." I grab a spider roll, dipping it in a mixture of soy sauce and wasabi. I'm not great with chopsticks, so I always end up shoving the whole piece in my mouth, instead of trying to take down the roll in bites. I figure I'd rather have a mouthful for a second than have dribbled sauce stains on myself all day.

Joanna's whole face lights up. "You're kidding! You found a place to sell your furniture?"

I nod, needing a second to chew before I can answer. "Yes! Laurie's sister Wendy's an artist and she's had a couple of shows at a gallery in Lake Forest. We were all at dinner and I showed her some shots of my newest pieces. Did you check out the Union Jack dresser I made for my office?"

"Yes, very cool."

"Wendy really liked my stuff, so she told the gallery owners about me. I went in to meet with them and the first thing out of my mouth was that I'm not an artist. I'm just a person who puts paint on furniture. But then I told them about how I salvage and refurbish pieces, and they explained that this dovetails completely into their mission statement. The place is called Re-Invent and it's all about finding new uses for old things. So I'm having an art opening in May. Because I'm an artist."

Joanna balls her fists in victory. "Congratulations! I'm excited to see what else you've been doing! I loved the pieces we saw in the

basement at your Christmas party. What's the gallery like? Are the owners nice?"

My words come out in a rush, because I'm so psyched about the show. "Kind of amazing. Aside from the actual gallery, there's a big retail operation with fun and funky pieces from more than a hundred local artists. One guy does sculptures out of old metal and there's a dinosaur made from bicycle chains. Fletch wants it, but where do we put a bicycle-chain dinosaur?"

"The yard?"

"Wouldn't it rust?"

"Good point."

While I talk, Joanna munches a smoked salmon roll. "Get this, the owners are a couple of women in their twenties. They both love art and studied it in college, so they decided to make a go at owning a gallery. They've each worked, like, three jobs apiece to get the place up and running, but now it's a viable business. Can you imagine being in your early twenties, owning a business, and meeting payroll? Wait, I'm sure *you* actually could, but I was still going to fraternity parties at that age. How could I have managed a business when I couldn't even manage to find my bra? Or could you imagine us partnering in a business back then?"

Joanna peels open a piece of edamame and plucks out the tender green peas. "Ha! I guarantee if we had, we wouldn't be having lunch together right now. Because I'd be dead and you'd be in jail."

I point out, "Unless the judge were sympathetic to people who snap when someone chews that much ice and keeps dropping the damn answering machine." We eventually had to tie our answering machine to the coffee table hostage-style after she knocked it onto the floor for the millionth time.

"If you'd gone to prison, then you could have written *Orange Is the New Black*."

I spoon a glob of wasabi into my dish of soy sauce and mix the ingredients together. I like my sushi spicy enough to invoke tears. "Right? Every time someone buys *Bitter* now, I wonder if they're reading it, all, *'When does she become a lesbian and go to jail?'*"

We both sample pieces of today's special roll—a concoction made of white tuna, cream cheese, and raspberry sauce. What initially sounded odd is actually fairly spectacular. With our mouths full, we both point at the plate. I nod and Joanna gives a thumbs-up.

"So is the gallery show part of your bucket list?"

I take a sip of my tea to stop the wasabi-based fire that's raging in my mouth and sinuses. "I wanted to start a business, so this totally counts." I amend my statement. "If people buy anything, that is. Otherwise, I'm still just a hobbyist. Oh, speaking of my list, I've got to head back home by one today. I have my first session with the nutritionist because developing healthier habits is on the list, too."

"Wait a minute; how are you seeing a nutritionist when you have a registered dietician right here in front of you? Plus, I'm free."

I look her directly in her eyes. "Do you really want to be the person who tries to come between me and my macaroni and cheese?"

She blanches. "I do not."

"I think over the last twenty-nine years of friendship, we've figured out our boundaries." Joanna, Julia, and I are going to the beach in September, after their kids go back to school. We could save two hundred dollars apiece if we bunked together, but we figure our friendship is worth more than that, so we'll each have our own rooms again.

Joanna snatches a raspberry off the plate of the day's special. "If you're seeing someone for dietetic counseling, then should we skip the mochi today?"

I put down my chopsticks. "Absolutely not. We're Team Butter and this may be the last time I'm allowed to have dessert."

My session with the nutritionist isn't at all what I expected. I thought Michelle would provide a rigid eating plan, cutting out all processed flour and dairy and refined sugar, and I'd diligently follow it until I couldn't take it anymore, backflipping into a vat of buttercream frosting.

Instead, she urges me to eat whatever I want, with the stipulation that I follow three simple rules.

First, I need to mindfully eat. Whatever I choose—and it can be literally anything my heart and palate desires—I need to pay attention to what I'm eating. I have to savor each bite. If I'm having, say, Port Salut cheese on a toasted crostini, I must be conscious of the interplay between the creaminess of the cheese and the tang of the sea salt and rosemary seasoning on the bread. I should note how the bite feels in my mouth. I should enjoy and appreciate every bite of every meal.

The second rule is to note my appetite cues, and quit once I'm satisfied. We discuss a hunger chart, where One is absolutely ravenous and Ten is beyond stuffed, ready to pass out in a food coma. As I learn about these cues, I can think of so many times I've proceeded past the point of satisfaction to uncomfortably full.

I learn that by taking a step back and really noticing my bad habits, it's easier to make changes. I realize that I often consume too much at dinner because Fletch is the world's slowest eater. (Seriously. He could win a competition.) He literally takes forty-five minutes to finish what's on his plate. Most nights, I'd find myself taking extra just to keep him company while he methodically chewed every bite nine million times. But now that I'm paying attention, I'm better prepared to stop once I've reached Seven or Eight on the scale. When I get to that point, I immediately put my plate in the dishwasher and I fix a decaf cappuccino. That way, I still have the enjoyment of sitting at the dinner table without feeling too stuffed to actually head down to the basement and work on furniture for my upcoming show.

Michelle's third rule is to completely eliminate any food-based guilt. She says the guilt is useless and just makes us miserable. The more we look at food as fuel and the more we take emotions out of eating, the more likely we are to moderate ourselves. I guarantee this is true and all I have to do is look at the times I tried the Atkins Diet. I remember once watching a kid eat a waffle and it was all I could do not to rip it out of his toddler fingers and run away with it. Every time I sit down to eat, I'm to tell myself, "I can have whatever I want."

Michelle bills herself as The Fat Nutritionist, as her mission isn't about making her clients skinny. Rather, her goal is to help people normalize their relationships with food.

She makes a lot of sense.

(Sidebar: She's Canadian and she promises me that the folks on *Love It or List It* aren't representative of her fellow countrymen. She also mentioned that maybe I'd be more mindful about my eating if I weren't shouting at the ridiculous home owners on television while having dinner.)

A few weeks into working with Michelle, I have to take an overnight trip down to Purdue because I'm speaking to a couple of classes. Along the way, I stop at McDonald's for a double Filet-O-Fish meal. For the first time, I notice that the drive-through has calorie counts posted and I'm shocked at how calorically dense the sandwich is. (I blame the tartar sauce.) But instead of feeling remorseful and overindulgent while I have my lunch, I mindfully eat the sandwich from Schererville all the way to Morocco. I finish when I feel satisfied and, because I've eaten the sandwich so methodically, for the first time in recorded history, I don't finish my fries. And because I'm satisfied, I don't stop later for a Dairy Queen butterscotch-dipped cone.

Granted, I won't ever be thin eating this way, but I suspect I could eventually be less fat.

It's a start.

I'm shocked at how the student body's changed since I graduated. When did kids become so somber and serious? I have a number of events throughout the day, from coffees to lunch to receptions, and I'm struck by everyone's intensity. My contacts in the Liberal Arts department confirm my suspicions that the good-time-party-uselessness of the eighties and early nineties has morphed into an ultracompetitive pressure cooker and that no one's allowing themselves any downtime. They're all driving themselves too hard.

(Sidebar: I also suspect that there's no way I'd get into Purdue if I were to apply now, but I don't mention this.)

I had a speech prepared, but I decided to freestyle instead because I'd written it based on wrong assumptions. My message to the students is that they're doing a great job at academics, but that they also need to cut themselves a break.

I explained how the most important thing I learned in college was to navigate the interpersonal aspect. I instructed them to, at least once a day, step away from a screen and sit down across from a friend to engage in conversation. Have fun. I landed my first professional job not because I was an academic trailblazer (clearly), but because I knew a ton of people from hanging out in the bars and one of these friends introduced me to her mom, who helped me get an interview. I took it from there, but if it hadn't been for how social I was, I'd have never had the chance. I explained to these students that they don't want to hit their forties and realize they've never cut loose or been irreverent.

In a world where every moment of these kids' lives has been orchestrated and micromanaged from the minute they could be taken from soccer practice to violin lessons to dance class to tutoring, they looked at me like I'd just revealed the Holy Grail. I came home feeling like I'd accomplished something important. I'm not sure what, exactly, but I imagine it was bucket list–worthy.

Although maybe the advice I gave them wasn't different from what Michelle's been telling me about finally, mindfully, giving myself a damn break.

I've lost five pounds in the six weeks that I've been working with Michelle. This is significant because I haven't yet actively tried to lose weight, as I plan to focus more on fitness over the summer. I've found that the more I allow myself to have what I want, the less I'm liable to take.

This spring has been hectic, as I've been hustling to complete my furniture collection. A week before my show, the paperback version of *Tao of Martha* comes out and I have to go to New York to attend some events.

I've just boarded the plane home. I'm all strapped into my seat and trying to figure out what movie I'd like to watch on my iPad (maybe *Wolf of Wall Street* since I'm in a New York state of mind) when I see a familiar face in the aisle.

Holy crap.

Rick Springfield's on this flight.

He's seated one row back and one seat over from me and I crack up every time a woman over the age of thirty-five boards the plane, spots Rick, and tries desperately not to lose her shit.

He's pretty nonchalant about the whole thing, as he's been causing this reaction for more than thirty years.

That's when I realize—this is it!

This is my chance to meet an icon!

I immediately download his book (having previously forgotten) so when I speak with him, I won't be lying when I say I bought it. I start working myself into a frenzy over the opportunity, but then I realize that's a mistake. I decide I'm not going to waste my time planning what to say when we're inevitably standing next to each other waiting to disembark. I don't want to sound phony and rehearsed. I hope to have a genuine, albeit brief chat while the ground crew attaches the gangway. I can't orchestrate a moment—I need to just let it happen.

To take my mind off of the general OMG-ery of the circumstances, I begin to watch my movie and . . . I quickly discover exactly how much gratuitous nudity *The Wolf of Wall Street* contains. There's a lot. So much, in fact.

Full frontal. Back frontal. From underneath frontal.

Perhaps Mr. Springfield and I will discuss my penchant for watching porn on a crowded airplane, as he has a bird's-eye view of my screen.

Nudity aside, the movie's kind of great and I spend the rest of the flight in a blind fury over Leo's never winning an Oscar. Good Lord, Academy, what does that poor man need to do to convince you he's worthy of a win? He *was* Gatsby, okay? *He was Gatsby.* And he's absolutely been Jordan Belfort, Howard Hughes, and Frank Abagnale, Jr. to boot. What of Romeo and of Jim Carroll and of J. Edgar Hoover? Why do you discount him so? Do you not want him to draw you like one of his French women, Academy members? Because at this point, y'all don't deserve it. I hope this kid somehow finds comfort in his millions and his supermodel girlfriends, because this shit is not right.

Our flight goes quickly, and before I know it, I'm standing next to Rick in the aisle. I smile at him, he smiles at me, and we have a quick chat about his new book, which was released on the same day as the *Tao* paperback. We speak briefly about publishing and writing and book tours and at no point do I come across as a screaming, seventeen-shirt-wearing fangirl. Instead, we're two peers ever so briefly discussing that which we have in common.

We have only a moment, but it's the right moment.

I don't ask him to pose for a selfie with me, because I want to act like I've been here before. I know the adage is "pictures or it didn't happen" but *I'll* know it happened.

Because I have the checkmark on my bucket list to prove it.

People not only attend my furniture show, but in the first two weeks, they buy up more than half my inventory. While I'm not going to retire early due to my sales, I've definitely recouped all initial investments and already turned a small profit. I'm not sure I have the means or wherewithal to become a Design Mogul, but I've definitely started something here. There's a photo floating around the Internet of the Beatles performing in front of eighteen people, with the caption that all artists have to start someplace.

This is my someplace.

Overall, I feel like I'm emerging from a long, bitter winter and I'm not sure if that's literal or figurative. I can't put my finger on how any one specific change has had an impact, but I feel like my whole trajectory is shifting and that I might finally be pointed in the right direction.

Which, right now, looks like Italy.

15.

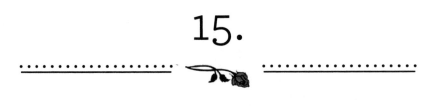

PARCHI E RICREAZIONE

I leave for Italy today.

By myself, instead of my original idea to travel with my Italian class.

And I'm so nervous that I may throw up.

I can't believe I'm doing this. Why did I consider this trip to be a good idea? I'm not someone who goes places just for fun. I was right not to have had wanderlust for so long. In fact, I'm *all about* the staycation. I enjoy being in my house to the point that I totally empathize with people who become agoraphobic. Like, I could see how it happens. Between pizza delivery, Peapod grocery service, and Amazon Prime, I find very few reasons to leave the premises and I'm fine with that! More than fine, even.

Content. Happy. Possibly even euphoric.

Nothing gives me greater pleasure than to say yes, only to have my plans fall through at the last minute and I can take off my regular-people clothes and redon my paint-splattered yoga pants. Dorothy Gale was onto something when she said that there's no place like home. Granted, I'm a nursery of raccoons shy of going

Grey Gardens myself, but, still, I feel like Big and Little Edie Beale were onto something.

(Sidebar: Although a "nursery" of raccoons is the proper term for a group or pack, a "gaze" of raccoons is also an acceptable expression. Look at us, learning things together!)

What the hell am I doing, boarding a plane that will take me five thousand miles away from everyone and everything I ever loved? What kind of Ambien-induced haze was I in that I considered foreign travel a good idea for a bucket list item? I'd like a bucket right now . . . so I can vomit into it.

Unlike so many others my age, I wasn't accustomed to traveling anywhere with Fletch, save for our recent trip to Florida and a couple of long weekends, because we were dead broke for most of the 2000s. When we were busy cobbling together mini-pizzas out of stale hamburger buns and canned parmesan cheese in an apartment where the lights had been cut off, jaunts across the pond weren't exactly at the top of our agenda.

Once we got our financial shit together, I suppose we didn't travel because trip planning seemed like such an enormous undertaking and I am, at my core, not always motivated to put forth the effort. Case in point? I used to suggest we keep a bucket in our old town house pantry to compensate for not having a bathroom on the first floor. For some reason, this bothered His Royal Highness very much, while I maintain it totally could have worked. Plus, we hated our neighbors, so sloshing the bucket on their patios could have been a rather elegant solution, you know?

(Sidebar: Fletch insists this is why we can't have nice things.)

Interestingly, planning this trip *has* been an undertaking, but I've actually relished the process. First of all, I've loved learning the language over the past year. The prospect of Italian travel as my end goal made the experience all the more meaningful. I paid attention to the language's nuances not because the difference between the formal and casual way to say "excuse me" would be on a test, but because I'm going to say this phrase to real people on Italian streets and I want to get it right.

Plus, I've had such fun poring over the Fodor's and Rick Steves guidebooks and running Google searches on stuff like "Ten Can't Miss Italian Destinations" and "A Beginner's Guide to Italy" and "Just Accept the Fact that You're Going to Eat Your Face Off, So Pack Elastic Waist Pants."

Actually, until now, I've been super-psyched for this trip ever since I booked it that miserably snowy day in winter. I'd been vacillating about specifically where to head because there's so much I want to see in Italy. Until I started my language class, I had no clue how diverse the different regions of Italy are. I assumed the country was one homogenous entity and figured anywhere I'd land would be representative. But that's like going to Fort Lauderdale and assuming the area will give you a taste of life in Seattle or Omaha or Dallas, when, really, the only commonality is our language and shared contempt for Katherine Heigl.

Although I desperately want to experience Venice and I'd love to trace my ancestral roots in Sicily (and hit the beach in Cinque Terre, shop in Milan, tour wineries in Tuscany, etc.), I decided to visit Rome first. I could fly there directly, so there'd be no chance of me causing an international incident in Berlin when I couldn't figure out how to change planes, plus I wouldn't run out of sights to see in a week. I found a reasonable air and land package, and before I could talk myself out of it, I made the nonrefundable purchase and then danced around my office for the next twenty minutes, so overcome with joy that I couldn't even sit down.

I originally planned to visit solo, as a character-building exercise, but shortly after I booked my trip, I realized that everything is more fun with Fletch. If I had him join me at the halfway point, I could still have my alone-in-a-foreign-country bucket list experience, before engaging in more couple-focused activities.

Because wasn't there something intrinsically *off* about going to the most romantic country on Earth without the person I love?

Plus, I figured if we went to Rome together, Fletch and I could have our picture taken in front of the Colosseum, which means I'd finally have the kind of photo that all my peers took twenty years ago on their honeymoon. Everyone I know has awesome shots of themselves smiling in front of the Eiffel Tower or Buckingham Palace or holding hands on a Balinese beach. When we got married, Fletch and I had two days together in Vegas after the ceremony and we didn't take a single picture, largely because everyone in our hotel was there for the Adult Film Awards and I really just wanted to forget the whole thing.

But I've yearned for my Kodak moment, too, damn it, enough to make **have a photo taken with Fletch somewhere recognizable** a bucket list item. So, I checked airfares and then I went downstairs to discuss the option with Fletch.

"Hey, how do you feel about coming with me to Rome for at least part of the time?" I asked.

Fletch looked up from his spot at the table where he was sketching out a fix for a broken dresser. Fletch accompanies me now when I go junking and his advice on what can and can't be repaired has been invaluable. This particular dresser had a wonky drawer, so he was trying to determine the best course of action. "Neutral?" he replied.

"What do you mean neutral? How is neutral an option?"

He tucked his pencil behind his ear while we talked. "I mean, in theory, it could be interesting. But if I could go anywhere, I'd pick Hawaii. I'd like to see the Schofield Barracks again."

"Are you kidding me?" I asked. "Given the opportunity, you'd rather see the place you were stationed in the army than one of the Seven Wonders of the World?"

"Yes."

"No."

Calmly, he replied, "Yes, and how is this an argument? You asked me my opinion and I offered it. I'd go to Hawaii."

What he failed to grasp was that this wasn't the answer I wanted.

"You'd prefer to visit the place you once did a whole bunch of push-ups and went thirty days without a shower rather than witness where the ancient Romans built aqueducts to bring water to a million citizens?"

Fletch rolled up the sleeves of his plaid shirt, which he wore layered over a thermal shirt over a T-shirt topping an undershirt because the house was still frigid at that point. Being so cold in my office was one of the reasons I picked Rome—all the guidebooks said it was sweltering in June and I longed to feel warm again.

Fletch explained, "We didn't shower when we were in the mountains doing a month of jungle ops. On base I showered every day. Sometimes twice if we were going out in Waikiki."

"Congratulations, Corporal Clean."

He returned his focus to his drawing, taking his pencil and tapping the diagram. "Hey, how do *you* feel if I were to replace the rotten drawer parts entirely? Just toss 'em because they're gross. I don't have the tools to do proper dovetail, but I can craft a decent routed lock joint with that leftover maple."

I swear some days I married Ron Swanson from *Parks and Recreation*. I know he's a fictional character, but every character has some basis in reality. I gritted my teeth as I answered him. "Neutral."

"Fair enough."

I sat down across from him. "You really wouldn't want to go to Rome? Even though they basically invented coffee?"

He glanced up from his plans. "The Ethiopians invented coffee."

Was that true? That sounded true.

Shit, I needed a new tactic.

"Okay, fine, maybe they didn't invent it, but they perfected it. They were all, 'Hey-a, Luigi, what if we put a little foamed milk in-a here-a?'"

"I'm sure that's exactly how it happened and I'm glad to see your Italian lessons have paid off."

"You have no curiosity about Europe whatsoever. Is that what you're saying?"

"Well, Europe *is* full of Europeans," he replied.

I feared this was the facial hair talking. He really didn't go The Full Swanson until he grew the beard and mustache a couple of years ago.

And did the *Parks and Rec* writers have a camera in my house? Granted, I'd never actually watched the show, but I'd seen enough Swanson GIFs to know that we may have had a case for likeness rights.

He continued. "Besides, if we have the cash to spare, I'd rather replace the carpet in the family room. Smells like the elephant house at the zoo in there. No, the *penguin* house, because it's wetter and more organic." He shuddered. "Awful. I'm embarrassed every time someone comes over. Bet we could knock that project out ourselves in a weekend."

That's when I lost it.

"No! No one puts replacing pee-stained carpet on their bucket list! A bucket list item is supposed to be *meaningful* and makes you put forth effort to learn and try and grow!" He started to say something, but I cut him off. "Don't you dare even draw a breath to tell me that replacing carpet takes effort. A bucket list item exists because once you check it off, you get to enjoy the memory of having done it *forever*! Plus, you'll have a shot of yourself standing in front of the Colosseum for perpetuity and YOU CAN'T DO THAT WITH BERBER."

He put down his pencil. "You already bought my ticket, didn't you?"

I couldn't hide my massive grin. "Let me just say this—we're both going to need a passport."

"Then I guess I'm going to Rome, too. But for now, I'm going to mend this drawer."

The best part of planning a trip like this is that there are a million little milestones to celebrate along the way. Take, for example, the day we went to Walgreens in Lake Bluff to have our passport photos taken.

(Sidebar: I'd planned to glam up as I do for any government ID, but at the last moment, I opted for a messy ponytail and a scowl, assuming that's how I'd appear to customs agents after an overseas flight.)

As soon as we told the cashier we wanted passport pictures, it's as though we entered some underworld crime lab. We were spirited away to the side of the store, where the employee flicked a switch that raised a background screen and closed the entire store's blinds. Start to finish, the whole process—which I assumed would be a bureaucratic nightmare—took four minutes. Then we went to the local passport office and filled out our forms, which took maybe ten minutes.

And less than two weeks later, my passport arrived, whereupon I whooped with such intensity that I lost my voice for three days.

(Sidebar: Thank you, US State Department, for not including weight on the passport application, as I'd prefer to not commit treason here.)

(Additional sidebar: Fletch said it would be a felony, not treason. Potato, po-tah-to. Either way, I appreciate it.)

For so long, I couldn't even imagine taking a trip overseas because I assumed the process was too daunting, but once I finally found my birth certificate (more on that shortly), securing a passport was easier than going to the DMV, especially the branch in Deerfield that accepts VISA but not MasterCard. How is that possible? I was unaware these two entities could even *be* separated. So, everyone who needs a new driver's license but has a MasterCard has to go down to the cigar store to use their ATM, whereupon they will immediately smell like a Macanudo for the rest of the day. The cigar store owner's delighted with the foot traffic and the fees, so he's happy to oblige, but that still doesn't explain what the State of Illinois's problem is with MasterCard in the first place.

Anyway, I even had an excellent experience applying for Global Entry/TSA Pre-Check status. After my passport was processed, I filled out my application online, and when I passed the initial screening, I had to go to the airport to meet with Homeland Security. I'd envisioned being chained to a table in a spotlit interrogation room where they'd grill me for hours. The reality was that I had a terrific chat with an officer who'd dated a friend of a friend. I didn't even have to write an essay on Why Terrorists Are Terrible. (Bit of a disappointment there, actually.) The only difficult portion of getting my Global Entry pass was figuring out where the office was located in Terminal Five at O'Hare.

(Sidebar: The Homeland Security office is downstairs, next to a McDonald's, and if you go at the beginning of March, you can get a Shamrock Shake to drink on the way home.)

Having put the pieces in place so easily, I was super-elated about the trip. Given the amount of research I'd done, and considering how smoothly everything had flowed thus far, I felt confident that I could handle any challenge that came my way. I didn't start to grow nervous until a few weeks ago at my last Italian class of the semester.

"You know Rome is the pickpocket capital of the world,

right?" one of the other students asked. (I'd been moved to a more advanced class partway through this semester, and regrettably, I hadn't learned anyone's names yet. And although I missed some of the other students I bonded with first semester, I appreciated the faster pace.) "You have to be on your guard every minute."

"But I travel to big cities all the time for work and I lived downtown for fifteen years," I said. "I know how to be on my guard. Italy can't be that different." I'd purchased an ugly black canvas purse with locking zippers and a cut-proof strap, figuring that would be insurance enough. I'd also made copies of all my documents, keeping one for myself, and sending one to Joanna for safekeeping, plus I burned the info onto a stick drive. I had a money belt, as well as a little envelope that attached to my bra to hold extra credit cards. I wasn't planning on wearing nice jewelry, either. Wasn't this enough?

"Oh, it *is* that different," another student intoned. "They'll bump into you and while they're apologizing, another person will be swiping your wallet, quick as can be. They work in teams. And all those kids running around who seem so cute? They're meant to be a distraction while their totally normal-looking parents steal your jewelry right off your arm. Boom. Gone. Gypsies. And don't even think about taking a bus or a train—they'll rob you blind."

"I had no idea," I admitted, my stomach beginning to twist.

"And make sure you have your RFID protectors over everything, including your passport. In Europe, they can use radio frequency to steal all your information—they don't even have to touch you. They can just pass really close by."

Panic began to creep in. "Shit."

"What about the store thing?" added the classmate sitting across from me. "You can't touch anything in a shop without permission. I learned that the hard way."

"What?"

What was going to happen to me in a store?

"It's rude for you to touch anything without asking. Also, you'd better make sure you greet them when you walk in or they'll yell at you."

"Is that insane? That seems insane considering what portion of their revenue comes from tourism," I said. The last time I actually left the country (1997, I think?) I remember Cancun feeling extra safe, like there was societal pressure to keep visitors secure to ensure the flow of tourist dollars. The Mexican people we met down there couldn't have been more solicitous or service-oriented. Maybe they hated us behind closed doors, but they sure were nice to us face-to-face.

My classmate shrugged. "That's Rome for you."

I began to worry that I'd prepared for the trip all wrong; instead of learning how to ask for directions or how to order in a restaurant, I should have been memorizing phrases such as:

Andare a farsi fottere, borseggiatore! (Go fuck yourself, pickpocket!)

Io ti schiaccerà il piccolo capo italiano come un brufolo. (I will pop your tiny Italian head like a zit.)

Sono una Americana, quindi ho una pistol. (I'm an American, so I have a gun.)

I figured the statement about the weapon would come across more menacing if I actually spoke it in low tones, so that's how I practiced.

Still, even with a semifunctional grasp on Italian profanity, the more I heard about travel dangers, the more I began to worry. I wish that I hadn't sought out advice, as I was much happier in my ignorance, but once I began to gather information, I couldn't stop.

I began cross-examining my friends, too, as they've all traveled internationally. (FYI, none of them has ever made Stale Bun Pizza or contemplated whizzing in a bucket. I feel these items may all be related.)

Tracey warned me of the dangers of pulmonary embolisms in

flight, so I had to buy compression socks. Gina cautioned me that I could be deemed an easy mark because I'm too polite. Stacey was the one who issued the direst warning. "No matter what, make sure you pack every piece of clothing you could possibly need. There are no fat Europeans and if you forget your swimsuit, you're fucked."

I was so busy heeding her advice and trying to Tetris-style every conceivable piece of clothing I owned into my luggage that it didn't even occur to me to wonder *why* they aren't fat. How are they not fat, living in the pasta and Buffalo mozzarella capital of the universe?

I guess I'll find out soon enough.

If I don't implode from anxiety first.

The few instances that Fletch and I vacationed in Las Vegas over the years, all we had to remember to bring was a credit card, as anything else was available twenty-four/seven in that city. In Vegas, you can literally call any hotel concierge and say, "Can I get a howler monkey wearing a tiny hat delivered to my room immediately?" and they'd be all, "Certainly. Fedora or fez?" And as for our one other vacation, to the Hamptons, that trip entailed nothing more than adopting a smug sense of self-satisfaction, which fit just fine in our carry-on bags.

So far the only hard part of going to Italy was tracking down my birth certificate. Of course, had Fletch mentioned that he kept a special binder of all our important paperwork BEFORE I tore through every single plastic bin in the basement, I might have been spared some aggravation.

Then again, I would never have found my name tag from when I worked at the Olive Garden in 1992, so my search wasn't a total loss.

I finished packing last night and I was completely taken aback by the profundity of my pretrip jitters. With the number of times I've toured promoting my books, I'm no stranger to the logistics of

getting from Point A to Point B, and I'm never nonplussed by travel. Aggravated, sure, but not flummoxed. Maybe it's that a trip to Minneapolis doesn't feel like A Date with Destiny the way going to Rome feels. (As an added bonus, everyone there is nice and it's Target's hometown, so what's not to love?)

Tired of my pacing and incessant hand-wringing, Fletch finally made me sit down with a glass of wine and *Parks and Recreation* on my iPad. (I wasn't sure about the show until the episode where Leslie Knope does the "Parents Just Don't Understand" rap. After that, I was hooked.) He then issues instructions to "Calm your ass down; you're making the dogs nervous."

So I tried, but as I watched *Parks and Rec*, I became panicky anew.

I paused my program and looked over at Fletch, who was busy mapping out an entirely new project to replace the screens on the back porch. "I was worried about you, but now what if *I* go all Ron Swanson over there?" I asked.

He knit his brows. "What do you mean?" he replied, glancing up from his graph paper.

I began to rock back and forth ever so slightly. "Like, what if I hate it there so much and I spend a week stomping around in impotent rage, complaining about socialism and government corruption and not being able to buy a huge soda?"

"Since when do you care about big sodas? The last time I asked if you wanted a Diet Coke, you said, and I quote, '*Pellegrino represent, yo.'* Because there's nothing more gangsta than a middle-aged lady with an e-reader sitting next to a pool. I blame BackSpin."

I considered this. "Well, it's just that I watched an episode where Leslie Knope tries to institute a soda tax and—"

"Nonsense," he interrupted, not even willing to entertain my anxiety. "You're worrying about nonsense from a television show that takes place in a nonexistent town."

"Oh, *really*? Mayor Bloomberg's fictional now, too?"

"Let me ask you this: When was the last time you felt compelled to order a dump truck full of Fanta in New York?"

The fact that the answer is "never" did not negate my point, but I switched tactics anyway. When Fletch gets all logical, it's very hard to derail him, so I felt like I should play to his emotions and sense of fair play. "What if all the horror stories I've recently read online are true and the cabdrivers rob me blind by taking endless loops around the city, thus turning a five-euro ride into a three-hour tour? A *three-hour* tour."

He shrugged, running a hand over his beard. "Then you'll enjoy seeing a new place from your favorite position—seated."

Ooh, had me there.

As I drank my wine and watched my show, I unclenched a tiny bit, much to everyone's relief. But now that I'm in the car on the way to the airport, my anxiety is back tenfold.

"Hey, slow down," I tell Fletch as we pass a Hyundai.

He glances at the speedometer. "I'm going the speed limit."

"You're in such a rush! Take your time. Smell the roses. Maybe we could find a more scenic route to O'Hare."

Fletch cuts his eyes over to me as he merges into the turnoff lane for the airport. "You'd like me to leave the highway despite our almost being there and then drive, say, twenty miles west, which is how far we'd need to go to get anywhere even remotely scenic."

"Yes. I'm not in a hurry." I fold my hands in my lap to demonstrate how very calm I am.

"Really? Because *I'm* in a hurry to get you out of the car at this point."

"Fine," I snap, gazing out the window at the dozens of trucks heading to and from all the cargo holds by the airport. Normally, I loathe driving next to semis with every fiber of my being, having once seen an episode of *20/20* in which an expert claimed that motorists would be safe to assume that every driver out there was hopped up on goofballs and delirious from having had zero sleep while hauling illegally large loads, one heavy-lidded blink away from jackknifing and causing a thousand-car pileup on the expressway. But today? Today the trucks seem like something I'll miss desperately while dodging Vespas and navigating the tiny, winding cobblestone streets of Rome.

"On a scale from one to ten, how likely is it that my flight will be hijacked? One being the least likely and ten being the most? Also, what if someone in Rome tries to sell me into white slavery? Like, this could be another scam the cabbies are running. They're going to take one look at me and be all, *'American woman sturdy like ox.'"*

"Why will they have Russian accents in Rome?" Fletch asks.

Ignoring him, I continue. "They'll be all, *'Many buckets she could haul!'* I fear my strong back will be my downfall."

Fletch inadvertently scrunches up his face in a manner that I call Muppet Mouth because it reminds me of a sock puppet tasting something sour and subsequently folding its lips back into its head. This happens only when he's simultaneously flabbergasted and frustrated by something extremely challenging. The last time I saw this look was when he discovered he'd measured all the screens wrong on this first iteration of the back porch project, after he'd already torn down the old ones.

(Sidebar: It's possible he went all Muppet Mouth because I'd said, "Wow, that seems like kind of a rookie mistake," as we surveyed the massive, gaping holes.)

Very deliberately, he takes a bracing sip of his iced coffee before telling me, "You must chill. Understand me? You. Must. Chill."

Yet. I. Can. Not. Chill.

"What if they lose my luggage and I can't buy a fat-girl swimsuit? What if the dogs miss me, or what if Hambone figures out how to scale the fence at the kennel? She has a four-foot vertical jump from a standing-still position! Remember when we found her on the counter that day eating hot dog buns? It's totally possible! What if someone really awesome dies while I'm gone, like Mary Ann from *Gilligan's Island,* and I never hear about it until well after the fact because the Italian news stations don't report it and then I'll be all upset because I won't have realized she'd already been gone for years? I hate that! What if there's an issue with the plane while we're in the middle of the Atlantic and we go down and, provided we don't go *kablammo* on impact, no one can find us? You always used to promise me that planes can't just disappear, but a whole bunch of Malaysians would beg to differ. Planes can just disappear now. It's a *thing.* What about that, huh? WHAT ABOUT THAT?"

Fletch patted my hand. "Stop it, Jen. I mean it. I love you, but you sound like a lunatic. All is well, okay? Stop trying to ruin this for yourself. Remember that you've looked forward to this trip every single day since you walked into your first Italian class in college. When was that, like 1994? This has been your dream for twenty years. You've plotted, you've planned, and I've no doubt you're going to surprise yourself at how well you do once you get there. So please do me a favor and take a deep, calming breath before I accidentally drive us into an embankment."

I process everything he's said and I try to get a grip on myself. He truly is my rock, my touchstone, my port in the storm.

"What if the Wi-Fi is as spotty as everyone says it is and I can't download episodes of *Parks and*—"

Fletch pulls up to the skycap in front of American Airlines. "Oh, look, we've arrived. I'll miss you very much but you should go now. Here, lemme help you with your luggage." He hops out of the car, after barely having put it in park, sprinting to the hatch. He kisses me good-bye and I keep him locked in a hug for long enough to attract the TSA's attention. "Time to go. You'll be great. Go eat gelato and get the lay of the land and I'll see you in a few days. Love you."

I reply, "I love you, too. But what if—"

Fletch tells the skycap, "She's all yours! Have a safe trip and *stop worrying!*"

And with that, he gets in the car and pulls away and I suddenly want to cry.

"Where to today, ma'am?" the skycap asks as I hand over my bags and my ID.

I tell him, "I'm going to Rome by myself like a big girl and I'm so nervous I think I may barf in my handbag."

He has the courtesy to not laugh at me and with a completely straight face, he replies, "Young lady (!!), that sounds like quite an adventure, so I'll make extra sure your bag is waiting for you at the other end. Don't you worry about a thing."

And with that, for the first time in weeks, I feel a tiny bit less tense.

All the guidebooks say to arrive at the airport early for an international flight, which is why I find myself with almost three hours to kill before boarding. I think the early-arriving rule must apply only on the way back *to* America, as there was nothing different about going through security. Because I have the Pre-Check, I was through security in less than five minutes and I didn't even have to remove my shoes. Plus, my flight's leaving from the regular terminal, not the international one, so essentially this feels no different from flying to Minnesota.

I sit at the bar in the Admirals Club and order a grilled cheese and a small ginger ale (I guess I really don't need to worry about suddenly wanting big sodas?) and I begin to think about my friend Angie. A couple of years ago, she traveled to China alone for two months to take a summer teaching position. I'm suddenly overwhelmed by how very courageous she was, considering I'm shaking in my boots about being by myself for three days in a place where I already know I love the food and I sort of speak the language. I'm staying in a pretty hotel with a rooftop pool and I don't have to worry about setting up a household or navigating a new job or, most important, dealing with the feeling of loss from being away from my children. I make a note to buy her something nice while I'm there, because bravery like that merits a reward.

The bartender who serves me has the most spectacular eyebrows I've ever seen, all clean lines and dramatic arches. He's also wearing glittery foundation and has long, black, perfectly mani-

cured nails, which causes the cowboy-types sitting next to me to giggle every time he turns his back. Really, assholes? You're drinking vodka-and-Diet-Coke and you have the nerve to laugh at anyone else? Not cool. I make sure to compliment the bartender on his whole look before leaving an extra-large tip.

After I finish my lunch, I settle in by the window to watch a few more episodes of *Parks and Rec* before boarding. I don't know if it's the dulcet tones of Ron

Swanson/Duke Silver's saxophone, the kind skycap, the distraction of directing my roiling disgust toward those in shit-stained
boots, the knowledge that I packed every item I could conceivably
need, or possibly the two Ativan I swallowed, but I'm now finally
a tiny bit relaxed and a whole lot excited.

Bucket list, I'm about to TREAT YO-SELF to the kind of
check that new carpeting simply can't deliver.

16.

SORRY I'M NOT SORRY

You know all those assholes who crowd the gate at the airport?

I can't mock them because I happen to *be* them.

I may even be their leader.

I'm fairly unapologetic about it, too.

I believe everyone's allowed one tiny aspect of their life where they're not on their best behavior. Maybe you're the finest person in America, tithing extra to your church, volunteering at a soup kitchen every single week, taking care of your elderly neighbor because he has no one else, and sending your kids to school with lunches that are both healthy and delicious, yet you still can't stop yourself from stealing *People* magazine at your dentist's office whenever Angelina's on the cover.

I think that's okay.

Or maybe you put your Ivy League law degree to work at Legal Aid, toiling eighty hours a week, choosing not to get rich, and instead concentrating on bringing justice to those in need. No one's going to judge you too harshly if you bring Tupperware to stash extra bacon at the all-you-can-eat brunch place.

For me, I'm beyond polite the entire year, save for those ten-minute increments leading up to boarding a flight. I mean, I'm all about thank-you notes and unexpected gifts. I let everyone cut in front of me at the grocery store, even when they're clearly violating the fifteen-items-or-less sign. I wipe pee off of whatever public toilet I've used, even what was there before I went. If there's ever a debate over who gets the parking space, I always defer to the other driver and God help us all if I wind up at a four-way stop with the like-minded because we'll be there all day, waving each other on.

I don't even yell at strangers anymore. (Much.)

Should I be nominated for sainthood given the above? Of course not, because it's all part and parcel of being a decent human being. No one gives out Congratulations on Not Being a Douche-Canoe medals, because good behavior is part of the social contract. I'm just saying that when presented with the opportunity, I do the right thing.

Except at the airport gate.

My rationale is that I'm an anxious flyer and being first at the gate helps me feel like I have a modicum of control.

Okay, this is mostly a lie.

Rather, I'm this way because I almost never check a bag, so it's very important for me to get on the plane before everyone else hogs up all the overhead compartments with bullshit that doesn't deserve space and can be sat upon or with, such as puffy parkas and pillows. (People, we are flying to *New York City*—I guarantee you they have pillows there. You needn't bring your own.)

Perhaps in the vein of full disclosure, or in case it wasn't already obvious, when it comes to air travel, I'm also pushy and petty and have a pathological need to win by being the first person on the plane.

There.

Now you comprehend why certain people crowd the gate and

you no longer have to stand there, boarding pass in hand, asking your-self, *"What's with* her? *We're all going to get to New York at the same time, lady, so there's no need to roll your damn luggage across our feet in your zeal to embark."*

(Sidebar: That happened only once and I swear it wasn't intentional.)

Are these valid reasons for us gate-crowders' collective rude-ness? No, but they're an explanation nonetheless.

Now that I've shared this insight maybe someone could re-turn the favor. Please explain to me why so few grasp the concept of emptying their pockets before going through the metal detec-tor, yes, of everything, yes, that includes the wallet, yes, all those nickels, too, yes, the cell phone, and no, they can't just hold it all in their hands instead of putting it in the little plastic bowl; I'd appreciate it.

Or maybe that's just the "one thing" for other people, too. In which case, cool.

We're likely all agreed that airports bring out the worst in us. Whatever bad behavior we're prone to is simply amplified in the presence of avionics. It's an altitude attitude, if you will.

I've had a lot of time to reflect about travel since I bought my ticket and why I've thus far been so hesitant to fly overseas, long after I had the means and miles to do so. Basically, I panic at the idea of being trapped in a tiny seat for so many hours, especially surrounded by all that water. When I was sixteen, I went to Eu-rope and I was somehow convinced we'd be flying over land. Yes, I *had* previously seen a globe, but the way it was explained, I un-derstood our trajectory would skirt Greenland and Iceland and Canadaland and the North Pole, so we'd avoid all the water.

In retrospect, I feel this yarn was spun to keep me quiet.

(Sidebar: I accepted our land-based flight path as fact due to having been more cute than smart in high school. Mind you, I was in my thirties before I realized that Mount Rushmore wasn't actually a natural occurrence. Somehow I fully believed that *God* was the one who put all those faces up there thousands of years ago, which is why I didn't understand why others weren't in a perpetual state of wonder, marveling over how it was both miraculous and prophetic. Two things to note here: One, Mount Rushmore is no longer on my bucket list, and two, I still harbor animosity toward the Indiana public school system.)

Anyway, because I travel frequently for book tours, I had enough miles to upgrade to Business Class, so I'm delighted by the prospect of not only putting my feet up on this flight, but also checking that item off my bucket list. In the course of this project, I've seen dozens of other people's lists and **fly First Class to Europe** seems to be near the top on almost all of them. I understand there's a difference between Business and First, but I figure Business Class is close enough. Apparently in First Class, you have both a seat and a bed, but that seems redundantly luxurious, like having a pool *and* a pond, when, really, either one would work for me.

(Sidebar: Congratulations to me for now having worked a *Caddyshack* reference into every book I've ever written. RIP, Harold Ramis, you magnificent bastard, and thank you for teaching an entire generation about comedy. You'll be sorely missed.)

When Fletch comes in a few days, he's in Economy Class, and again, no apologies. When he accumulates all his miles on tiny prop planes where he has to duck his head upon entry, mashed shoulder to shoulder with the only other fat person on the flight, or whiles away endless hours drinking shitty coffee while sitting on airport floors waiting for his flight to Birmingham, Alabama, to be rerouted, he'll have earned this indulgence, too.

When I booked my trip, I was content just taking Economy Class to Italy. Going there was reward enough. It wasn't until after I traveled to Richmond, Virginia, a couple of months ago that I decided to upgrade because this was truly the worst trip ever.

(Sidebar: Yes, even worse than the flight to Raleigh last year

where the pilots completely missed the runway on our descent—
largely because we were *flying in sideways*—and then the stall warnings kept buzzing when we lost altitude on our emergency
diversion to Greensboro. Even the atheists on that flight found
religion by the time we landed safely.)

What's ironic is that the day started out so well. I arrived at
the airport far before my departure time to Richmond and totally
breezed through security, as it was my first time with TSA Pre-
Check/Global Entry.

Ah, yes, I thought, watching all those suckers retie their shoes
and adjust their belts, *the Travel Gods are smiling upon me.*

I was so damn smug, tweeting my record time from car to
gate. Yet I should have known to never be smug on social media
because it comes back to bite me in the ass every single time.
Karma, if you will.

I was supposed to arrive in Virginia by ten a.m., with seven
full hours to relax and practice my speech before dressing for my
first event, but the universe had other plans. As I prepared myself
to crowd the gate, my flight was delayed due to weather. No one
could give us a straight answer on how long we'd have to wait, so
our delay was doled out in fifteen-minute increments.

Something had happened to the original flight that was to
take us to Richmond (I believe it, too, disappeared, as that is
clearly a *thing* now) so we were rerouted to a plane that was coming from Louisville, except the flight from Louisville had been
diverted to Indianapolis due to weather so they were maybe going
to find us a third plane.

Are you keeping track of this? Because it was certainly problematic for the fine folks at American Airlines.

(We *not* in a fight, though; I can't stress that enough.)

The night before the trip, Fletch had cooked a stir-fry that
hadn't sat well with me. My stomach hurt, so I really wasn't hun-

gry while I waited, despite not eating any breakfast. Plus, I figured I'd get room service upon arrival, positive they'd have grits on the menu. (Grits are like catnip for us Yankees. Ditto for sweet tea.)

Because our delays were meted out as they were, I was worried that if I wandered all the way down to the food court I'd miss my flight. We were departing from L Gate in O'Hare, a neverland so far from the beaten path that I didn't know it existed until that day, so there wasn't anything remotely appetizing remotely close.

Finally, after five hours of fifteen-minute delays, we boarded. Or, the rest of the plane covertly boarded while I was in the bathroom. Damn you, stir-fry! I was assigned the bulkhead on this itsy-bitsy plane, so I didn't have under-seat storage. Plus, everyone had already stormed the gangway and taken all the prime real estate with their pillows and parkas, so I had to stuff my carry-on in a bin half the length of the plane away from me. At this point, I felt the first twinges of hunger, possibly a four on the scale, which was no problem because grits were a-waitin' in ol' Virginny.

(Sidebar: I should mention no one actually speaks like this in Richmond.)

Also, I travel with an ample supply of protein bars, peanut butter packets, and trail mix in case we ever do crash-land à la *Lost*, wherein my hoarded Biscoff cookies will be our island's only form of currency; ergo, I would be queen.

Seriously, it could happen.

The more likely scenario is that there's some sort of debacle with my flight and I arrive at my hotel after room service shuts down and I make a meal out of whatever I'm carrying.

Either way, I'm prepared.

We finally loaded up all the angry travelers and as soon as we shut the doors and prepared to pull out from the gate, the sky opened up and began to hurl fist-sized chunks of hail down upon us. We were absolutely pummeled for a solid ten minutes, causing another delay. The pilot told us not to leave our seats for our own safety; thus my PowerBars were just out of reach. The airport closed down, with us trapped on the tarmac in a minuscule sardine can.

Mmmm, I thought, *sardines.* I was down to a two on the scale, meaning I was hungry enough to have happily woofed down a briny plateful of Nature's Boniest Mistake.

Once the airport reopened, we had to wait for the plane to be inspected to make sure there was no hail damage. As every jet in the airport had to be scrutinized, this took a while, and apparently required us to remain in our seats. I suspect our needing to sit down was less for our safety and more to keep us all from badgering the flight attendant are-we-there-yet style. (To be clear, I have no complaints here because I'd rather wait than take unnecessary risks.)

An hour and a half later, when I was at zero on the scale and ready to chew off my own arm for sustenance, we finally pulled away and began to taxi. But instead of going to an actual runway where we may have, say, built up enough speed to become airborne, we instead took a slow, steady, sightseeing cruise around the periphery of the airport, much like how I used to aimlessly drive around the McDonald's parking lot in high school, as that's what passed for entertainment in 1980s Huntington, Indiana, home of the subpar academic curriculum.

Oh, God, *McDonald's.*

At that point I would have done unspeakable things to that creepy redheaded clown for a single McNugget.

Unspeakable.

We putted along for so long that I assumed the new plan was to simply *drive* to Richmond. The pilot finally announced that we were cleared for takeoff and everyone in the plane let out a collective cheer. Our glee lasted for all of two minutes when the pilot made a second, decidedly more sheepish announcement that *some-*

one hadn't gotten the requisite hail-damage sign-off, so we had to pull over until a dude in a van could drive up and deliver the paperwork.

I didn't know who *someone* was, but I suspect he or she was in for a stern talking-to.

At this point, I was ready to pass out from hunger, but I still wasn't allowed to get up from my seat. I was so close to my pistachio nuts and dried cranberries, yet so very far.

I was my own personal O.Henry story.

The notion of O.Henry made me think of an Oh Henry! chocolate bar, which almost brought me to tears.

That's when I noticed there was a bulge in my sweater, ironic because that meant that *I* was the asshole going through the metal detector with loaded pockets.

When I reached in, I realized why I hadn't set off an alarm. I wasn't carrying coins or keys or Krugerrands; instead, I had a pocketful of dog food pellets. I don't remember the whens or wheres of having loaded up with kibble, but that certainly sounded like something I'd do, as I'm always using food to bribe the dogs to behave.

(Sidebar: With this technique, I would have very fat children. Very fat.)

I've been buying the guys this fantastic, organic, grain-free, superhealthy stuff, chock-full of delicious and nutritious antioxidants, manufactured in a human-food-grade facility. As I held up these concentrated bits of beefy protein, I swear my mouth began to water.

But, come on, it's not like I didn't have some damn pride.

Besides, we'd be in the air soon enough, where magical carts full of pretzels and Pepsis abound and salvation was mere steps away. I began to plan my snack—I'd smear Justin's Vanilla Almond Butter on crackers as an appetizer (or perhaps I'd go all tequila-shot with it, squeezing it directly into my mouth; I was still deciding), followed by a satisfyingly chewy main course of Trader Joe's Turkey Jerky, with Nutella-dipped Biscoff for dessert. I would feast like the King of the Minibar!

The minute the wheels left the ground, however, it was clear this was to feel less like a "flight" and more like "a lone tube sock sloshing around in the washing machine's spin cycle."

Our plane was a toy boat bobbing atop a roiling ocean, so no one was getting up, not for love, money, or Trader Joe's Turkey Jerky. When we finally had respite enough to be served drinks, I was trapped in my spot by the beverage cart, where my only option was water without benefit of pretzels.

Suddenly, the concept of air rage made sense. Whither hast thou gone, honey-roasted nuts? Ginger ale, where art thou? WHY ARE WE BEING SERVED ONLY WATER?

Then I realized I'd been awake for almost twelve hours without a single morsel of food and it would be another two hours before I could find any.

As it turns out, I . . . have considerably less pride than one might imagine.

Yeah. Went there.

When I relayed this story to Stacey after the fact, I explained my actions by referencing the reality show *The Colony*.

"You're saying that TV encouraged you to eat dog food?" Stacey asked. As part of my policy of saying yes, we were having lunch at The Bagel. Apparently my story impacted her enough to cause her to set down her Reuben.

"No," I replied. "Well, actually, yes, a little bit. See, the premise was that the Colonists were in a postapocalyptic world and this diverse group of people, each with very specific skills, like mechanics and nurses and engineers, had to find a way to build a vehicle that would take them to safety."

"I never heard of the show. Is it like *Survivor* only where everyone is smart instead of hot?"

I nodded and dunked my crisp, salty French fry in a puddle of cool ranch dressing. If America had a flavor, this combination is exactly what it would taste like. Mmmm, patriotism!

I'd been back only a couple of days and I was still making up for the trip's caloric deficit. I had a wonderful stay once I landed, with really lovely hosts devoted to a worthy cause. However, I was so busy with the various charitable events the entire time, either giving speeches or signing books or Enlightening Tomorrow's Leaders, that I barely had a minute to ingest anything, let alone find and savor me some grits. (Praise be for carry-on Biscoff.)

I chewed thoughtfully before answering her. "Basically, yes. Thing is, everyone understood they were on a reality show, but they were encouraged to *believe* the false circumstances, and after a bunch of simulated attacks and positively grim living conditions, their fantasy really seemed like reality."

Stacey nods affably. "Ergo, you ate dog food. Makes perfect sense."

"You're going to be so embarrassed when I get to my point. You're gonna be all, *'Jen, you are actually kind of brilliant.'*"

"Undoubtedly."

My sarcasm detector was pinging but I went on anyway. "These guys were stuck in this New Orleans warehouse in an area that was never fixed after being devastated by Katrina. The producers had planted useful items here and there within a mile of where they were, but some of the stuff they scavenged was simply what was left when the area was abandoned. It was amazing to see them build combustion engines out of nothing but junk."

"That actually doesn't sound like complete Bravo nonsense," Stacey admitted. Although we both love all things Bravo, we're aware that it's ridic. Case in point, I'm extraordinarily volatile, and yet I've never once flipped a table or yanked a bitch's weave.

Stacey was having a potato pancake with her sandwich. I watched as she delicately spread thin layers of sour cream and applesauce on her bite, which seemed kind of wrong. And yet, I was the one who ate dog food, so I didn't share my musing.

I deliberately chewed another fry before I continued. "Right? Anyway, this old physicist found a few tins of cat food and after so many days starving, he relished the opportunity to eat them. Everyone asked him, *'Does it taste like chicken?'* and he laughed and said no, it was more like low-grade tuna, but he was so hungry that to him, it was delicious. And that is what was in my head when I found the dog food."

"Was the dog food delicious?"

I tried not to retch at the memory. "Oh, God, no, it was pretty horrible. Grainy. Bitter. Left an oily residue in my mouth, too. I guess I have different taste buds from the dogs, because they seem to love it."

Despite having lived in Chicago her whole life, Stacey can dole out the super-Southern-bless-your-heart-slow-blink like she'd been raised by the O'Hara clan at Tara herself. "Your dogs also love the taste of tossing their own salads."

"True. Plus, I had a tummy ache for the next three days, but I don't know if it was because I didn't have time to eat while I was there or if it was the kibble. Maybe it was the stir-fry?"

Stacey blotted her lips with a paper napkin. "Do me a favor?"

"Of course!" I quickly agreed.

"When you tell everyone the story of eating dog food—and I guarantee you will—be sure you include the TV part, too."

"Because it makes more sense that way, right? Like, it was a good rationale," I said, pleased to have convinced her of my great pragmatism.

"Yeah," Stacey said, "let's go with that."

"And the dog food? Wasn't even the funniest bit!"

Stacey places her hand over mine to reassure me. "Don't sell yourself short, peanut. It's plenty funny."

"No, see, I had to go Enlighten Tomorrow's Leaders while I was there. The charity had me talking to a couple of groups of high school kids as part of their community outreach. An English class, I think. Anyway, I had a whole lesson plan devised, but the kids were not into what I had to say, like, at all. I thought they'd dig me because the Purdue thing went so well, but no. Not the same. I kept telling these kids that their moms would love me, but apparently, not a selling point."

"This is brand-new information to you?"

"Actually, yes. See, I thought they'd participate and answer my questions and we'd all leave, believing we'd learned something from one another. I was all set to *Stand and Deliver*, but really I was more *Bad Teacher*. I figured I could fill the fifty minutes, but no. Not even a little. Twenty minutes in, I'd breezed through all my points and then we were all sort of looking at one another in this really fancy private school theater."

Stacey began her career as an educator and was already familiar with the fact that kids will not give you an inch. "Awkward."

"I'll say. You know how I get that nervous talking thing?" Stacey flinched and nodded, having witnessed this firsthand on a number of occasions. "I ended up babbling about all kinds of stuff—like, telling the kids how I flunked out of college and how I lost my job and had my car repossessed and how forty girls in my high school got knocked up my senior year because there was no Planned Parenthood in Huntington County in the 1980s. My plan was to tie all these stories into a redemptive arc about not giving up, also contraception, but then the bell rang and they all left believing my life was a country music song."

She clamped her hand over her eyes in a show of secondhand

shame. "How many sets of parents would you estimate called the school later that night? Five?"

"That's my best guess," I admitted. "But that's not the bad part."

"Sweet Jesus." She slow-blinked again.

"I had another class come in. And this time, they weren't a bunch of quiet freshmen. These kids were all seniors and some of them seemed into having me there—they'd even read my books, so I really wanted to be able to connect with them. Drop some knowledge bombs, yo."

Stacey sipped her diet black cherry soda and slow-blinked some more. "Really, LL Cool Jen? Do continue."

(Sidebar: I admit BackSpin is becoming unduly influential.)

"I wanted them to take something away from the experience. Like, teaching the youth of America something useful could be my legacy. Years from now, one of them could win the Pulitzer and during his acceptance speech, he'd say that a chick lit writer who visited his English class back in 2014 inspired him. Let's be honest—that's the closest I'm coming to any Pulitzer who isn't Lilly."

I took a bite of my tomato and bacon–enhanced grilled cheese, again pleased at the opportunity to savor something that nine out of ten veterinarians hadn't recommended.

I continued. "Having learned from my last class, I decided to prompt participation by calling on them. Had 'em all go around the room and tell me something about themselves."

"Which killed two minutes." Stacey blotted a stray bit of Thousand Island with a paper napkin.

"That's two minutes I didn't blather, so, victory. As we were talking, I noticed this group of six kids sitting in the back, giggling and grab-assing. They struck me as ringleaders and I decided I'd need to keep my eye on them."

"They were the John Hughes movie villains? *'What about*

prom, Blane? What. About. Prom?'" Stacey banged the table for emphasis, causing our drinks to ripple.

"Exactly. When it came their turn to talk, I noticed most were sucking out of sport water bottles. Didn't read too much into it, assuming they'd just come from doing some rich-kid sport, like lacrosse."

"Perhaps they were playing polo or racing their Ferraris."

"Right? But then one of the girls held up her lidded paper cup when it was her turn to speak. I could hear the ice rattle and she exclaimed, 'I like coffee!' and then cracked herself up. That seemed odd. As I talked, they kept interrupting and trying to go off on nonsensical tangents. That's when I realized, *these kids are fucked-up.*"

"As in troubled? As in poor James Spader who could buy anything he wanted, save for Molly Ringwald's love?"

"As in *full of booze.* They were day-drinking! Think about it. They were seniors at a private school, minutes away from graduation, all enrolled in college—they didn't care about rules because they're at the age where they believe they're invincible."

She grinned at the familiarity of this story. "Sometimes I miss the high school kids I used to teach and . . . sometimes I don't."

I shifted in my seat, reflecting on how very awkward the whole scene was. "Clearly they were new at drinking in class, seeing how they were terrible at it. But it was obvious and disruptive and I was pissed at their level of disrespect. I thought, *'I ate dog food to come here and interact with you little shits.'* Uncool. Sure, I screwed up the first hour, but I was ready to kill it in the second. I was getting my redemptive arc, damn it, and I was not about to let the gin-soaked Plastics throw me off my game."

(Sidebar: My streak of referencing *Mean Girls* in every book I've ever written is also intact.)

"Devil's advocate here—how can you be sure they were drinking? That's a hefty accusation."

"Stacey, I was in college for *eleven years*. Trust me, I know what drinking in class looks like. The ice was a dead giveaway."

She nodded, satisfied. "Point taken. You say anything?"

"Hell, yes, I said something! I go, '*Are you guys cocktailing back there?*' And just like that, these six smug little bastards went pale, suddenly realizing the potential consequences of their actions. Busted."

"Did the teachers intervene?"

"No, at that point I'd already lost all credibility with the grown-ups in the room, but *I* knew. That was enough. I suspect I put enough fear in them that they won't do it again, though. So I added **scare kids straight** to my bucket list."

"Does it count when you retroactively add something you've already accomplished to your list?"

"Yes."

"Then you're a true American hero."

"Damn skippy. Someone should carve my face on a mountain in a national park. Hey, did you know that Mount Rushmore isn't a natural formation?"

"I feel like I should be concerned that you didn't." She took another small bite of her potato pancake, dabbing a bit of stray applesauce from her lip. "So, what's your takeaway from all of this? What was the big announcement you wanted to make when you invited me to lunch?"

"My takeaway is . . . I'm upgrading to Business Class on my flight to Rome! I figured if I'm going to be stuck on a plane for an undisclosed amount of time, I should at least be able to recline."

"Sometimes you're a genius," she said, before quickly amending her statement. "Not about geography, though. You know you'll be flying over water this time, right?"

"Sort of?"

And so that's why I'm now here, crowding the gate, waiting

to steamroll my way to my very first international Business Class seat.

Sorry I'm not sorry.

When I board the plane, the flight attendant instructs me to cut through the galley to get over to the left side of the plane. I crane back to see if there's a curtain on the other side, but I can't actually tell if there's a First Class section on this flight or not. If it's here, it's hidden, which is kind of badass. They don't need to mix with the hoi polloi that is us. So I make my way back to 5G.

I'd hoped this was to be one of those two-story planes, but no such luck. Stacey said she flew on one once and it was glorious, so perhaps I'll add that to my list at some point. (Again, retroactively counts.) Yet because this is such a special experience and since I waited so long in my life to do this, I don't want my thoughts muddied by wishing for something else in the middle of what's already a dream coming true. I just want to be in the moment.

I'm immediately taken out of the moment when an angry old lady with a battleship gray perm rams her plaid carry-on into my spleen as I lift my own bag into the overhead compartment. And she's not sorry she's not sorry. I guess I'm not proceeding quickly enough for her and she huffs with rage at having to wait for me to get out of her way. Listen, Betty White, crowding is acceptable only *at the gate*. Now that we're on the plane, you need to check yo-self; otherwise it's going to be a really long eight hours.

The old woman is traveling with her entire extended family— multiple kids and adult children trail in her wake, followed by a beleaguered older gentleman who I can already tell has taken more than his fair share of blows to the spleen. He looks to be plotting his escape. He and I exchange glances and he offers me a shrug of his defeated shoulders by way of apology.

The family has assigned seats in the pods all around me, but that doesn't stop them from halting the boarding process for everyone else at the gate while they allow the children to try out each and every seat in determining which one they want. I watch as the tormented grandfather of the group sits as far away from his wife as humanly possible while still technically being a part of flight 110.

While the family continues to gum up the works for the other passengers, I inspect my home for the next eight hours. My seat reminds me of those old eggshell chairs from the seventies. It's not a private pod like First Class is rumored to have, but the shape boasts definite noise-blocking properties, and it affords some privacy.

The tension I felt earlier has completely lifted. This was such a good idea! I monkey with the controls of my seat to find it not only reclines almost flat, but also raises the legs. I already predict I'm going to spend the whole flight trying to figure out the best position.

Each seat is stocked with a few supplies, such as a toiletry bag with a toothbrush, toothpaste, lip balm, socks, and an eye mask. There's also a down blanket and a thick pillow, so it's a shame that most of the Annoying Family decided to bring their own, which they summarily shove in the overhead bins. As it's only five p.m., I'm not exactly ready for bed, so I stuff all these items under the seat in front of me while I plug my iPad into my DC adapter. While the Annoying Family continues to jockey for position, I catch another episode of *Parks and Recreation*, which has *literally* become my favorite sitcom. (But, Rob Lowe, why are you leaving now that I've just found you?)

The middle-aged dad of the group decides to sit next to me and I watch as he fumbles everything he touches. Down go his blanket, his pillow, his toiletries, his laptop, his earbuds, etc. I sure hope Captain Butterfingers doesn't have a job that requires he keep a grip on anything important.

Captain Butterfingers's scantily clad Trophy Wife keeps jumping out of her seat to take pictures of her whole brood. She's sporting a sheer sleeveless blouse and sporty-shorty-short shorts. Despite the plane being plenty bright, she insists on using the flash, thus blinding everyone in a three-row vicinity who happens to glance in her direction.

I should mention the entire rest of the plane is *still waiting to board*, which is made far more difficult as ninety-six pounds of sleeveless soccer mom insists on Instagramming every single moment that passes. Finally, one of the flight attendants has words with her and she grudgingly returns to her seat, which she then kneels on to continue with her photojournalism.

I know I said that everyone's allowed to have "one thing," but I'd wager this family indulges in more than their allotted share of annoying habits.

Captain Butterfingers then dumps his Diet Coke, thus necessitating more stopped traffic while the flight attendant mops him up, as Trophy Wife preserves the images for posterity. I would not like to be whoever's forced to watch this family's slide show upon their return home.

After spilling a bag of trail mix, Captain Butterfingers decides he's going to watch a movie on his laptop. I'm really sad to be traveling alone because I have no one to whom I can whisper, "Just wait, he's going to jam a regular plug into the DC adapter." He bashes at his outlet like a baboon trying to start a Jeep with a stick.

I can't stand to watch him struggle for so long, so I show him the package my new adapter came in, explaining that because this is an older plane, he'll need a DC plug—which is basically a car cigarette charger. I tell him I'd read that the flight attendants have extras for those who need them, so he just has to ask. (As he's an American, I assume he understands my use of the English language, but in a pinch, I could have told him the same in Italian.)

He nods and drops his plug back in his bag. I assume he's going to hit his call button, but no. Instead, and I swear I'm not making this up, he begins to try again, only this time with a flat USB adapter, which is honestly and truly the old square peg–round hole conundrum.

At that point, I put my headphones back on, as you can lead a horse to quantum mechanics, but you can't make him accept Feynman's path integral formulation. Eventually, the old lady leans across me to yell at him that he's doing it wrong while the Trophy Wife captures the moment and his sucker-holding children leave sticky snail-trails everywhere their fingers linger.

We have not yet even left the gate.

The couple to my right is the polar opposite of the Annoying Family. Upon boarding, I note their stylish yet practical travel garb—cute, wrinkle-free pants with numerous pockets, slip-on shoes, and lots of layers, with a pashmina for the lady. With the precision of an Indy pit crew, they ready their area before takeoff. I watch as they refuse the preflight champagne, instead swallowing sleep aids with their bottled water. They wrap themselves in blankets and dull their senses with noise-canceling headphones and eyeshades.

As soon as we're in the air, they turn off their overhead lights and fully recline, preemptively shutting down jet lag before it even has a chance to set in. These two have to be old pros at this international travel thing, unlike me, who is now so excited I'm practically levitating out of my seat, or the Annoying Family, who've clearly never traveled without the warden before.

The eight hours pass largely without incident. Funny how you never remember the flights that go well and you never forget the ones that go awry. As I relax in my seat, I'm so grateful to have been able to get into Business Class and I appreciate having the extra space and the little courtesies. All those miserable flights were worth it because they're why I'm here. I've not only had eight hours of comfort, but I also had a month and a half of blissful anticipation of it, which is just as valuable.

After dinner service, when I eat the best pretzel roll of my life, I settle in to watch movies. I'm not able to sleep, largely because Trophy Wife keeps waking up fellow travelers with her incessant flashing, passing out mini candy bars, and her loud complaints of being cold. (Hint: It's called "clothing"; look into it.) Just desserts will likely be served tomorrow when she drags five sugar-addled, jet-lagged children around the city.

At one point in the evening, I glance down at Captain But-terfingers's choice of reading material and I silently laugh myself into an asthma attack when I realize he's perusing a professional medical journal. Specifically, he's reading about new techniques in urological surgery. And according to the label on the front, I note that he's actually a physician.

Let's milk this, shall we?

Captain Butterfingers is a *surgeon*.

I quickly write down his full name because I want to make sure I eliminate him from our list of participating heath care providers.

An hour before we land, I wash my face and brush my teeth after being served a light breakfast. Then I fix my makeup and review my itinerary so I know what to do once I'm on the ground. I'm supposed to meet a driver out past baggage claim. Normally, I'd have just taken a cab, but today's a national holiday and I un-derstand transportation is scarce.

I disembark easily and am waved through Customs without even having my passport stamped. I choose to believe that this is because I look like I belong, although the more likely scenario is that the Junior Varsity squad's working today due to the Festa della Repubblica and it's a free-for-all.

I quickly locate the driver and the last thing I see before we exit the airport en route to the parking garage is Dr. Butterfingers and his Annoying Family trying to figure out how to get to their hotel because there are no available cabs.

Sorry I'm not sorry.

17.

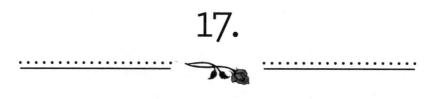

JULIA ROBERTS LIED TO ME

My first impression of Rome is . . . that it looks exactly like Houston.

I'm sorry, Rome, but it's true.

Between the heat, the industrial areas surrounding the airport, and the sparse yellowing vegetation, I'm having a hard time believing I'm not in Texas right now. Even the signs on the highway look similar, save for being written in Italian.

The only real difference on this stretch of road thus far is the size of the cars—my goodness, these are the cutest things I've ever seen. So wee! So bite-sized! Most of them seem to be two-seaters, but we've passed a few that accommodate only one person, which are roughly the dimensions of my ex-tricycle, if it had doors. Rome must not have a Costco because no one could fit a bulk-sized pack of paper towels in one of these vehicles.

We arrive in the city proper in about twenty minutes and this is where the similarities with Houston end. I truly have a sense of *other* now, for the first time. Elaborate fountains abound and the streets are topped with square paving stones. The buildings are all low, not more than three or four stories tall, all stucco, in various shades of gold, coral, and salmon, each with massive painted shutters. These structures appear to have been here for hundreds of years. The roofs are covered with brown or orange tiles and there's very little green space on any of the main drags. Everything's close and tight and I have approximately twenty-six consecutive heart attacks as three-wheeled death machines and Vespas dart in and out of traffic. I catch myself thinking this city looks just like a Vegas theme hotel, before I remember this is the real deal.

We wind through streets that are in no way linear, going up and down hills, so I haven't a sense of north or south. I arrive at my hotel, which is a bit off the beaten path, in the northeast corner of the city. I'd decided to stay at a place close to the train station, just in case I want to take a day trip to Florence. My teacher assured me I'd not be bored in Rome, but I always prefer to have options. Also, there's a rooftop pool, which was what sold me in the first place. I figured if at any point I become overwhelmed, I could take a swim and regroup. My mantra has always been—find a body of water or find a body; your call.

A bellman greets me at the entrance and, in my best Italian, I tell him I'm checking in. He immediately replies in English that he'll have my bags sent up to my room. I reply thank you in Italian, because I'm here, damn it, and I plan to practice. The same thing happens at the registration desk: I speak Italian; the clerk replies in English. And when I say *buongiorno* to a hotel employee in the elevator, she also replies in my native tongue.

So it's going to be like *that*, is it?

I realize I don't look European, but with my snappy travelin' scarf and my stylish shoes, I don't appear to be overwhelmingly American, either. I mean, I'm not draped in the stars and stripes, clomping around in a cowboy hat or sparkling white sneakers, demanding ice in my drink. I could easily be British or Australian. Fine, both these countries speak English, and, granted, I appreciate everyone's trying to make everything easier for me to understand, but I studied really hard to be able to navigate without assistance, so I'd like to try.

I take the elevator up to the third floor. The door to my room is massive and solid wood, glossy to the point that I can guarantee these are rubbed with lemon oil daily. Inserting the key card, the first thing I notice upon entry is that instead of a full king bed, I have two large twins pushed together. While I should be disappointed at how not-romantic this is, I'm actually pretty psyched to have my own covers. Fletch is a known blanket thief and does this hugging and spinning move in his sleep that leaves me perpetually chilly.

The room's on the small side, with only a tiny desk and a single chair, but the ceiling's easily fifteen feet high, so it feels airy. The walls are padded and lined in fabric, and the draperies are heavy, so the whole place is cozy, too. I don't hold out great hope for my view, and when I part the curtains, I see industrial air conditioners, exactly what I expected. Although I'd love a balcony with a view of the Piazza della Repubblica, I'm not paying for that luxury. Generally when I travel, I go for the least expensive class of room in a higher caliber property, as the overall amenities will be better. (Basically, this is the same theory as owning the worst home in a nice neighborhood. Case in point, my house.) At one point, the hotel was an actual palace, but this room indicates that even the maids had to sleep somewhere. Regardless, I'm happy to call this home for the next week.

As I'm a little delirious from not being able to sleep on the plane, despite a liberal dosing of prescription pharmaceuticals, it's all I can do not to fall face-first into bed before my luggage is even delivered. Stacey says the best way to fight jet lag is to take as brief a nap as possible and then go to sleep at what would be a normal bedtime there, so that's the plan.

I can't inspect the bathroom yet, as I'm not sure how to turn on the lights. I bash a bunch of buttons, with no luck. (Times I've bashed things = one hundred thousand; times bashing has produced the intended result = one.) (Figure this must have worked at some point; otherwise why would I continue to bash?) Then I realize that none of the lights function in the room, either. There has to be a trick here; I just have to figure it out. I'd call downstairs and ask, but imagine I'll be annoyed when they reply in English.

When my luggage arrives, the bellman sticks my electronic key into a slot on the wall, which powers everything. Oh. I guess this is how they conserve electricity here, by not allowing the wasteful Americans to run the television and lights when they're off walking the Forum. Makes sense. I'm an energy Nazi at home, perpetually following Fletch around to flip off switches, but when I travel, all bets are off because I hate coming back late to a dark, quiet room.

Still, if my hotel wants the lights off while I'm gone, that's what I'll do. My goal on this trip is to not be an Ugly American. I realize fellow countrymen don't always have the best reputation overseas, so I feel like it's my duty to be an ambassador of sorts.

Also, I'd prefer not to be mocked in Italian, particularly because I understand a lot of the derogatory terms.

I even tried to pack in a way that was more European, with non-tennis-shoe footwear and cotton skirts for the days we visit religious sites. Instead of my usual summer uniform of alligator shirts and khakis, I've brought lots of light, gauzy peasant tops and airy Capri pants. Right before I left, I watched *Roman Holiday* and asked myself, "Would Audrey wear this?" about every item I chose. I even went so far as to buy a colorful dress to sport over my swimsuit, instead of my everyday choice of paint-splatted cutoff sweatpants. (Fancy!) And I brought a bunch of long scarves. Thus far, every single woman I've seen on the street has been wearing something draped around her neck, so I'm pleased at having gotten it right.

Now that there's light, I can finally see the bathroom and I'm thrilled that the horror stories of a hole cut in the floor are untrue. (I still have a purse full of Kleenex in anticipation of the "You won't find toilet paper in any public Italian toilet" warnings, though.) Mine's a standard-issue, made in 'Merica-type hotel bath with an updated toilet, sink, shower, and bonus bidet. The counter's plenty wide for all my makeup and the hair dryer is powerful. I'm missing washcloths, but I can work around that.

(Sidebar: I receive a washcloth on the second day when I put my Italian to use to ask the housekeeper for a "tiny towel for my face." For some reason, they don't use them here. No idea why.)

I flip on the television as I unpack, and immediately become entranced by the show *Guardia Costiera*, which is an outstandingly cheesy program about the Coast Guard. I'm already making a rule to limit my time with the television, lest I waste the whole trip mesmerized by dubbed reruns of *Friends*, which I didn't even watch in English.

Thus organized, I inspect the minibar, opening a package of shortbread cookies with big discs of chocolate baked in the middle. Is there anything more exciting than an exotic minibar? (No. No, there is not.) Then I put on my pajamas, draw the shades, and set my alarm for two hours later.

I figure if the rest of the city is as good as these cookies, then I'm in for a treat.

I've now been wandering around Rome for about two hours looking for the Trevi Fountain, finding myself utterly and completely lost because I'm incapable of reading a map. I'd ask Siri, except my cell phone won't work because either I didn't buy the right international data package or I don't have the Wi-Fi set up properly.

Somehow I suspect this is all Rome's way of paying me back for saying she reminded me of Houston.

I'm not stomping around angrily, though. I'm trying to take

in everything I see and I keep bumping into unexpected land-marks, like the Spanish Steps. History exists on every corner here. I can't go more than a few paces without discovering an ornate fountain or ancient church or a remnant of the old baths. And, my God, the people-watching! Every Roman woman is the physical embodiment of Sophia Loren, with elegance and confidence to spare. And Stacey was right—no one's wearing shorts. They're all in little sundresses or skirts or—please don't let this be a thing—elastic-bottomed harem pants. The Roman men are equally dap-per and completely gorgeous, but for some reason, they're all shorter than the women.

When I was in my twenties, I was afraid of Rome after Jo-anna graduated and spent the summer with a Eurail pass. She said the Roman men were butt-pinchers, calling, *"Bella, bella!"* while they followed her down the street.

Clearly, that's no longer going to be an issue, at least for me.

Not sure if I should celebrate the victory of becoming invisi-ble or mourn the loss of what made me visible. But at least I don't have to bust out the Italian insults, so perhaps it's a draw.

The saying is that all roads lead to Rome. While this may be true for others, for me, all roads apparently lead to snacks. As lost as I've been in this magnificent city, I find myself standing in front of the Gelateria della Palma, which is the exact gelato shop my Italian teacher told me to visit because they have something like one hundred and fifty flavors. Never one to ignore serendipity, I step inside and order a cone topped with almond tiramisu mousse and pistachio gelato. And with my first bite, I can already deter-mine that this trip has been worth it.

Real Italian gelato is both heavier and lighter than American ice cream due to being made with milk and eggs instead of cream. (Kind of like our version of frozen custard.) Gelato's also distinc-tive because there's less air pumped in while it's being made and it's served a few degrees warmer than ice cream. The amount of sugar seems different, too, as I taste more of the actual nut and coffee flavors rather than an overwhelming cloying sweetness. But none of the specifics matter as I plant myself on the bench in the middle of the shop, trying not to make om-nom-nom noises as I watch a tour group shuffle in, each wearing earphones and receivers in order to hear their tour leader.

As I've marched around the city, I've seen lots of groups being led here and there (wait, why didn't I follow any of them?) but this is the first time encountering a pack of Americans. Although the loud English is a heavy clue, I could have quickly identified them as fellow citizens by their fanny packs, cargo shorts, cowboy hats, and logo tees alone.

I make a mental note to tell Fletch not to pack like a jackass. I said this before I left, too, but it bears repeating.

I'm not sure why I believe I'm all EuroJen after having staked my flag in the gelato shop no more than five minutes prior to this group's arrival, yet here we are. But these people aren't following their tour guide's instructions on how to order and I'm bothered. Instead, they're barking commands at the nice employee who suddenly . . . doesn't seem to speak any English, despite our having the very conversation where I learned the difference between gelato and ice cream moments earlier.

Well played, gelato shop kid. Well played.

But I guess the Americans receive their just desserts (pun intended) when the tour leader apologizes for not turning off his mike while he used the restroom.

Ten euros says this was deliberate.

Before I exit the gelato shop, having finally figured out my location on the map, I buy the greatest possible Italian souvenir anyone could ever purchase. My new prize possession is a giant rainbow sucker with a picture of Pope Francis on it.

I call it a Lolli-Pope.

I walk for hours and for miles, trying to figure out where all

the points of interest are because I don't want the city to feel confusing for Fletch. Even after I bought the plane ticket, I had to sell him on the idea of leaving his comfort zone. Right before I left, he spotted a note my friend Jenny sent me about places to eat. Her husband, Jason, recommended we try the restaurant Il Pagliaccio, saying:

The food was tremendous, service awesome, and the setting was in a pretty sunken room with domed ceilings. They also serve an overpriced coffee that uses a bean that was partially digested and shit out by a rat. Not kidding. Of course I tried it. And, yes, it was delicious.

"Are you going to try to make me drink rat-shit coffee?" Fletch demanded, pointing at that line in the e-mail. "Because those are exactly the kind of stunts they pull over there to make Americans uneasy."

Wearily, I replied, "No one's making you drink rat-shit coffee." Although that was exactly my plan, had I not been busted. Now he doesn't entirely trust me, with good reason, so I want to smooth the way for his arrival as much as possible.

Anyway, what surprises me most so far is how these tiny cars drive everywhere, even down the alleys that are filled with sidewalk cafés and in no way resemble roads. For years, I thought my Sicilian grandfather was a menace behind the wheel and only now do I realize that he was simply an Italian driver.

Around dusk I decide I'm hungry, so I find a picturesque outdoor café right around the corner from the Spanish Steps. I'm as intrigued by their menu as I am by the promise of free Wi-Fi, as I've been radio silent for the past six hours. But because I'm not online I have no way to check out whatever the Italian version of Yelp is, so I take my chances.

I start with a glass of wine and ask for the prosciutto and buffalo mozzarella dish as my *primi piatti* (first plate), followed by the spaghetti carbonara, which is a creamy pasta dish—similar to an alfredo—made with pancetta. Years ago, when I worked at the Olive Garden, they occasionally had carbonara as a special and I was apeshit for it. I'd spend the whole shift annoying the cooks, making sure they'd have enough ingredients left over for my order at the end of the night. Magically delicious as carbonara was in Fort Wayne, Indiana, in 1992, I can't even imagine the majesty about to appear on a plate here where pasta was born.

I feel like I have to pinch myself, sitting at an outdoor table on a Roman side street, Vespas zipping by, with accordion music in the background, about to try the authentic versions of the cuisine I already love so much. I congratulate myself on having made travel part of my bucket list; otherwise I might never have come here.

My appetizer's served and I can't stop staring at my plate, trying to figure it out. Even though prosciutto and buffalo mozzarella appear to be exactly the same as the stuff I buy at the grocery store at home, I'm sure that the looks must be deceiving. Maybe Italy's more about the local, rustic ingredients and doesn't get all wrapped around the axle about the presentation like in American restaurants. This plain white plate, the same you'd find in any greasy spoon, is neither twee nor artisan. Maybe food in Italy is all substance, and who cares about style?

I slice off a tiny bite of the mozzarella, wrapping it in a bit of prosciutto before popping the delectable morsel in my mouth. I follow Michelle the Nutritionist's advice, chewing slowly and deliberately for maximum impact.

Turns out the looks are actually not deceiving.

In fact, what I buy at the Sunset grocery store is actually a lot better than what's in front of me. The dried ham lacks any discernable flavor and has the consistency of old Bubble Yum, while the buffalo mozzarella is a lump of bland, served on a plate of apathy.

I take a bite of the bread, which is grainy and stale and ever so slightly pungent.

WTF, Italy?

But afraid of seeming like an Ugly American, I don't want to complain. Maybe prosciutto is *supposed* to taste like under-salted shoe leather and I've just been eating candy-coated, super-spiced American versions at home. I have a few more bites before giving up. Doesn't matter if this is the authentic Italian way—I simply don't like it.

My carbonara arrives and it's . . . not a color I've ever been served before. Sometimes carbonara contains an egg stirred in at the end, so the dish can be a pale golden hue. But what's in front of me is the bright yellow of a bottle of French's mustard. I poke at the pasta, searching for the pancetta, wondering if I've been served the wrong item. When the waiter comes to check, I explain that I don't see any pancetta and he points to something the size of a micro-grain smeared on the side of the bowl, rolling his eyes as he saunters off.

I take a bite and taste what's absolutely, positively, without a shadow of a doubt boxed pasta mixed with canned cheese . . . and now I'm mad because this means I've literally had better meals at the Olive Garden, especially because back in 1992 they made their pasta from scratch.

How is this my luck? Not only did I have the one Italian nonna who couldn't cook, but now I've apparently stumbled into the place that taught her everything she knew.

I feel like Julia Roberts lied to me.

Did she not run around Italy in that movie, eating in places exactly like this, right in front of the perfect photo op, losing her mind over all the food?

This is the exact moment I realize what I've done wrong. I'm sure Julia Roberts (really, author Elizabeth Gilbert) didn't go to restaurants a stone's throw from a massive tourist attraction, because *her* phone probably worked and she could pull up Italian Yelp. You know what you get in Chicago when you eat by the Ferris wheel at Navy Pier?

Bubba Gump Shrimp.

So, I'm dining at the Italian version of Bubba Gump Shrimp. *Damn it.*

This restaurant has nothing to do with good food and everything to do with proximity and I vow to not make this mistake again.

Then, having given up on all things food-related at this particular little bistro, I decide that I can at least end the night with my first Italian coffee.

I order a cappuccino, which is apparently a crime against humanity, on par with the atrocities in the Sudan.

Damn it again.

My waiter literally winces in pain when I order, much as I winced when tasting his subpar prosciutto. I find out later that cappuccino's considered a breakfast drink and if you insist on having afternoon/evening coffee instead of wine—like a savage—then ordering a macchiato is de rigueur.

Listen, if I wanted to be scolded and dismissed and condescended to in English, I'd have just gone to Paris.

Equal parts discouraged and aggravated, I pay my bill and head to the cab stand. I tell the driver where I want to go. *Of course* his English is better than my Italian. However, he immediately recognizes me as having Sicilian ancestry, so we chat as he takes me back to the hotel. I relay my dinner experience and he cracks up.

"Ugh, terrible place. For tourists," he tells me. "Your thumb rule is '*if monument, then no you want.*' Do not eat anywhere looking at anything pretty. They cut the corners and they charge too much money. How much you pay for dog's dinner?"

"About forty euro?" I say. I still can't grasp the conversion rate, so this could be twenty bucks American or sixty. (Their Wi-Fi didn't work, so I couldn't look it up.)

He snorts. "Is the robbery of the highway, as you Americans say. Beautiful dinner is sixteen euro, eighteen euro maybe. *I ladri.* Crooks. You go back, get refund."

"I'm probably not going to do that," I admit.

"Next, you go to neighborhood, maybe Trastevere or Testaccio. Still tourists, but food is better. I promise."

"Well, thank God," I reply. "Because finding and then punching Julia Roberts really shouldn't be on my bucket list."

18.

················ ⬤ ················

Ugly Americans

Rome redeems herself at breakfast.

Big-time.

I'm spending the morning at the Galleria Borghese and need to be properly fueled, so I head to the restaurant downstairs in the hope of some decent bread and maybe some fruit. The moment I take in the buffet spread, I feel like Charlie Bucket upon seeing the Chocolate Room for the first time. There's a towering display of gorgeous fruits and fresh juices right as I walk in. Then I spot a yogurt bar with a dozen varieties of European flavors, surrounded by heaping bowls of nuts and seeds and granolas for toppings.

The breakfast offerings are arranged in stations, and with each bend and curve in the room, I find new nooks of nirvana. Although the Italians aren't huge on eggs for breakfast, they are tremendous proponents of breakfast meats, with platters groaning under the weight of the salumi like sopresatta, bresaola, mortadella, and prosciutto. Ten kinds of braided, seeded, and swirled breads spill from baskets, buffeted by muffins, scones, and croissants, with every type of jam and curd imaginable offered along-

side. Across from the Bread Barge, there's a whole array of buffalo
mozzarellas, including its milkier, even more delectable cousin
burrata, alongside fresh ricotta.

Oh, my God—cheese
for breakfast? Is that even
legal?

And, wait, what is this?
A whole section of the room
filled with plate after plate
of fifteen kinds of breakfast
cake?

When I look back at
the end of my life, I will
least regret the day I ate cake
with breakfast in Rome.

I do concentrate more
on the meats and cheeses,
however, because they are
brilliant. Each bite of mortadella (a pistachio-studded type of bo-
logna) is an aria, hitting every high note in the opera of my mouth.
The tomatoes taste like they were picked five minutes ago and the
multigrain roll I choose is so dense with the flavors of barley and
malt and honey that to mask it with butter or jelly would be a
travesty.

Classmates kept telling me to order the *spremuto* (fresh-squeezed)
orange juice, so I pour myself a glass. I take a sip and it's the naturally sweetest thing I've ever tasted. I'm not sure if I can use words
alone to describe the spectacular-ness of this experience—I think
I need hand gestures, too. When Fletch arrives tomorrow, this is
the first place I'm bringing him.

I'd literally stay here and graze until the staff has to roll me
out like Violet Beauregard, but it's time for my first real excursion.

Before I left for Rome, I was warned about the extensive lines to Roman attractions, so I preordered all my tickets and I'm due at the gallery by nine o'clock.

(Sidebar: If you ever come to Rome, *please* buy your tickets early/with the skip-the-line option, as it's the difference between three hours in the Vatican Museum and three hours *waiting* to get into the Vatican Museum in the punishing sun.)

I decide that today's an Immersion Day and I pledge to speak only Italian, which was why there was some confusion at breakfast when the host asked me for my room number and I told him I was well, thank you.

Hey, the Roman language wasn't built in a day.

After a quick cab ride, I arrive at the Galleria. After I check in, the employees confiscate all bags, including purses. I immediately comply, not even thinking to place my wallet in my pocket, because I'm a dumbass. For all my safety concerns, for all my posturing and learning to spew insults, apparently all anyone in this country has to do to get my purse is hand me a chit.

(Sidebar: The purse thing turned out fine. Also, I don't understand why everyone was so rabid about my being safe with my belongings. Rome's no different from any other city: Don't be stupid, have situational awareness, and you'll be okay.)

The museum's breathtaking, with massive portraits displayed in rooms illuminated by windows three stories tall. The ceilings are covered in trompe l'oeil clouds and angels, with a plethora of statues between the pictures. The statues are simply amazing due to the level of detail, right down to the veins running through forearms. Seems like the one area that gave sculptors difficulty was the hands, though. They're all huge and out of proportion with the rest of the statues' bodies.

Or is it possible all the ladies had man-hands back then?

I'm awed to be standing in the presence of all this history. But

I'm reminded of my friend who's a high-up in a museum in Chicago, where she's responsible for keeping the art safe. She once even worked on a film set where her job was to prevent the actors from bringing beverages or pens within fifty feet of the paintings. (FYI, she and Hugh Grant in a fight.) So while I stroll from room to room, I imagine the hair on the back of my friend's neck rising from an ocean away as visitors put their grubby fingers on everything.

Every damn thing.

To be clear, this is not an *interactive exhibit*. All the statues I pass have something broken on them, which I imagine is because no one here's being told to keep their mitts to themselves. Please explain to me why it's okay for patrons to run around with Sharpies and sketchbooks and water bottles and I'm not allowed to carry a tiny handbag. How, exactly, would I steal a Caravaggio painting that's two stories tall? I mean, (a) I'm honest, and (b) even if I weren't, I don't speak the kind of Italian I'd need to get myself out of Roman jail.

I learn that being drawn or sculpted nude was among the highest honors in the 1600s. Only the wealthiest citizens and most important politicians were allowed to be captured in the buff. Judging from the naked ladies, gravity was not a factor, so, good for them. And maybe big hands on the statues were a sign of virility/fertility?

Because I'm clearly a Philistine, the art isn't what moves me most. Instead, I'm entranced by the walls' faux finishes and the gilding on the furniture, so essentially I'm the kid who cares less about the expensive toy and more about the big cardboard box it came in.

After a few hours in the museum, I head to the snack bar to order an iced cappuccino and I sit outside in the sun to drink it. There's a lion-headed fountain with a basin to the left of me and people keep filling their water bottles from it. This city seems to have a one-to-one ratio of fountains to citizens because they are *everywhere*. The thing is? I can't tell which ones are for drinking and which ones have been shat in by pigeons for the last three hundred years, so for now, I'm buying my water.

I hop in a cab and in my best accent ask to go to the Campo de' Fiore, an open-air market, where I haggle for scarves to bring home to my friends. By "haggle," I mean "pay full price" because I'm clearly not just the worst negotiator in America, but also in Europe. Still, I conducted the transaction entirely in Italian, so this feels like a win.

Rome quiets down between two and five p.m., with many shops closing. How does this make any sort of business sense? However, as it's very hot and I've completed my day's itinerary, I decide to spend some time at the pool.

My plans for Italian immersion are shot when I discover that the only people up on the roof are either from New York or Texas. One of the Texan women has an actual paw print from her now-dead dog tattooed on her shoulder. Let's just say it's a good thing I didn't know this was an option when Maisy was still alive.

The New Yorkers at the pool are mad at the father of one of the Texas clans, as he'd earlier admonished them for using profanity in front of his sixteen-year-old daughter. The New Yorkers' stance is, she's sixteen and these are not the first f-bombs she's heard, and if they are, then the family should probably subscribe to HBO. So, every time the Texas dad turns his back, the New Yorkers flip him off and mouth, "We hate him." I don't think the New Yorkers give a shit whether or not they're being good American ambassadors, so the whole scene's actually pretty funny.

The view from the top of the hotel is spectacular, with vistas of tiled roofs and little courtyards in every direction. Building restrictions prohibit historical sites from being blocked, so there are no skyscrapers in this part of the city. Save for the satellite dishes and tiny cars, the view can't be much different from when this outdoor deck was part of an actual palace.

Unlike a *Bachelor* contestant, I actually am here to make friends, so I talk with the other Americans. When I ask the other (temporary) ex-pats where they've been eating, one of the women says her family's had dinner at the Scottish pub around the corner for the past few nights, a statement that seems so illogical all I can do is smile and nod.

Why would . . .

How could . . .

Does not compute.

The New Yorkers said they saw a sign for an American breakfast yesterday, so they went inside to order and were served twelve partially cooked scrambled eggs, which then caused the wife to barf.

None of them seems terribly intent on experiencing what Rome has to offer. They're all more well-traveled than I am; is this all old hat to them? They're spending all day at the pool and their nights trying to find food that's familiar, so really, they may as well be in Vegas. Personally, I didn't want to take a vacation so much as I wanted to experience Rome, so I eventually excuse myself; even though the pool is lovely and the company affable, I have homemade pasta to find and Italian to *parlo*.

"So, the Pantheon is over there and the gelato shop's back that way. Which would you rather hit first?" I ask. Fletch arrived this morning in high spirits, despite not being able to sleep on the plane either.

So far, I've taken him for breakfast and coffee and a brief detour to Testaccio instead of Sant'Eustachio, as the Senegalese cabbie spoke neither Italian nor English, which reminds me of the time at home when the taxi driver had never heard of Wrigley Field. Anyway, now we're trying to determine what to do next as we loiter in the piazza halfway between the grand Corinthian columns of the Pantheon and the less historic palm trees on the sign for the gelato shop.

"Well," Fletch says, "the Pantheon's been standing for thousands of years, so it can probably wait a few more minutes while we eat gelato."

The Pantheon does, indeed, wait for us. The ancient Roman temple is amazing and guess what—it's free! What a gift that is for anyone with an interest in history, religion, or architecture.

We take our time to explore, gawping up at the oculus—a central opening up at the top that floods the room with light. We learn that the oculus is the world's largest unreinforced concrete dome, commissioned by Marcus Agrippa in the time before Christ. We're floored by what Man could accomplish long before benefit of machine.

The longer I'm here, the more I feel a connection with Italy, and I marvel at having come from such industrious people. Until now, I always identified more with the English side of my heritage, mostly because of the history behind my last name. Rumor has it we're descended from the Lancasters who date back to the War of the Roses. Then again, my paternal grandfather used to swear that every time any toilet flushed, the contents went to Moon Island, so it's possible he wasn't the most accurate steward of family lore.

We tool around the city with no particular

agenda, taking pictures of fountains and browsing in shops for a few hours until Fletch tires and needs to rest.

I want Fletch to have the best meal tonight, so we decide to visit the Trastevere neighborhood across the Tiber. I dress and touch up my makeup quickly and am halfway through an episode of *The Good Wife* in Italian (screaming with glee when Julianna Margulies says the name of the town where I live) when Fletch begins to pace between the closet and his suitcase.

"I don't have anything to wear."

"How do you not have anything to wear? You brought two huge suitcases. For four days. You have stuff to wear. I'm sure of it," I reply.

He begins to pull inappropriate choice after inappropriate choice out of his bag. For some reason, he brought nothing but ratty old polos and weird T-shirts.

"Seriously? *Seriously?* You brought your *El Pollo Loco* shirt? You thought, 'Hey, I'm going to one of the most elegant cities in the world, so I'll be sure to bring my chicken T-shirt.'" I'm shaking my head as I dig through his baggage. I hold up a faded gray offering. "Johnny Cash? You brought a Johnny Cash shirt? What part of '*Don't pack like a jackass*' was problematic for you?"

"I was confused. I didn't know what they wore here," he argued.

"So you erred on the side of *Johnny Cash*? Where are all those nice polished cotton oxfords I bought you last summer?"

"I didn't think they'd be appropriate."

"But a *chicken shirt* would be?"

"Shit. I don't know. We probably need to go shopping. It's still early so I'm sure the stores are still open," he says.

And just like that, for the very first time in our relationship, Fletch actually Tom Sawyers *me*.

• • •

"You look very handsome."

"I do, don't I?" Fletch admires himself in the hotel room mirror because over the past couple of days, he's learned that European-cut shirts fit him as though custom-made.

"You Tom Sawyered me. You packed like a jack- ass on purpose." Much like Tom suckered his friends into whitewashing the fence, I have a rather unfortunate history of doing tasks wrong in front of Fletch so that his impulse is to jump in and take over, which is often my endgame.

"I didn't pack badly on purpose," he lies. (Such lies.) "Fitting so well in the shirts here is a happy accident."

"Right. Like me convincing you to 'teach me' to paint the trim in my office was a 'happy accident.'"

"Yeah. So now we're even."

Because we did budget for shopping here, I'm not mad. In- stead I'm charmed—who'd have guessed the old dog had a few new tricks in him?

(Sidebar: You know who didn't anticipate me shopping here? My credit card company. Despite calling card services before leav- ing, and verifying all purchases via their app, every single charge I attempt is declined, to the point it becomes comical. I return from Italy having purchased only a new lipstick and a pair of sunglasses for myself, whereas Fletch comes home with a veritable trousseau because there's no problem with his card.)

(Additional sidebar: I guess the lesson here is to pack like a jackass.)

We take a taxi across to our new favorite place. Trastevere is only a mile away from the center of Rome, but must somehow be the difference between Brooklyn and New York. It's blocks away, yet oceans apart. The buildings are smaller and closer together and it's much more of a hotspot. Tons of bars ring the square and all the European kids in their twenties are drinking beer in the court-yards, while the older generations are sitting in overlooking cafés with their bottles of wine. The whole place feels like a polite fra-ternity party,

We pass by the street vendors and they all try to catch our attention as they hawk their wares. We walk up to a display of woven leather bracelets and the vendor says to Fletch, "Hey, Brit-ish guy, you like?" At the next table, he's mistaken for French. Fletch decided to go Euro on his first day here, so he's been buying bracelets, saying that they'll remind him of the feeling of being relaxed and on vacation once he's back in the States.

I can't argue with his logic, yet this is so out of character. He is not a man who wears jewelry. He also isn't one to roll with the punches or enjoy adapting to his surroundings, but there's some-thing magical about this place that's making him loosen up.

(Sidebar: Cute as he looks in his new accessories, my only regret is that I can't mock him by saying, "Hey, Johnny Depp, nice arm party," having already used that line in *Twisted Sisters*.)

Another table vendor starts speaking to Fletch in Spanish, assuming he's a Spaniard. Argh. No one's assuming I'm from any-where but the US of A, I assume because there are no fat women here. I can't buy any clothes because no one sells plus-sized items, so I decide to pick up the aforementioned sunglasses. I head into a nice designer optical boutique off the square and begin to peruse the selection. I want something Fendi because I'd like to support their efforts to repair the Trevi Fountain. Also, anything Fendi costs half as much here, so, when in Rome . . .

The owner's helping me select the right pair. At least, I assume she's the owner as she's the one in all the pictures on the wall. In each shot, she's posed with a celebrity, some of whom I recognize. Those who aren't familiar are likely European movie stars. I'm really taken by how service-oriented shopkeepers are here, and not in a way that's pushy. Employees everywhere really take the time to figure out what's best for the customer, offering honest critique on what works and what doesn't.

After we find an extra-cute pair, I'm in the middle of paying (yes, in cash because my credit card company has somehow decided they're my parents now) when an American kid wearing cargo shorts, a fraternity shirt, and a backward baseball cap bursts in the store.

"Y'all got Ray-Bans here?"

No *buona sera*, no hello, just a blatant interruption delivered with the absolute confidence that not only does the store owner speak his language, but that she's simply dying to stop what she's doing to assist him.

Far more politely than the situation merits, the shop owner points him to their selection and offers to assist the moment we complete our business.

The kid says, "Yeah, but how do I know they're *real* Ray-Bans. How do I know you're not trying to cheat me? See, I bought some Ray-Bans before in another place and they were fake. I still wear 'em, but I don't like being faked out. I don't want you faking me, you feel me?"

I want to shake this kid, saying, STOP BEING A CLUELESS ASSBAG; YOU'RE MAKING OUR ENTIRE COUNTRY LOOK BAD. Though he appears to be college-aged, he's acting like he just downed fifteen Pixy Stix before breaking away from the rest of his class on a field trip to the Children's Museum.

"I assure you, sir, I am not a street vendor and I only sell authentic designer sunglasses," the owner says. Never will I be able to muster similar amounts of forbearance, but something tells me this isn't the first assbag in her night, let alone her career.

"I don't knoooooow," he singsongs, crossing his arms over his Theta Chi shirt. "How can I be sure? You guys can be pretty sneaky over here. Like, oily and stuff."

I hold up my bag, glare at the kid, and tell the shop owner, "Thank you for including this certificate of authenticity. I really appreciate your service and I'll surely enjoy my authentic Fendi product for many years to come."

My words fly right over the kid's head. He pokes around at the Ray-Ban selection, smudging up a whole row of lenses as his fingers are damp from holding his beer. "Your prices are kinda high. I can get these for a lot less outside."

The owner shoots Fletch and me a resigned look, like, *can you believe this shit*, while in Italian, I promise the owner that we aren't all this stupid.

We step outdoors, both of us incredulous, and Fletch says, "So *that's* why they call us Ugly Americans."

"I never knew it could be like this," Fletch moans through a mouthful of pasta. "I want to bury every other spaghetti I've ever had in the backyard."

We're sitting outside at an unassuming pasta place somewhere in the Santa Maria area of Trastevere, eating one of the best meals of our lives. My driver from the first night has been spot on with his recommendation to cross the Tiber to find restaurants. Our whole dinner, including two courses each and a bottle of wine, will run a couple euros north of what my first terrible meal did. Our pastas have been simply prepared, his with tomatoes, basil, and pancetta, and mine with Parmesan and pepper. What takes this repast from a meal to a memory is the quality of preparation and the freshness of the ingredients—that's a theme we're finding over and over in Rome. Nothing is complicated or overwrought, topped with foam or served with attitude. Instead, the food truly speaks for itself.

I've already inhaled my first course and I'm fighting the urge to lick my plate. I've always heard the term *al dente* in regard to making pasta, but I've never sampled an actual example of it before Rome. The firmness of true al dente is way chewier than I would ever imagine serving, but it really is perfection. The next time I make spaghetti at home, I'll have to remind myself that what seems wrong is actually right.

After the waiter brings our second course, Fletch says, "How nice is it to finally have a meal without dogs staring up at us?" He slices off a piece of his steak, fragrant with garlic, oregano, and rosemary. When the waiter carried the still-sizzling dish out, we could smell it from halfway across the patio.

The universe must have heard us because at this exact moment, I notice a rustling in the bushes next to me and a pointy face appears on the other side of the fencing. "Oh!" I exclaim. "Look at you!"

A little fox dog is panting up at us in the way that almost seems like a smile.

"Clearly I spoke too soon." Fletch laughs.

"Well, of course he smelled your steak. There's a meat cloud of deliciousness hovering over our table. I'm surprised hungry people aren't lining up at the fence, too." I turn my attention to the dog. "How cute are you?" I ask. Fox Dog bats his long lashes in response, giving me that nose-down, eyes-up look that slays me every time.

I've noticed that the Italians have a different relationship with their dogs than I do with mine. At home, and like many Americans, our dogs are our babies, our sweeties, our little girl or our big man. We hug them and kiss them and love them and never quite let them grow up. Over here, no one seems to infantilize their pets; dogs are treated more like companions and pets act much more independent.

For example, Fox Dog belongs to someone at one of the tables across the alley from us. This guy's allowed to range freely without someone like me hovering over him, trying to determine whether or not hims needs him sweater. Also, because Italians will drive on any surface large enough for a Smart car to pass, there's the occasional vehicle coming down this alley, and still, no leash. I would be having a million panic attacks right now, but it seems like all the Romans are having is wine.

"Look at him! So fluffy! Such big eyes! So hungry!" I exclaim. None of the dogs here are chunky, either. How is that possible? I have to monitor Libby's every bite to keep her from turning into a full-on Macy's Thanksgiving Day Parade balloon.

"Do not feed the strange dog," Fletch warns me.

I say, "I would never," which means, "I absolutely will." Because hims very hungry! Hims has to keep up all him fluffs!

Although the dog is paying strict attention to us, particularly since I started doling out scraps of pork chop fat, he's got one eye on the alley behind us and we begin to notice a pattern. Vespas can whiz past, go-cart-sized cars, folks on bikes, etc., but the only time the dog barks is when a person of color passes.

"He's barking at all the Moroccan men! This dog is racist!" I say.

"No, he's probably just an all-around jerk," Fletch argues. "Watch."

A group of rowdy Aussies comes down the alley and the dog has no reaction. Then a chick on a scooter goes past us so closely she practically clips his puffy tail. Nothing. A restaurant worker dragging garbage cans along behind him produces no reaction whatsoever, but when a Moroccan passes us, the dog loses his shit.

"I'll be damned," Fletch admits.

Fox Dog blinks up at me but I'm resolute. "No more chops for you, bigot."

"Have you been slipping him food?" Fletch asks. "What am I saying? Of course you have. *You* are why our dogs are fat."

He's not wrong.

Fox Dog eventually loses interest in us when he realizes the Pork Chop Express has pulled away from the station. He wanders off to perpetrate his xenophobia elsewhere.

Fletch and I linger over dinner, enjoying our wine and each other's company.

I say, "The longer I'm here, the more I understand the Roman way of life. When citizens go out here, that's the whole plan for the night. They don't run out to dinner and rush home to make sure they don't miss *Real Housewives*. Donatella says they'll sit at the table for hours."

"Waiters make a living wage here, none of the two-dollar-an-hour-booshit like we used to deal with. I imagine that's why there's no pressure like in US restaurants to turn the table ASAP," Fletch replies.

"And it's so pleasant, right?" I toy with my glass of Chianti. "I'm starting to figure out that in Rome, there's a time for everything, like with the cappuccino." Again, coffee is for the morning.

No one drinks coffee at night because that's the time for wine. "Seems like at home, no one ever has enough hours in the day to allot for each activity, but here, they have time in spades."

Fletch sighs with contentment as he checks out our surroundings. There's a quiet buzz of conversation and clink of glasses and silverware, but the overall vibe is serene. "You're checking off your bucket list items right and left here, but I think what you're learning most in Rome is to slow down."

I nod. "Like, Romans move with purpose on the street, but otherwise no one's in a hurry here. There's no panicked sense of urgency like I always feel at home. I wonder how much of this dovetails into our consumer culture."

He tilts his head and sips his wine. "How so?"

"Here, I don't have a sense that people are rushing off to work a twelve-hour day, coming home and popping a Lean Cuisine into the microwave before doing more work and checking in on Facebook before going to bed so they can do it all again in the morning because they need to pay for their houses they never enjoy and the fancy cars they use almost exclusively to get to their jobs that allow them to buy all the trappings they're a slave to in the first place."

"Whew, now *I'm* exhausted."

"You know what else I haven't seen? Home stores. I've not passed the equivalent of Restoration Hardware or Crate and Barrel or Pottery Barn, so I get the feeling that no one's killing themselves working double shifts so they can consume stuff to make their homes Pinterest-perfect. Maybe the Roman message is to not let your stuff own you."

Fletch smiles. "Are you suddenly advocating socialism?"

"Of course not, plus a country on the verge of financial collapse might not be the best example, but there *is* something to be learned about easing my pace. Maybe Americans stick out here so much not because of the wardrobe or language, but because of our

frenetic energy. Like, *that's* what makes us ugly. We're not good about taking the time to just be and do. We make everyone else tense."

When I was planning this trip, I'd originally had every minute orchestrated, but Stacey warned me that was a bad idea. She said I'd regret not allowing Rome simply to reveal herself to me, so I cut my scheduled activities to no more than three hours per day. Yesterday, we visited the Colosseum but then we had the afternoon free to enjoy a leisurely lunch in the Campo de' Fiori. We won't get to see all of Rome this way, but that just means we'll have to come back.

"I bet having enough time is why no one's fat here. Stands to reason everyone would be beefy because of all the wine and pasta, but they're not. Here we are, lingering over dinner, and we've actually eaten less than we would have at home in front of the television. Where are you on your hunger scale right now?"

I try to get a sense of where I am. "Maybe a seven? I'm satisfied, but in no way uncomfortable. I'm not in the kind of food coma that'll keep me up all night like when we go to Italian restaurants at home."

Fletch does this move I call Dinosaur Finger when he's making a point. He'll tap on the table with his first, second, fourth, and fifth fingers, while holding up the one in the middle. Reminds me of a little brontosaurus. "That's what I'm saying. Here, having dinner is the end goal. Italians are not wolfing down Monster Thickburgers in their massive SUV as they haul their kids from soccer to Mandarin to ballet so the kids have fully rounded résumés in order to go to college so they can graduate and repeat the whole cycle."

"They've stopped the insanity."

"Exactly."

"Doesn't seem like a bad life," Fletch replies. "Not a great way to run an economy, but a relaxed way to live."

"No wonder Americans get here and lose our minds. Without the day-to-day pressure of a rigorous daily schedule keeping us reined in, we go careening all over the place like a rapidly deflating balloon."

"Nice visual."

I nod. "Thanks. Professional writer."

He says, "Too bad we have to go home on Sunday. Given enough time here, I believe we could solve all the world's problems."

19.

IL CAVALLO

"You know what no one ever says about the Vatican?" I ask. *"'Wow, what great air-conditioning they have here.'"*

"How much water did you drink?" Fletch replies.

"Four bottles, easily." I was so thirsty shortly into the tour that I actually filled my bottles at one of the decorative fountains, and I'll be damned if this wasn't the freshest, most pure-tasting stuff I've ever had. At first I didn't want to drink anything because our guide said we wouldn't have access to a bathroom for two hours, but then I sweated so profusely that excess fluids weren't an issue.

Fletch says, "I can't get over how rude everyone was in the Sistine Chapel. We had two rules to follow. No talking, no taking pictures. Yet everyone was talking and snapping photos. They didn't even shut up when that cardinal came out to bless us."

"I sort of get the photo part. When you come face-to-face with such an iconic piece of art, I understand the motivation to capture the moment. I do. How many times have we seen the hand of God on coffee mugs and posters and T-shirts? Then to finally witness the real thing in person? I can understand the rule break. Me, I was too busy being the Sleeve and Shorts Police. Every guidebook says that you have to cover your shoulders and knees, and that you'd be asked to leave otherwise, but no one there was acting as a bouncer. Had I known, I wouldn't have worn this heavy-ass skirt."

We're currently attempting to exit the Vatican grounds after spending hours touring the museum and St. Peter's Basilica. This is easier said than done because this place takes up miles of real estate. Not coincidentally, the thousands of the faithful who'd also been having their day o' religion are seeking taxis to return to their hotels for some downtime before dinner alfresco, so we encounter a highly unfavorable cab-to-Catholic ratio.

Having lived in the city of Chicago for so many years, we understand that the best way to get a taxi is *not* to stand in a line that is already nine-billion deep with sweaty papists. The better strategy is to walk a couple of blocks away from the venue where the competition will be less intense; see: *Every Professional Ball Game, Concert, and Play I Ever Attended.*

"What was your favorite part?" I ask. I'm still bowled over by the level of detail in every nook and cranny of the Vatican and Basilica. There's not a single surface that's unadorned, because everything's either frescoed, marble-covered, or gold-plated. Maybe this is where I get my decorating style, reasoning if one vintage trophy on a shelf is good, then ten are so much better.

"I was impressed by the

hallway of maps," Fletch says. "I had no idea the old Popes were more like kings than religious leaders." When we went down one passage, the guide showed us intricate maps on which the Popes commissioned artists to note every single aspect of their enemies' defenses, down to where they kept their beehives.

"My favorite part was when the guide rushed us through the contemporary part of the museum. She was all, *'Don't worry about this bullshit. Is nothing important.'* We were passing paintings by *Matisse* and *Dalì!* Only in a place with this much Michelangelo can the modern guys be considered bullshit."

(Sidebar: I had no idea Michelangelo was not only the most interesting man on the planet, but also the most beleaguered. Our guide, the same one who told us to "Push gypsies out of your way," then added, "with manners," called Michelangelo a "bitchy old queen." I'm getting the idea that Romans haven't much of a conversational filter, which may explain my lack of one as well.)

(Another sidebar: When Michelangelo initially declined a Vatican commission, the Pope said, "Sure, that's cool, no probs, Mikey. But I hope you don't mind if tomorrow we burn down the city you're from in retribution." Really puts my former bad bosses into perspective.)

Fletch and I both agree that the Vatican's absolutely a once-in-a-lifetime experience, which neither of us expected. Before this trip, I didn't have a grasp of any history outside of what happened in my own country. But compared to Italy, the US is like five minutes old. For some reason, I always assumed history was dry and boring, nothing but a collection of dates to memorize. I could not have been more wrong and I'll be returning home with a burning desire to learn more.

I had no idea of the drama and corruption behind the Borgia Pope's reign. I didn't realize how Julius Caesar was responsible for the rise of the Empire on the heels of the demise of the Republic, dying on the Senate steps after being stabbed. *Say what?* Sure, I'd heard of the Ides of March, but I had no clue as to what actually occurred that day. And who could have guessed that gladiators were the ancient equivalent of rock stars, with clever vendors selling bottles of the sand on which they sweat and bled. The Colosseum was Beatlemania BC.

Basically, I'm here wondering WHY WAS I NOT INFORMED THAT HISTORY IS THE BEST REALITY SHOW OF ALL TIME?

Or is this yet another fact everyone else knew and, as usual, I'm the last horse to cross the finish line?

Fletch and I stroll for a bit, mulling over our dinner options, deciding not *if* we should have *cacio e pepe*, which is now my favorite dish ever, but *where*. Satisfied that there's no dearth of places to find Italian macaroni and cheese, we move on to discussing if this is the best day we've ever had. Fletch thinks it's possible, but I'm not sure I can agree until I remove my sweaty girdle and voluminous eyelet cotton skirt. Then we debate if it would be weird to convert to Catholicism simply because of the magnificence of St. Peter's Basilica. At this point, the heat or jet lag catches up to Fletch and he declares that he can't go another step without coffee.

Unfortunately, we have no choice but to take many more steps because there's no coffee shop to be found.

We continue shuffling down rustic cobblestone streets, in

fine spirits, but tired, hot, and desperate for something caffeinated. We keep hearing Rome referred to as the eternal city. Now that I've been in the city for a while, I suspect this has to do with the fact that everyone here is eternally broiling and exhausted from enjoying its many treasures.

We're not so beat that we aren't mesmerized at how incredibly picturesque everything is, though, and each moment we've spent feels like a gift as there's so much to appreciate. For example, I love that there's not an inch of Rome that hasn't been embellished for the better. Even the doors are works of art.

Design is so prevalent and inspirational in Rome that all I want to do is go home and paint murals across my monotonously white ceilings and slap gold leaf on every dreary chair in my dining room. I mean, the *garbage cans* are decorative, for crying out loud!

Architecture aside, the light itself is magical. At this time of day, the sun's no longer pounding relentlessly down, incinerating everything it touches, turning me into a human dress shield. Rather, it's a benevolent warm glow in the sky, casting a rosy gold radiance that illuminates the ancient stucco buildings, which are all adorned with bright wooden shutters and festooned with window boxes groaning under the weight of all their fuchsia flowers.

Every inch of the narrow *strada* we're currently on is picture-postcard–worthy, with fascinating vignettes as far as the eye can see. To our right, there's a couple of grizzled old priests smoking, laughing, and drinking red wine at a little iron bistro table. There's a joke here, I think, and it begins, "Three priests walk into a bar." What's their story? Did they just get off work? Are they employed by the Vatican? Does that job come with dental? Are they friends with the new Pope? (I suspect yes—Francis seems kind of awesome.) Do they desperately miss Saint John Paul II or are they frankly just relieved to be done with the interim guy who was so scowl-y?

To our left, a skirt-clad, scarf-wrapped Roman mama purposefully pedals her bike with an adorably pink-cheeked toddler in the seat on the back. She has a basketful of gorgeous produce and fine bread balanced in front. (No one wears bike helmets here. *No one.* It's like Milwaukee!) It's all I can do not to follow her home and beg to eat whatever she's cooking for dinner.

Please, God, let it be eggplant.

Plus, it's jasmine season, so the blooming flowers provide a heavy perfume that blankets the city, mingling with the scent of thousands of years of sandalwood and frankincense emanating from all the old churches. Someone should bottle the fragrance of Rome in June; they'd make a fortune.

In terms of sensory overload, we're still reeling from the perfection that is the Sistine Chapel ceiling, even if its magnificence renders everyone incapable of shutting their yaps. I still can't believe we're surrounded by the kind of splendor that assaults every single sense.

Still . . . the coffee thing is getting to us.

"I feel like you pulled a bait and switch," Fletch says, as we plod down the street, two pilgrims on a quest for liquid salvation. We both heeded everyone's advice and are wearing fine walking shoes, and thus far, no one's turned an ankle or formed a blister.

(Sidebar: Another Roman observation? You can't buy a pair of stilettos in this city. Impossibly high platform sandals abound, but there's nary a spike or kitten heel to be seen. I like thinking that I can't manage heels because my ancestors never walked in them, even though it's more likely due to my comorbidity of poor balance and weak core muscles.)

"How so?" I ask.

"You lured me here under the pretense that I'd spend my days swilling java, but they make it almost impossible." He qualifies his statement. "It's worth it, but it's still hard."

He's right, too. Who knew coffee would be such a challenge in Italy? I mean, isn't this the birthplace of the modern espresso machine? A couple of days ago, before Fletch arrived, I found a Nespresso shop by the Spanish Steps and I was so excited that I had to take a picture for Julia, who fell in love with my unit last Christmas and finally had to get one of her own.

Coffee is not easy here. In fact, coffee is so freaking hard. (One could argue that coffee is for closers.) For some reason, I assumed Rome would be an enormous Starbucks, only a million times better. My best guess was that espresso would be as free-flowing and abundant as the fountains dotting the streets. There'd be coffee places on every corner and we'd stroll around the city with our giant cups, admiring the scenery while we sipped the finest brew on Earth. And, because we're a tiny bit smug now—like no one saw that coming—we'd be laughing about all those unenlightened saps at home drinking their stupid, subpar American coffee.

Ha, ha, ha, no.

Easy access to coffee is not the case in Italy.

At all.

The whole getting-coffee process is incredibly complicated, at least for the first-timer. Coffee procurement is an entire procedure and there are distinct rules. And no one tells you the rules; they expect you to know them already. For example, there are scads of cute little outdoor cafés (except, apparently, in this ten-block radius on the wrong side of the Vatican), but you don't usually see anyone except for tourists sitting at them because the real Italians are all inside crowded at the bar.

To order coffee in Italy, you have to master the steps. First, you go inside and you place your order with the cashier, where you'll note that Starbuck-y tweaks such as half-caf-soy-extra-hot-skinny-shot-of-hazelnut are not even a consideration, let alone a viable option.

The cashier will grudgingly take your money, but he won't actually hand your change back to you, instead depositing it in a small dish, even if your hand is right there and in position. I've yet to figure out what purpose the dish holds, but maybe in a city where the plague was an actual thing, they don't touch people when not absolutely necessary?

After you pay, the cashier gives you a chit and you take said chit over to the baristas' area. This separation of church and state makes sense in terms of sanitation because they don't want the people who handle the money to also put their paws on the food and drink. (Again, plague-related?)

As Chief Watch Captain of the Health and Safety Patrol, I'd be one hundred percent behind this system, except that at any point in time, there will be eight thousand people crowded around said coffee bar, because (a) the cashier is super fast, what with throwing your change in a bowl instead of counting it back to you, (b) the baristas are in no hurry whatsoever because this is Italy and, for better or worse, they take their damn time, (c) they serve your beverage in real cups; ergo, you have to drink it inside the shop, unless you want to pay more to have your coffee outside, and (d) Italians are not big on the concept of "lines" so there's a mass of humanity all clustered together on the floor of this very small shop, with no rhyme or reason as to traffic flow.

See? The coffee process is already unduly complicated.

Because there are dozens and dozens of other patrons between you and the barista, you have to wait for one of them to finally acknowledge you. And as there's no line, there's no set way of deciding who's first and whoever receives their coffee next is based on a completely arbitrary and capricious set of rules. I've found that if you give them a really big, creepy, toddler-beauty-pageant smile, they go faster, largely because it's so off-putting.

So, when you and your chilling rictus finally get the barista's attention, you hand him your slip, which is when you specify if you want your drink served with or without sugar, which is yet another mystery.

Is *il zucchero* a precious commodity in Italy? I suspect it may be; otherwise, why wouldn't they let you sweeten your coffee yourself?

(Sidebar: This is also my problem with the Dunkin' Donuts corporation. I guarantee you I know how to lighten and sugar my coffee better than the surly person behind the counter who looks at my cream consumption as both an insult and a challenge.)

(Additional sidebar: Last year I went to Dunkin's on Memorial Day at ten a.m. to buy doughnuts and they were sold out. How do you sell out of doughnuts? The cashier suggested that I might rather have ice cream from the attached Baskin-Robbins. Hell, no, I don't want ice cream! Not eating breakfast ice cream is the only thing that stands between me and not needing a crane to knock down a wall so that I can leave the house! I mean, breakfast cake on vacation is one thing, but breakfast ice cream? No. If it's ten a.m. on a holiday weekend, I want crullers and bismarcks and fritters, damn it! Come on, Dunkin' Donuts, you had ONE JOB here.)

Ahem.

Anyway.

So, you've finally run the order decathlon and oh, happy day, your coffee is coming! When it arrives, don't expect a big paper traveling cup or even a standard-sized mug. Instead, your coffee will be served in a delicate little demitasse the size of an eye bath. I'm not kidding. Even if you order something other than espresso, you get maybe six ounces, as opposed to the Starbucks Trenta, which is thirty-one ounces of pure USA! USA! USA!

Then, you'll stand there and imbibe your thimbleful of coffee, which is the greatest possible thing you'll ever put in your face, thus making the entire tribulation worth it. The full-bodied richness of this heady concoction commingles with the smoky undertones, somewhere between chocolate and tobacco, melting onto your tongue, without even a thought of bitterness or acidity.

As you sip, the woodsy notes become more defined, with hints of the same florals so perfuming this ancient city. The regular old milk from Italian cows is far richer and more resplendent than any heavy cream from Wisconsin's finest and the barista was right to portion out your sugar for you, as he's stirred in the perfect proportion, down to the very grain.

The reasons Italians make the best coffee in the universe are a subject of much debate—some say it's because they hand-pump the espresso shots, while others argue it's the roasting process, which allows the beans to caramelize. Perhaps it is the minerals in the water that turn an average breakfast beverage into alchemy. Others will insist that half the battle is the scenery surrounding the coffee shop. My guess is it's all these factors combined.

One could argue that the Italian cup of coffee is proof that God exists.

I won't disagree.

Anyway, your impulse will be to savor this nectar of the gods, this potable ambrosia, to take each sip and hold it in your mouth while it warms your soft palate, allowing the rich goodness to penetrate every taste bud and fill your sinus cavities with delectable, aromatic steam.

Instead, you'll have to swill it down as quickly as humanly possible in order to make way for the hordes of impatient Italians behind you, who are all staring holes in your back, you slow-sipping-doughnut-munching-Rockport-wearing-fanny-pack-having-sugar-hoarding-spaghetti-cutting-American-motherfucker.

Mind you, you could have this same exact experience outside at a table, without all the dirty looks and elbows to the kidneys and plague fears, except the waiter has chased a pretty girl from Singapore down the street in order to flirt with her and it's going to be next week before he even acknowledges your existence, let alone takes your order.

Still, and I can't stress this enough: The coffee is worth it.

We continue to traverse the little cobblestone streets and we're just about ready to give up and grab a cab when we spy a glint of a copper espresso maker inside a restaurant on the corner across from a gelato shop. We step inside the pristine storefront to order, finding it delightfully empty. Noting how hot and haggard we are, the barista suggests we sit outside and enjoy our drinks, sending a non-Singaporean-chasing-waitress to seat us immediately. Fletch asks for a *caffè macchiato* and I order a *caffè freddo*, which I assume is an iced coffee.

I assume wrong, but this is yet another in a series of happy Roman accidents. Instead of receiving a big glass of coffee over ice that I can doctor with the Italian version of Splenda and milk, I'm served what's essentially a straight-up, shaken coffee martini, less the liquor.

This turns into one of those moments on the trip when we've inadvertently veered off the beaten path, only to discover something we never expected yet suddenly can't imagine ever living without. Somehow this barista managed to compile everything that's remarkable about a big-assed iced coffee, and compress it into one simple drink that is espresso at its very essence.

Fletch raises his miniature teacup at me. "If this macchiato is any indication, then we definitely need to eat something here," he declares.

We order a couple of pizzas—Fletch has his with prosciutto and I get the one with bresaola (slices of air-dried, salted beef), rocket, and Parmesan. While we wait for our food, we continue to bask in the scenery.

He asks, "Have you decided if this is your Best Day yet?"

I'm not hot to the point of expiration now, thanks to the power of my chilly glass of miracle juice, so I'm able to better consider his question. After arriving on Italian soil, I amended my bucket list to **have a go-to greatest day of my life for when people ask**. Seems like everyone has an example, like, "That time we were scuba diving in the Galapagos Islands and narrowly escaped the Great White," or "When my son was born," or "Our wedding day," but I'm not PADI certified, we don't have kids, and our wedding? Was an unmitigated disaster. Thus far, I've had an awful lot of nice days in my life, but I'm not sure I can say that any of them have qualified as The Best.

The Best Day doesn't necessarily have to be conflict-free or picture perfect from start to finish. Rather, said day should contain a variety of experiences and sensations. Plus, the day's events could illuminate an answer to a long-asked question. A Best Day definitely will provide the fodder for a story I can tell for the rest of my life.

So far, today's been pretty damn good. Our morning began with another wonderful breakfast, including mortadella, buffalo mozzarella, and fresh blood orange juice so sweet that you'd swear it was Hawaiian punch. Then, I was still tired, having finally succumbed to the jet lag, so I sent Fletch out on his own while I rested. I watched Italian television and couldn't believe my fine fortune upon discovering *Vecchi Bastardi* (Old Bastards), which is essentially their version of *Jackass* meets *Betty White's Off Their Rockers* with oldsters pulling pranks on young punks.

Fletch returned to the hotel a couple of hours later with more new clothes, delighting again in how everything here fits him perfectly. Plus, this was the first time he tried to find his way around the city on his own. He went out with the intention of buying a couple of ten-euro belts he'd seen, but instead he allowed a salesman to talk him into a sweet pair of navy blue loafers.

I've been shocked at how easily Fletch has been trying new things and calmly navigating all that's uncertain. When at home, he's not so great about relaxing, but here? He is Mr. Chill. He is Dr. Cool. Twenty years after we first met, he's still able to surprise me! That alone practically qualifies as Best Day material.

Add the Vatican trip into the mix, with the agony of sweat rolling down the crack of my ass while coupled with the ecstasy of a once-in-a-lifetime experience, and we may well have a Best Day contender.

"Maybe," I gamely reply.

He smiles and holds my hand as he takes a sip of his macchiato. The foam sticks to his mustache, which is apparently by design. Honestly, I suspect he likes having his whiskers trap the flavor for a future savor.

"Maybe? What are you talking about, *maybe*? We've seen everything good. We've seen the whole city! We went to a museum—we saw priceless works of art! We ate pancreas!" he says, quoting one of my favorite lines from *Ferris Bueller's Day Off*. "Screw your *maybe*. Today's a keeper for me."

We content ourselves with our drinks as we look around. "You know, this area feels like what Rome really is," I say. "We've seen so many monuments and so much tourist stuff that I'm not sure we've gotten enough of a taste for what it's like to actually *be* Roman, to live *here*. Like, when people come to Chicago and they check out the Bean and go to Navy Pier? Yeah, the sights are land-marks but visiting them doesn't give you a sense of what it's like to *live* in Chicago. Do you understand what I'm saying?"

Fletch nods, and catches his upper lip with his lower lip, checking for stray foam. "Sure, it's the difference between eating lunch at a nice chain restaurant on Michigan Avenue versus having brunch outside at Lula's in Logan Square. One isn't better than the other, per se, but the latter is where the actual Chicagoans are. When *you* go somewhere new, you want to get an idea of how they live."

He's right; I'm perpetually fascinated by how other people go about their lives, especially in new places, to the point I wish I could peek in their windows in a nonthreating-or-illegal way. I'm desperately curious whether they know something I don't, and if so, can they teach me? And what makes them tick? What guides their choices? Why *this* house, *this* neighborhood, *this* city, *this* job, *this* spouse? What's important to them? How do *they* avoid regrets? In what ways are they trying to live their lives to the fullest?

(Sidebar: I suspect these questions are why I'm so fascinated by reality television. Yeah, I'm a small enough person to admit I enjoy seeing the bitch who's not here to make friends have her extensions yanked in a pique of rage, but that doesn't negate how fascinated I am with what happened in their lives to lead them to the extensions-yanking portion of the show to begin with.)

So, naturally I have to wonder what it's like to live in the very cradle of civilization. Do the Romans exist in a perpetual state of wonder, all, "My God, this is freaking stunning!" upon seeing the Trevi Fountain on their way to their jobs as legal secretaries and orthodontists every day? Does it take their breath away to stroll the very paths that Julius Caesar once walked? Or is it human nature to become immune to one's surroundings after a while? If so, is that the case for both beauty *and* misery—does everything eventually all become familiar to the point of forgettable?

When I lived in downtown Chicago, I valued having art and culture at my fingertips, but I never really dwelled on what that opportunity meant. Instead, what truly lit my fire were the new and often benign happenings, like when the three-story Whole Foods opened up on Kingsbury Street. Sure, I was grateful to have the option of gazing upon a non-bullshit Matisse painting whenever I wanted, but, honestly, buying organic Rainer cherries had a much larger impact on my day-to-day life.

(Shameful. But honest.)

While we eat and ponder, I notice some action about halfway down the block. "Fletch—check out those guys over there, smoking while they paint the shutters. I love that there's nothing here that can't be done with a lit cigarette. I wonder why the smoking doesn't bother me? Remember the last time we went to Vegas? I wanted to buy a respirator!"

Fletch cranes his head around to see what's happening behind him, appraising the two men in the distance at their outdoor workstations. One looks to be in his fifties, and the other one is probably in his seventies. Maybe they're father and son? They're standing in front of a shutter repair shop, putting the finishing touches on a recent job. Although they're doing manual labor, they're both wearing tailored slacks and dressy leather shoes, which neatly encapsulates everything that's charmed me so much about this place. Rome engenders a certain level of formality and elegance. I bet, unlike me, no one here even *owns* a pair of yoga pants, let alone spends seventy-five percent of their non-yoga-doing lives in them.

"I've noticed that," he says. "The cigarettes don't stink. I wonder if the Italians do something different during the manufacturing process? Or the filters are different?"

Given the quality of everything else we've experienced so far, I guess it stands to reason the Italians would rule tobacco, too.

The gentlemen have a couple of battered sawhorses set up, with two of the same large shutters that we've seen all over the neighborhood placed on top of them. They wield two crusty cans of forest green paint, which they slowly but meticulously apply with wide, worn brushes. They take a few strokes and then pause to raise their faces to the sun, inhaling the sweet Roman air.

And just like that, any question of whether or not the Romans appreciate their surroundings is answered.

I continue to watch them paint, their practiced hands performing the same operations so deftly that they don't even need to look at their work. They smoke, they laugh, and they chat with such enthusiasm and familiarity that I'm suddenly transported to the back room of my Sicilian grandfather's shoe repair shop. In this moment, these men remind me so much of my grampa Vitale that it hurts my heart.

While they labor, a small dog wanders out of their shop, thus snapping me out of my melancholy because he's the most ridiculous creature I've ever seen. The dog is some sort of black-and-white terrier, deep-chested and extra long, but with stubby little legs. What's incongruous is that he has the head of a horse. It's a miracle of physics that he's able to support his enormous melon with his tiny body.

"Look at that little guy!" I exclaim. At this point, Fletch is accustomed to me pointing out every pup in the city. I can't get over how different the dogs are here, from their personalities to their relationships with their owners to their level of independence. Their physicality is the biggest difference, as they're all so squatty. There has to be some kind of story why they're such low-riders. I assume these breeds were the best at catching rats, which would have been abundant because of the plague.

BTW, does everything here relate to the plague? I make a mental note to find a book about the Black Death when I get home, as clearly this was a *thing*.

(Sidebar: At home, I learn the Black Death killed more than two hundred million Europeans in the most gruesome and painful way imaginable, so yes, (a) this devastating pandemic was more than a *thing*, and (b) I am an asshole who's clearly never taken a history course on anything other than Lewis and Clark. But that's going to change soon.)

"That is the ugliest dog I've ever seen," he says, not unkindly.

I reply, "Yet somehow he's possibly also the cutest."

A complicated set of body harnesses completes Ugly Dog's ensemble, giving him the appearance of a tiny leather daddy or a miniature Hannibal Lecter. The dog circles each of the sawhorses,

as though inspecting his masters' work. Satisfied with their progress, and that they did not, in fact, miss a spot, he settles into a sunny patch a few feet in front of them.

Our pizzas arrive and we dive in—they're just as good as we'd hoped! Fletch takes an enthusiastic bite of his pizza, hoovering in an entire slice of prosciutto in one mouthful. The downside of this trip is that I'm going to be ruined for regular pizza, particularly Chicago-style, which I never quite liked. The crust here is so thin, and the cheese so sparse, with but a spoonful of tomato sauce. There's only a couple of ounces of thinly sliced meats on top, so technically, their pizzas are inconsequential, but each bite is so fresh and packed with flavor that there's no need to go over-the-top with the toppings. Plus, I like that this pizza hasn't been dusted with cornmeal to keep it from sticking in a not-hot-enough oven—somehow cornmeal feels like a shortcut.

While we cram in as much pizza as our mouths will hold, a trio of floppy-hat-wearing Chinese girls walks down the street. They look to be in their late teens to early twenties. I wonder, what would it have been like to come here while I was still that age? How would that have affected my life's trajectory? Would I have fewer regrets now? I couldn't understand how travel broadens before now, because the only travel I'd ever done has been of the off-to-work or sit-by-the-pool variety.

But this?

This is addicting.

I never wanted to go anywhere before and now I want to go everywhere.

Two of the Chinese girls peel off to hit the gelato shop across from us, while the third waits for them in the sun. She spots Ugly Dog and tentatively approaches him. She bends down, offering her hand, and the little fella horse-head-butts her leg in a show of affection. Her whole face lights up and I watch as these two fall immediately and profoundly in love. Little cartoon birds busy themselves carrying hearts back and forth between them.

"Ooh, look at Ugly Dog!" I squeal. (I suspect I'm really missing my own pups right now. According to the photo updates we received from the kennel, they're having a wonderful vacation, too, but still.) "Hims love her!"

She pets the homely boy, who couldn't be more effusive or

demonstrative. As a dog fanatic myself, I can tell that she's already taking measurements, trying to figure out if this handsome bloke will fit in her carry-on bag. The Italian men are charmed by the instant bond between man and beast, and they exhale lots of smoke and gesticulate in approval, as they don't speak a common language with their soon-to-be new daughter-in-law.

Her friends finish buying their gelato and walk back out into the street. The two Chinese girls sit on a bench to eat their treats so the third reluctantly looks back at the dog, before walking away to rejoin them. Ugly Dog trots behind his new girlfriend, only to be summarily yanked back by the younger man.

The two girls are taking their time with the gelato, so the third wanders back over to the dog, an action that is clearly the greatest thing to ever happen in his entire canine life. Their reunion is that of two long-separated lovers slow-running through a field of flowers in a sun-dappled meadow. The tenderness between them is inspiring to watch.

"Are you paying attention here? That girl is about to steal the dog," I say, gesturing over Fletch's shoulder. "They're going right back to the Vatican to solicit the Pope to make a decision on interspecies marriage. And the new guy is really progressive; I bet he'd consider it."

Fletch brushes stray crumbs off of his new shirt. "No, that girl is about to do something stupid, which will make the dog nervous. Just watch. Trouble is brewing."

"Impossible," I reply. "They're soul mates. Besides, you see trouble brewing everywhere and I guarantee this isn't one of those times."

Convinced I'm wrong, Fletch turns around to watch. We witness the girl lifting the dog up in order to get closer to him.

"Aw, she's going to kiss hims' sweet, sweet face!" I cry.

She places him on one of the sawhorses, which immediately begins to wobble.

"Trouble," he counters. "Mark my words."

Before I can even roll my eyes, what happens next unfolds like a terrible silent movie.

The short version is that Fletch, as always, is right.

The long version is that Ugly Dog begins to panic as the shutter wobbles, so the girl swoops in to rescue him. But he doesn't see her as a liberator. Rather, she is the asshole who caused the problem in the first place.

Having quickly tired of this ill-fated intercontinental romance, the Ugly Dog demonstrates his displeasure by solidly biting the Chinese girl on the hand while she's placing him on the ground. She yanks her hand back so fast and with such force that she knocks off her own sun hat, while the older Italian man throws up his arms in a gesture best described as that of a caricature of an old Italian man in distress.

Her two companions, who I strongly suspect would be my friends if I lived in China, don't rush in to help. Instead, they begin to point and to laugh so hard that they knock their own behatted heads together on the bench. The younger Italian painter simply takes another puff of his smoke before he picks up Ugly Dog by his BDSM harness and hauls him back into the shop.

The look on the dog's face transmits exactly what he's feeling: *I regret nothing.*

The folks at the gelato shop become involved when the bitten girl runs in and points at her hand. Wads of napkins are passed over the cooler and there is much pointing and blotting on her part, even though there's no blood or discernable damage. I'm not sure she's hurt physically so much as she is damaged emotionally.

Her hand will heal, but in her heart, she may well become a cat person.

She and her friends walk away and I watch as the Italian men shrug and smoke and commence sunning themselves again, like nothing ever happened. I suspect this is not the first time this odd little dog has behaved badly, nor is it the last, thus proving my theory that the dogs here are jerks.

Fletch wipes his mustache with his napkin. "I told you so. Saw that coming a mile away."

I feel really sorry for the girl and yet there's a part of me that's grateful for having witnessed the whole scene. Because now I have my go-to story about the best day of my life.

20.

RUN FOR YOUR LIFE

"More prosciutto?"

"Yes, please!"

"You want any of the nice buffalo mozzarella?"

"I do."

"There's homemade ricotta and sunflower seed rolls, too. You interested?"

"Definitely."

I load up our plates and return to my seat with the breakfast offerings, setting our breakfast in front of our cups of morning-only cappuccinos. We're dining alfresco again, taking advantage of the break in the weather. I gaze out at the surroundings, a riot of green grass and fuchsia flowers, illuminated by the morning sun.

I say, "Looks like we have a beautiful day on tap. But I think it's supposed to storm later."

Before Fletch can reply, Hambone farts with such intensity that she propels herself forward. She whips around, brow furrowed, searching for the source of the noise.

Glancing down at Hambone who's now bent herself into the shape of a doughnut in her zeal to inspect her noisy posterior, Fletch replies, "Yeah, I'd never guess we weren't in Rome anymore."

"Hey, at least our dogs aren't jerks, even if they lack Roman dignity," I argue.

"True enough."

Ever since we've gotten back, we've tried to implement all that we enjoyed about Italy, starting with cheese for breakfast. Instead of wolfing down a microwaved breakfast burrito in front of the computer, we're both taking the time to sit together outside to start the day. Maybe we don't arrive at our desks quite as soon this way, but is the world really going to end if I respond to an e-mail at eight thirty-two a.m. instead of eight?

Even though we ate like kings in Italy, I returned about five pounds lighter, due to walking for hours every day. But having been home for almost a month, I'm pretty sure I gained everything back . . . and then some. I need to weigh myself, but I'm afraid to confirm my suspicions. Last I checked, the number on the scale was fantastic for a bowling score, but not so much in terms of living without regrets.

Of course, if anyone asked what this number was, I'd lie, much like I've been lying for the past thirty years, starting in 1985 when I did a local pageant. Some sadist found it necessary for the emcee to announce our weight alongside information about our families, our hopes, our hobbies, and our college prospects. I couldn't fathom why my plans to study tele-journalism at Purdue were given no more import than whether or not I might be carrying three extra pounds of water weight.

I remember my naked shame at clocking in at one hundred and thirty-five pounds back then, despite being almost five-foot-eight. Ironically, I wasn't stressed about slicking Vaseline on my teeth, parading around in a bathing suit in front of an entire auditorium, or being judged on nothing but my looks, which is odd. Yet hearing the actual number was too much to bear, so I shaved off ten pounds from my total. Then I figured the whole audience would be hip to my fib, so I ended up bungling the swimsuit portion, desperately struggling under the weight of my ten-pound lie.

How fucked-up is that?

Hold the phone—I vaguely recall having to stand with my knees bowed so it wouldn't look like my thighs touched each other. So I guess standing thigh gaps have always been a thing.

I wish I knew how skinny I was back then. If I could talk to seventeen-year-old Jen, I'd say, "You look great, okay? And even if you were fat, you'd still be fine. You won't even know you're funny until you gain weight and can't skate by on cuteness alone, so it all works out. P.S. buy another bike now because that shit is hard to relearn."

At this point, I don't need or want to weigh one hundred and thirty-five pounds, because have you ever seen what happens to the people on *The Biggest Loser* when they hit their goal weights, especially when they're over thirty years old? They shrivel into human raisinettes! They look like dehydrated versions of their former selves and all I want to do is offer them a glass of Gatorade. I'm way less concerned with the state of my ass than that of my face, where the key to not going full-on Shar Pei is a little extra fluff. Not bowling-score-worthy amounts of fluff, but some.

Still, one of my bucket list goals has been to drop twenty pounds, not for vanity so much as health. My gynecologist told me that the heavier I am, the more likely a return of my uterine squatters and I'd rather not pay another visit to the OR. Also, because I'm carrying too wide a load, my knees constantly ache and I've been experiencing a weird numbness in my hands and arms when I lie down. That can't be healthy.

My plan was to hit the gym hard this summer, all Jillian Michaels–style, but other priorities keep popping up, such as eating breakfast cheese and putting on a second furniture show. The first iteration went so well that the gallery's asked me to do another.

I want to up my game in terms of new products, so I've spent the past week trying to paint a Union Jack on the front of a dresser, which is so much more math-y than I ever imagined due to how the piece curves. (BTW, if the fate of Earth depends on my being able to divide by three, be sure to kiss your loved ones good-bye.)

There's no way I can charge enough to recoup the cost of the twenty-plus hours I've put into it, yet I've been determined to get it right. I finally finished last night and I'm elated with the results.

So, as I sit here eating breakfast in the morning sun with my kind husband and flatulent dog, I'm concerned about my weight, but not quite concerned enough to actually go to the gym.

Story of my life.

The least I can do is to weigh myself after I've finished eating, just to get a baseline.

In which case, I may as well have another slice of prosciutto.

I'm tidying up my work area when I hear Fletch let forth a professional-grade string of profanity. As he's been operating the table saw, my assumption is that he's cut off a finger, hailing as he does from a long line of nine-fingered Fletchers. But then I remember this past spring when he debated whether or not to upgrade to the SawStop with the electronic sensor that brakes the blade within five milliseconds of detecting anything even vaguely organic, such a hot dogs or thumbs. He wasn't sure he wanted to spend the additional money, but I said if we amortized the cost of keeping all his digits over the next thirty years, it worked out to sixteen dollars a year to continue operating a remote control and not give a really creepy handshake. He agreed and made the buy.

(Sidebar: I could totally have a second career selling Saw-Stops.)

Anyway, the swearing's not a lost-finger thing; that I can confirm. In terms of being shout-y, Fletch trends toward the far end of the bell curve, particularly when inanimate objects are involved, so I've long since learned to tune him out. His loudly grousing about something is benign background noise at this point, much like when people live by the airport and don't even notice the planes anymore. Plus, years ago, an army dentist tore a piece of the inside of his cheek and he's perpetually accidentally catching the loose flesh in his teeth, so that accounts for about seventy-five percent of the outbursts. In short, I'm sure he's bitten himself again while eating his "secret" stash of peanut butter M&M'S, so I pay him no mind.

(Sidebar: There's no such thing as secret chocolate in this fat chick's house. I have the snout of a truffle pig.)

We've both been in the basement all night, readying my pieces for the show later this week. Having weighed myself this morning, I'm loath to sit in front of the television, assuming my inactivity coupled with a newfound love of breakfast cheese and pork is why I've hit a new all-time high. I suspect the Roman way of eating works only when coupled with the Roman lifestyle. (I imagine this is why Italians aren't usually fat, while Italian Americans are, at least if my extended family is any indication.)

To avoid dwelling on the numbers, I've been working on the finishing details of my pieces, such as adding a second coat of wax, or gilding the raised portions of the hardware. Really, though, everything's done and our only crucial task is to move the twenty new pieces from the workshop to the gallery.

The cursing on the other side of the basement continues.

"You should stop biting yourself," I suggest.

When I hear him charging up the stairs, I mosey over to his side of the workshop, more curious than concerned. I don't see any evidence of M&M's. I spot a little trail of fluid leading to his fancy new saw and I trace the line back to its origin, where I expect to find a Hambone-based puddle. Instead, I see that the window well in the basement is not only filled with three feet of water, but the glass is bulging. I guess we've had so many thunderstorms this summer that I didn't realize it had been raining, let alone pouring.

(Sidebar: I really am immune to loud noises at this point.)

One of the reasons we bought our house is that the basement is supposedly flood-proof, with its watertight system of checks and balances, such as a fail-safe drainage system, cement walls and floor, and triple sump pumps with bonus backup battery power. Then I realize that none of these precautions actually work if the window well glass breaks, in which case . . . every damn piece of furniture I've slaved over in the past month will be soaked in storm sewer runoff and I won't be able to sell any of it.

Shit! God save the Queen (dresser)! I can't do that kind of geometry again!

With power and speed I didn't realize I possessed, I immediately go all Noah's Ark, hoisting up all twenty desks, dressers, bookcases, and tables onto our workbenches. I throw an old piece of plywood onto a couple of sawhorses in order to provide more stacking space and I start rehoming other basement items.

I'm in the process of unplugging everything when the glass in the window well shatters. I witness hundreds of gallons of water pouring through the gaping hole, with a handful of very confused toads riding the crest of the wave as it sweeps across the entire basement.

Flood-proof, my ass.

As the water begins to rise, I slosh around, rescuing anything of value (including toads) before using a broom to direct the water flow over to the sump pumps.

Any sensible person would have likely retreated to the first floor after the initial tsunami, but no one ever accused either of us of prudence. Fletch, who'd been outside trying to unclog the French drain in the backyard, returns to take care of killing the gas to the water heater. Our furnace is seated on cement blocks, so we have about six inches of leeway before it's destroyed. Between exorbitant homeowner's insurance deductibles, paying for our trip, and covering our property taxes, we currently don't have the funds to replace an entire heating and cooling system.

So, if I want to keep my furnace, I need to save it my damn self.

We strap on our headlamps and cut the power to the basement. I use my broom to deflect the water away from the HVAC system while he guards the water heater and his precious finger-eschewing saw.

I manipulate giant swaths of mulch-studded water to spread the tide across the basement in order to engage all three pumps and keep my Trane running. I throw some spare screen material on top of the sump pumps so they don't fill with debris. I feel like I'm suddenly Patrick Roy defending my net for the Montreal Canadiens and I'm not stopping until I bring home the Stanley Cup.

After about forty-five treacherous minutes, my hands are blistered from my fancy broom maneuvering when the water finally recedes to below the lip of the window in the well and stops gushing in. Within the hour, we're able to remove the whole window housing and block the massive hole.

Through teamwork, we're able to protect everything of value. What's funny is that, save for Fletch's initial outburst, we handle this emergency in calm, rational tones. As both of us are so loud when it comes to petty annoyances, all the hollering must be out of our systems when we deal with what's important.

I shudder to think of the damage wrought had we been in Italy during this storm and I'm so thankful. I'm not at all aggravated by the extra effort we have to put in sanitizing the basement on top of prepping for the show and working on a novel deadline. I'm far too relieved at having been spared to grouse.

What does chap my ass, as always, is social media. Last week, I'd found a disgusting old horsehair footstool and perpetrated a fix that was nothing short of miraculous, even going so far as to learn how to reupholster with furniture tacks. I'm so proud of the craftsmanship and I want to show others that there's almost nothing that can't be brought back from the brink with due effort, so I post a before and after shot on Facebook. Lots of people are engaged and I happily talk them through how to make something similar.

The comment that makes me want to say, "Screw it all," and delete my stupid profile is someone named Lorraine, whom I've never met. Her response is, "Oh, *nice*. The idle hobbies of the idle rich. I used to like your writing, but you're all privileged now and I can't stand you anymore."

Mind you, I'm all about free speech and have no issue with folks sharing opinions in public forums. Others' thoughts and feelings are none of my business, and not within my purview. But what gets me is when others decide to take their ugliness to *my* page. Not cool.

When, in polite society, did it become acceptable to walk uninvited into someone else's virtual living room and piss all over the sofa? And then for said urinator to feign indignation at the sofa owner's shock and dismay at having been the victim of an unprovoked attack? I could understand if I were posting hate speech or spreading false, inflammatory information. But putting up a picture of a lemon-yellow footstool covered in fabric boasting cartoon frogs and goats?

Really, Lorraine?

This is what sent you over the edge?

A *frog footstool?*

Personally, I dislike car-away seeds. In my opinion, caraway seeds mar otherwise delicious sausage links and slices of bread. Because I don't en-joy caraway seeds, I avoid eat-ing caraway seeds. That's it. I just don't eat them.

What I don't do is invite myself into caraway seeds' social media presence to renounce caraway seeds to caraway seeds' de-voted following. I'm not looking to negatively influence caraway seeds' fans, nor am I hoping to fight with them, because who cares if someone else loves caraway seeds? Personally, I'd never actively try to derail caraway seeds' ability to conduct business. I'm not storming the caraway fields of Egypt because I feel these terrible seeds (technically bits of fruit) shouldn't exist. I *simply don't buy caraway seeds* because engaging in any other sort of action against that which has no impact on my life is as fucked-up as a soup-sandwich, *Lorraine.*

Moving past the general rudeness of her commentary, what I want to say is, "Lorraine, feel free to grab a broom and stand next to me, ankle-deep in toad-infested water after putting in a month of fifteen-hour days worked for the express purpose of guarantee-ing I can cover my mortgage and then please tell me exactly how idle and privileged *you* feel. By the way, you should wash your feet with soap before getting into bed because I'm not one hundred percent sure the water doesn't contain sewage overflow, too."

Instead, because I'm a decent person, I delete her comment. I don't need a hundred people ganging up on her, regardless of how satisfying that might be to witness.

So, between catching rogue toads, scrubbing every basement surface with a bleach water solution, prepping for my show, and actively restraining myself from signing Lorraine up for the NAMBLA newsletter, I don't have a moment to dwell on what the scale read after my ham-tastic breakfast a few days ago.

Once the opening is over, however, I feel I have no choice, so I weigh myself again.

That's when I realize that maybe the flood of toads wasn't an indication that we need to have our backyard drainage system inspected so much as it's a sign of my own pending personal apocalypse if I don't get my weight in check.

I have to do this.

But how?

In 2007, I dedicated six months of my life to document the experience of losing fifty pounds in a memoir. The resulting *Such a Pretty Fat* was a huge success, spending six weeks on the *New York Times* bestseller list.

Except at the end?

I didn't actually lose fifty pounds.

And now, almost eight years after conducting my initial experiment, I'm bigger than ever. The only difference now is that when I searched for quotes about being overweight, I found that *I'm* now a source that others quote.

So I'm famous . . . for being fat. In fact, I was recently approached for an interview about how fat writers are generally funnier than their skinnier counterparts—in all seriousness, and as though this wasn't the most insulting proposition I'd ever encountered.

I declined.

In the proposal for *Pretty Fat* (the original title before I discovered the URL linked to a big-girl-fetish site), I pledged to do the following:

Stop sweating while I eat.
Stop driving one block to Starbucks.
Stop having cookies for dinner.
Stop promising to go to the gym instead of actually going to the gym.
Stop treating my body like a fraternity party.
Start growing up.

I largely failed at keeping those promises, save for not eating cookies for dinner, mostly because I learned how to prepare home-made, Martha Stewart–style fettuccini Alfredo and cheesecake and pulled pork instead.

Also, breakfast cake. This, in the scheme of things, is worse.

What bothers me so much is that despite the effort I've put forth to attain professional success, the first thing that strangers notice when they look at me isn't the cute bag or the flattering haircut.

What they see is my size.

Regardless of my achievements, I still note the panic in people's eyes when they think they're going to be stuck next to me on an airplane. Despite my upgraded circumstances, the second I clash with a stranger—and regardless of my being in the right—I'm still called a "Fat Bitch."

I'm finding it harder and harder to laugh off these instances. I'm tired of being pitied for my perceived lack of self-control. I'm weary of feeling like I have to apologize for something that is no one's business but my own. I'm sick of cringing every time I see a full-body photo. I'm at the point where if I hear I have "such a pretty face" one more time, something very bad is going to happen.

Most of all, I'm so very over having others on social media speculate that there's something very wrong in my life simply because I haven't managed to conquer this weight business . . . largely because a part of me wonders if they're not right.

Fortunately, I did keep the most important promise I implicitly made when writing *Such a Pretty Fat.*

I grew up.

So, in the past year, I've begun therapy to discuss the kind of issues that have no place in a humorous memoir. (Sorry. Not that kind of book.) I've learned about emotional eating and I've had nutritional counseling. Overall, I'm in a positive mental state. The more I pursue my bucket list items, the better I feel about life in general. I'm sure I'm on the right track, as I've laid bare my problems and rebuilt my whole self on a more solid emotional foundation.

Truly, my regrets are few. But *I'm still as fat as ever.*

Really, what's twenty pounds? A couple of bags of flour? A few gallons of milk? A bag of kitty litter? In the scheme of what I have to lose, it's really not that much; why can't I just do it already? Losing twenty pounds might not make a big difference in my appearance but it would sure help my aching knees and, just maybe, give me a jump start that spurs healthier actions.

(Sidebar: I'm especially frustrated because I visited the doctor when it occurred to me that I've never had my thyroid checked. I mean, what if something chemical has been keeping me fat this whole time and I didn't even know it? How great would that be? I blew it with not having a cyst the size of a football, so a thyroid dysfunction seemed like a real second chance. Too bad my doctor ran every test imaginable and . . . THERE'S NOT A DAMN THING WRONG WITH ME. Except for high cholesterol, every single one of my levels is fine—optimum, in fact. All of this extra weight I'm carrying around is entirely my doing, my fault, and my responsibility.)

Earlier this year, when I told Julia about my plan to complete a 5K, she said she wanted to do it with me. We made plans to run together on our upcoming girls' trip in September. I told her that

I was tired of being Team Butter and I wanted to merge with Team Lettuce. Julia replied, "That's awesome because butter lettuce has always been my favorite." But now I have fewer than two months to try to go from couch to 5K.

I decide I'm not going to let her down.

I decide I'm not going to let myself down.

I decide I'm not going to keep making excuses.

Nothing's going to change until I lace up my running shoes, channel the energy generated from haters hating and just freaking do it already.

I'm going to need all my friends behind me here—Ice Cube, Chuck D, LL Cool J, and the whole damn Sugarhill Gang. I put together the greatest old-school hip-hop playlist of all time and then, for the first time in far too long, I cart my big ass downstairs to the treadmill. I'm beginning my training right now. Period.

I start with a brisk warm-up walk while Hambone stares me down, completely confused as to why I'm moving but not actually going anywhere. Eazy-E's "Gimme That Nutt" plays first, a song that's so unbelievably filthy and wrong it's actually funny.

(Sidebar: This is exactly how I feel about *Fifty Shades of Grey*, too. In my opinion, it's not erotic; it's *hilarious*.)

"Nutt" is only three minutes long and I feel . . . okay by the end of it. So I press on to De La Soul's "Me, Myself, and I" and I'm puffing fairly hard by its finish. I may well be panting and my heart's beating out of my chest. I think I've gone deaf in my left ear, too.

I'm already tired and I feel like quitting. Then I realize that it's my *mind* telling me that this is difficult, rather than my body.

I have strength.

I have endurance.

I can hump a hundred-pound dresser across a Wisconsin county fairground. I can lift and move twenty pieces of furniture in the time it takes a window well to burst. I can stand on my feet and paint, buff, and polish for twelve hours straight. And in terms of tapping into my "stored energy," also known as fat, I could likely power Toledo based on my reserves.

I can do this.

I just have to quiet my inner critic, whom I've thus dubbed Lorraine.

Next up on the playlist, I "Fight the Power" with Public Enemy. I always feel like a massive poseur when I listen to this song. What power am *I* fighting against in my suburban-dwelling, college-educated, conservative-news-watching world? The power baked goods hold over me?

To truly relate, the song would have to be rewritten thusly:

Salad was a hero to most/But lettuce never meant shit to me/Straight up tasteless that arugula was/Simple and plain/Motherfuck endive and John Wayne.

I want to send Chuck D a note telling him that I'm so sorry about co-opting his struggles to meet my own purposes. Gina's friends with him and she promises he's just happy that I'm paying to download his stuff on iTunes. I hope so.

As I chug along, I hear Lorraine tell me that I'm tired and that I'm destined to fail, that I'll always be fat, and that I need to just accept it.

Lorraine is a punk-ass bitch.

I'm as warmed up as I'm going to be, so it's time to start alternating jogging with walking. According to the Couch to 5K app, I'm supposed to alternate sixty seconds of jogging with ninety seconds of walking, and I'm to keep doing this for twenty minutes.

I look to Eazy again for inspiration and I complete my first sixty-second run to "Straight Outta Compton."

Much to my surprise, I do not die.

Take that, Lorraine.

I run another sixty seconds. Then I run again. Eminem helps, as does Run–DMC, and I find myself changing the lyrics to:

Whose house?/JEN'S HOUSE!

I power through the end of the training session shouting along with LL Cool J about not calling it a comeback, 'cause I been here for years.

Hear that, Lorraine? I BEEN HERE FOR YEARS.

Fueled by spite, I reach my goal.

Turns out the actual act of trying to run wasn't so terrible. The hard part was getting out of my damn head and finally starting.

I *can* do this.

And I *will* do this.

21.

SEE YOU IN HELL, BETTY SPAGHETTI

I'm surprisingly spry the first morning after running.

If I were starting the Couch to 5K program cold, I imagine I'd be in pain, but between walking the length and breadth of Rome and carrying furniture up and down the stairs, I'm more prepared than I hoped. In trying to build a new business, I'd already set the wheels in motion toward success in fitness and I didn't even know it.

My first month of training progresses so smoothly that I've decided when we run our girls' trip 5K, I want a medal at the end. We're not participating in an actual race because there isn't one where we're headed, but that doesn't mean we can't still award ourselves upon completion. As I'm vehemently against "trophy culture" where everyone wins, of course I'll be eligible for my medal only if I complete the race. I believe when everyone's guaranteed the same prize regardless of performance, the efforts of those who actually won are discounted.

Of course, if I were someone's mom and saw my little kid standing there crushed and empty-handed at the end of the game despite giving her or his best effort, I'd surely be ringing the TROPHIES FOR ALL bell. It's easy for me to suggest that children have to learn to deal with disappointment when I have nothing at stake, but in practice it's got to be so damn hard.

Making judgment calls as a mom or dad has to be the toughest job in the world, especially with us childfree types on the sidelines, quietly judging.

I'm so sorry if I've inadvertently contributed to anyone else having regrets.

Because, honestly, what do I know about raising kids? I can barely discipline my dogs. (But I do keep my opinions off everyone's Facebook page, so there's that.)

Anyway, I'm planning to eat some Yoplait between now and my trip. I'll use the lids to make medals, like they did on *The Office* in the Olympics episode. Should I complete this event, I'd also appreciate if someone were to craft a crown of wildflowers and ivy leaves. I don't know who or how, but again, I'm putting that out there à la *The Secret*.

Probably won't happen.

I'd request that the girls carry me on their shoulders like a conquering hero, but I'm still way too heavy and also, I won't have cured cancer or brought about world peace. But I'll have done something so outside of my comfort zone that I'll definitely be proud of myself.

#WINNING

I practice jogging every day, so by the time my girls' trip rolls around, I feel ready to complete my 5K.

The universe, of course, has other ideas.

Our original plan was to run on the beach but somehow the Savannah-bad-travel-juju rears its head again. What's supposed to be a relaxing seaside vacay turns into a flea-bitten (literally), roach-infested (again, literally), stray-dog-ridden, non-toilet-flushing nightmare that is so aggressively unpleasant that my friends and I end up abandoning our group tour three days into it, heading to the nearest big city.

Although we probably could have stayed and tried to make the best of the Worst Tour in Christendom, we decided that we'd have the fewest regrets if we simply charted our own course, which is why we now find ourselves about to run crowded city streets, instead of the beach where we were supposed to be staying on our tour.

Julia, Alyson (a friend from Dallas), and I are all geared up in our moisture-wicking running clothes, with bills stuffed in our sports bras so we can buy bottled water along the way. Joanna, having recently completed her own first 5K, decides to cheer us on from her spot in the café with free Wi-Fi. She and Alex, Julia's mom, promise to have cappuccinos ready for us on our return.

We take the elevator down from the little apartment we rented on the fly and hit the street. We start out slowly, intending to add speed once we're properly warmed up. But within the first five minutes, we realize that our goal of running on these old cobblestone streets is not only impossible due to all the pedestrians, but also quite dangerous.

Instead of giving up, we choose to adapt.

In lieu of running a 5K, we end up speed-walking for 10K.

Never saw that coming.

Later in the evening, when Julia places the completion medals around each of our necks, I truly feel like I accomplished something significant. While walking a 10K wasn't my original goal, without having trained, I could never have powered through.

Never one to allow a triumph to go to waste, I immediately add **walk a 10K to my list**, taking great delight in immediately crossing it off.

Which feels terrific. And that's enough for me . . .

. . . or is it?

Once I return home (and after all the flea bites heal), I still feel like there's something left to check off my list, so I lace up my shoes and head down-stairs to the treadmill.

No one's here in the basement to cheer me on (or offer me a cappuccino) and there's no prize at the end, but that doesn't stop me from trying anyway.

I cue up my best hip-hop running playlist and put a muted episode of *Jersey Belle* on the television, so I have something to focus on other than the numbers.

As always, I start off slowly, allowing my muscles the time to warm up. My knees feel better than they have in a long time. I was always so hesitant to work out for fear of injuring them, but it turns out that the more I exercise, the better they feel.

Yesterday when I undressed for my shower, I noticed some-thing odd going on with my butt. It's . . . a little bit higher than it used to be, and now there's some distinction from where my thigh ends and my glutes begin. In no way am I ready to pose for a swimsuit calendar, but that I've actually worked hard enough to see a difference is incredibly motivating.

As my muscles begin to loosen, I quicken my pace from 2.5 mph to 4.0, which is not terribly fast. At all. In fact, I can speed-walk more quickly than I can jog.

I crank up the speed some more and within the first ten min-utes, I'm so hot that my whole shirt is damp and clingy, to the point that I have to take it off. I pray that Fletch doesn't come downstairs to see me running in my sports bra because I suspect he'll never stop laughing.

I chug away for an embarrassingly long time, feet thudding on the moving belt beneath me, heart pounding so hard that I temporarily lose hearing in my left ear again. Maybe it's all the sweat pooling in my ear canals? I eventually find a rhythm and my task becomes slightly easier.

I have to break up my jogging with frequent bouts of walking to keep myself from hyperventilating. But in the end, I manage to complete the full three point one miles in . . . well, more minutes than you'd think. I'm not about to go posting this Personal Record anywhere because it's nothing to be proud of.

And yet.

I really did a full 5K, which is why I feel completely justified in donning my medal again.

For I am a champion.

A very, *very* slow champion.

Delighted with my 5K checkmark, I feel ready to embrace all sorts of healthy habits, so I don't laugh when Fletch suggests a juice cleanse. (Although I do highly suspect he's been reading the lifestyle magazines I leave in the bathroom.) Gina does cleanses before every bikini-based vacation, and each time, I've questioned her sanity. But now a cleanse doesn't seem like the craziest idea in the world, especially when I hear that some guy made a movie about losing one hundred pounds in sixty days by juicing.

A hundred pounds? In sixty days? Sign. Me. Up.

"How does a cleanse work?" I ask. "Do we buy premade juices?" Every time Gina's on a cleanse, she shows up with cute little bottles of clever-sounding drinks.

"Of course not. Why would we buy anything when we can

do it ourselves so much better?" Fletch asks, handing over a stack of diagrams and recipes. "We'll do it at home. We make five juices a day and we can eat fruits and vegetables for dinner."

Two months ago, I wouldn't even have considered such an idea due to my deep and abiding love of dessert. When I started the 5K training program, I noticed how much more energy I had on the days I avoided simple carbohydrates, so I decided to cut out sugar entirely to see what happened.

What happened is I dropped ten pounds in a week.

A freaking week.

It's no hundred pounds in sixty days, but it's certainly a start.

For years, Fletch and I have been trying to get to the bottom of why I weigh too much. He eats every meal with me and can see that I'm fairly cautious about calories and serving sizes, save for Italian food, such as when I turn into Betty Spaghetti on Bolognese Sauce Night. But since working with Michelle the Nutritionist, I learned to stop piling up my noodles in a big bowl, instead opting for a plate that I fill with an equal amount of fresh vegetables. Same deal with pizza—now I have a salad and I eat one slice instead of my half of the pie. As for the Roman breakfasts, I'm doing more fruit and less cheese. (My new motto is What Happens in Rome Stays in Rome.)

I thought the issue could be that I was an emotional overeater and I explored this possibility in therapy. My therapist gave me tons of literature about it and the more I read, the less I identified with those ladies in the books who hide in the closet with a bucket of chicken, alternating finger-licking and crying because they hate the fact that they have to eat in the first place. If I want fried chicken, I'll order it, without a side of histrionics. No judgment on those who do struggle, because I know it's hard, but for once, this isn't my actual problem.

But all summer I regulated my portions and came to terms

with the difference between hunger and boredom, and I still couldn't figure out what I was doing wrong.

What I was doing wrong was consuming far too much sugar.

To be clear, I'm not anti-sugar and I'm definitely still a fan. I happily ate a piece of cake at Laurie's son's engagement party, but that's all I've had this entire month, having decided to save treats for special occasions. So, for now, it's no cupcakes, no gelato, no brownies, no pie, no kidding. I even refused my favorite Momofuku blueberries and cream cookie when I was in New York on business and had only a single cup of gelato on my girls' trip. I find the fewer sweets I eat, the fewer sweets I want to eat.

I understand moderation works well for many people, but I'm not someone who'll ever be satisfied with a single bite of cheesecake, regardless of how slowly I savor it. I either want the whole piece or I want nothing. Honestly, having nothing is easier and I'm all about easy.

Looking at my food choices through the scrim of therapy and nutritional counseling, I realize that dessert is more than just flour and frosting. For me, dessert represents the few golden hours in the evening when we've both finished all the day's tasks and we're finally able to hang out together on the couch in the TV room. Dessert is my reward for having met my goals during the day. Really, dessert is an event rather than a specific item.

Turns out I'm fine subbing a bowl of raspberries with a splash of cream for a pint of Graeter's Black Raspberry Chocolate Chip during *So You Think You Can Dance*. This way, when I do have something like special-occasion engagement cake, I can enjoy the whole damn thing without a twinge of remorse. I can't say if this approach would work for anyone else, but for me, that I'm actually amenable to a juice cleanse is evidence of stratospheric progress in all things food-related.

"Since when do you want to do a cleanse?" I ask.

"I read about how cleanses are supposed to reset your metabolism and enhance your taste for fresh food. Sure, you're eating better, but now I'm sucking down everything you left behind. At this point, I've had so many Grasshopper cookies that I'm going to turn into a Keebler elf."

(Sidebar: I prefer the Keebler Grasshopper cookies to Girl Scout Thin Mints because (a) they're better and, (b) I'm not a fan of tracking down little girls for any purpose.)

I say, "Fair enough. Want to start tomorrow?"

Neither one of us has reason not to begin, so we head to the grocery store for supplies. The list of fresh ingredients fills an entire sheet of notebook paper and by the time we reach the cashier, our cart is overflowing with beets and Swiss chard and sweet potatoes. As we fork over what we'd normally spend for a week of food on three days' worth of fruits and veggies, a thought occurs.

"Do we need a juicer?" I ask.

"We have one," he replies.

"No, we don't."

"We do."

"Believe me, nothing happens in our kitchen I'm not aware of. I assure you, we are juicer-free."

He insists, "We have a juicer. You used to use it to make that banana ice-cream stuff."

He's referring to the Yonanas ice cream maker I bought a couple of years ago when we attempted the Paleo diet. The device turns frozen bananas into creamy soft-serve, which sounds really healthy until you do the math—one non-sad-sized serving of banana ice cream takes four to five bananas, which is almost five hundred calories. For that many calories, I may as well have regular ice cream.

Or a Burger King Whopper.

"That's not a juicer," I say.

"Then what is it?"

"Basically, a waste of fifty bucks."

"Oh. Do we need to buy a juicer or can we just use the Vitamix?"

I do a quick Google while we wait in line and confirm that our Vitamix should work. "Says we're fine, particularly because we'll get the benefit of all the fiber, too."

"Then I guess we're juicers now."

I'm in charge of making the first round of juice because Fletch has a conference call. Our fridge is overflowing with produce and I have to open a dozen plastic grocery bags to find the carrots, apple, and ginger for the first drink. Although the instructions say to juice and pour over ice, I core the apples, dice the carrots and ginger, and dump the whole lot in the blender. I press the ON button and wait for the magic to begin.

I envision sitting at my desk, quaffing delicious and nutritious smoothies, as my body becomes stronger through the antioxidant intake, all my excess poundage simply melting away.

What I don't anticipate is the logjam all the carrots create in the Vitamix. Smoothies normally blend nicely because they contain milk or other liquid, whereas this is nothing but a pile of choking hazards. I spend the next twenty minutes poking at the cache of veggies with the end of a wooden spoon. The Vitamix makes terrible noises under the strain of trying to liquefy the carrots, so much so that I receive a text from Fletch asking, "That your friend in the wood chipper?" I end up pouring a little water into the mixture to prevent motor burnout.

When the first drink is finally blended, the sheer volume of it all takes me aback. I figured I'd be left with about ten ounces once everything processed, but what I have here is a quart of . . . homemade soup? I take my first sip, expecting the cool, creaminess of a regular smoothie, slightly sweet from the apple, which is very exciting. Because I've had so little sugar, even blueberries taste like Jolly Ranchers to me right now.

The flavor isn't what's disturbing, largely because the front of my tongue is numb, having scorched my taste buds earlier on the boiling glass of required hot lemon breakfast water.

The problem with this "smoothie" is twofold: First, the texture, which is somewhere between baby food and oatmeal-laden vomit, and second, the temperature. Instead of being frosty, the concoction is lukewarm from having run in the blender for so long.

I deliver Fletch's bucket-o-juice just as he's hanging up the phone.

"What is this?" he asks, his eyes growing wide.

"Breakfast," I reply, spinning on my heels before he can argue with me.

I spend the next two hours trying to choke down my "juice," finally employing a straw. I feel like I'm drinking from a trick glass as I can't seem to pass the halfway mark, although that's probably because I have to keep adding water to thin it out enough to operate the straw.

Fletch is convinced that I somehow read the instructions wrong, so he volunteers to make the midmorning juice, which is a blend of cucumbers, celery, apples, ginger, lemon, and kale. Save for the kale, which is my favorite salad addition, I've enjoyed many fine beverages from these ingredients. Bloody Marys are brilliant with the addition of a splash of celery juice. (But not Clamato. Never Clamato.) Cucumber martinis could not be more light or zesty or refreshing. I'm mad for all things lemonade, and you can't go wrong with apple juice, so I anticipate the next round will be better. Besides, I probably did do it wrong, as I'm not the best at following directions. I always get dyslexic reading recipes and then end up trying to stir in baking powder after I've already poured the cake batter in the pan. (I bet this is what went wrong with my Christmas cookies.)

Fletch is in the kitchen for at least as long as I was, Vitamix churning away, and when he comes upstairs with thirty-two ounces of fibrous army-green juice in a massive tumbler, I fear for the worst.

I take a sip, swishing the juice (which is the consistency of lumpy toothpaste) from one side of my mouth to the other in an attempt to identify the overpoweringly familiar flavor.

"Did you . . . wash the kale leaves first?" I ask.

"Was I supposed to?" he replies.

Argh.

"We need to buy a juicer," I reply. "Like, today."

After adding a pinch of salt, I manage to put away a decent portion of the midmorning juice, profoundly confused as to how the ingredients that mesh so nicely on a salad plate can go so horribly awry in a glass. When I pull in a mouthful of grit, I decide I'm done. Libby, normally so anxious to bat cleanup, slinks away when offered the remains of the dirt daiquiri.

The lunchtime gazpacho juice is what breaks me. Normally, I'm never one to shy away from an onion. A big red Bermuda on my backyard barbecue burger? Yes, please! Diced and tossed with balsamic, feta, watermelon, and tomatoes? My favorite! Nestled in sour cream on top of a bowl of chili? The best! Fried, sautéed, or au gratin? I live for you. But blended into a diarrhea-colored sludge with parsley, red peppers, and cucumbers?

I can't. I try, but I just can't.

Fletch can't either. He starts to research juicers and ends up in such analysis paralysis that we miss our afternoon snack of pureed clementines and Swiss chard.

Damn.

Desperate to get as far away from our Vitamix as possible, I head down to the treadmill and jog, the whole time pretending I'm running away from a river of hot, roiling compost water.

When I come upstairs an hour later, I find Fletch in the kitchen, marveling over a partially eaten apple.

He holds the Golden Delicious up to me, all Garden of Eden–style. "You can just eat the fruit. Did you know that? You can just bite it and chew it and it tastes really good," he tells me.

We end up ordering a Hawaiian pizza for dinner and it is freaking delicious.

We regret nothing.

"So the next day I go out and find that I can purchase premade cleanse juices, which is actually cheaper than getting a juicer, buying all the veggies, and trashing my kitchen," I tell everyone. "Plus, the juice tasted like cocktails. Win, win."

"Why do you never ask me about these things before the fact?" Gina queries.

"Because it's impossible for me to learn any way but the hard way," I reply.

"How much weight have you lost so far?" Tracey asks. "Your face is definitely thinner. I can tell."

I sit up very straight in my chair. "As of this morning, thirty pounds!"

I receive a round of high-fives from everyone at the table.

"Glad you're here to celebrate with us," Stacey says.

"Right now, the difference is barely noticeable, but my pants are definitely looser and my arms aren't going numb in my sleep anymore. I totally see more definition in my calves and around my chin, too. Thing is, I *feel* like I'm different, not just because of diet and exercise, but from everything. It's like speaking Italian actually *did* make my ass smaller. The other times I've tried to lose weight, I was never in the right mental mind-set."

While I was on my girls' trip, I looked at a bunch of shots

from Savannah last year and I noticed how much fatter I was back then. But for the first time, this observation came without feelings of guilt or inadequacy.

Really, looking at my shape was more of an observation, kind of like, "Huh, I had a better tan back then," or, "Wow, I really needed to have my roots done." The key has been taking responsibility for my own weight loss. Instead of relying on a trainer or a diet plan, I've been in charge of my own destiny; ergo, the success is all mine.

"Sometimes it's just time," Stacey says with a shrug. She's lost quite a bit of weight herself in the past year, not by making drastic changes, but by adding healthy habits here and there.

I think the older we get, the more we learn to moderate our moderation. Thus far, it's working for all of us.

We place our orders and instead of my usual breakfast burrito with extra sour cream, avocado, and floppy bacon, I choose the watermelon gazpacho and kale and beet bruschetta, not because I have to, but because the dishes sound appealing. Juicing really made me appreciate the fresh taste of these ingredients when not blended into a vat of tepid, unseasoned stew.

"You haven't been down here all summer. We've missed you," Tracey says. Between travel, the furniture show, due dates, and Hambone, I've not had a minute to spare. "How's Hammy doing?"

At the beginning of the summer, Ham got into a huge fight with Loki. She didn't start it, but she certainly finished it. After that, she became really aggressive and started to attack Libby and Loki, to the point we were worried the dogs would become seriously injured. (By the way, I could check off the **break up a fight between two pit bulls** item on my bucket list now, except that was never anything I'd wanted to do in the first place.)

As soon as we had the second dustup, I realized the fighting wasn't just an anomaly and I began to research specific steps I'd need to follow to help my baby. I immediately began to investigate what had gone wrong and one of the first resources I turned to was Cesar Millan.

I perused his Web page, with poor little Ham clinging to my legs under my desk while the other dogs were downstairs with Fletch, and I ran across a few products he sells on his site. Where there should have been product reviews, dozens of people were instead telling their stories about the problems with their dogs, each desperate for Cesar to respond and tell them what to do, begging him, pleading with him, saying he was their only hope.

This broke my heart.

Instead of figuring out how to implement solutions to save their dogs—with much of the needed instruction posted elsewhere on this very site—these owners instead opted to do nothing but write their stories. I hate to imagine how many of these dogs will be put down when the nothing their owners tried doesn't pan out.

If anything, this year's taught me that the key to living without regret is to take immediate action.

You see, I'd already lost one pit bull before her time and I'd be damned if I was about to lose another.

Thing is, I *knew* Hammy wasn't mean or evil and I'd trust her in a room full of babies. After each of the fights this summer, she'd been so frightened, trembling for hours, even though she was the instigator. I quickly discovered that hers wasn't the behavior of an aggressive dog; it's what happens when a dog is scared.

Sweet Hammy has always been anxious and I now realized that we'd been dealing with her angst all wrong, like when we'd come home and she'd lose her mind. We were taught to ignore her and to discipline her into submission either through yelling or shaking a can of pennies at her, but that's the opposite of what she needed. An anxious dog requires reassurance, so now we greet her and find a way to redirect her nervous energy. We have her cycle through her retinue of tricks until she's calm, and for this, she's richly rewarded.

Over the course of the summer, we've seen our vet and a board-certified behaviorist to help us take the steps needed to give Ham a long, happy life. One of my tasks is to walk her every day for an hour to burn off her nervous energy. The walks are of huge benefit to both of us.

Now she's calm enough to be left in a room alone for the first time in her life, and I can be left alone in a room with a cheesecake for the first time in my life. And she and I have an exceptionally tight bond now because I feel like we're both tearing ourselves down to the studs and starting over. She'll never be Maisy, but I've discovered that her being Hammy is pretty darned good, too.

"Hammy's working so hard," I say. "Yesterday we were on our walk and we passed a couple with two badly behaved beagles. They were yipping and pulling and lunging and basically pushing all of Hammy's buttons. So I put her in a sit and let the beagle owners walk past and that little champion didn't even blink an eye. I could hear the owners asking their dogs why they couldn't behave like the nice red dog over there. Sure, mainstreaming her back into the pack is going to be a process, but I believe we're all up for it."

"Glad to hear it," Gina says. "Hammy's such a little peanut."

"Now, what are you having done today? You're down here for some reason, but I forget what," Stacey says.

"My first laser tattoo removal session! I thought that getting rid of this thing"—I point at the letters on my ankle—"would be a great way to finish up my year of eliminating regrets. Because you know who doesn't have tattoos? Every middle-aged person in the entire town of Lake Forest."

"Won't that be ridiculously expensive?" Tracey asks.

"Yes, if I went to a plastic surgeon. But I found a place called Vamoose, which is catty-corner from where I lived in Bucktown and only costs seventy-nine bucks per session! They can't say how many sessions I'll need until after we begin, but at the most, I'm looking at three to five times, which is a massive savings."

"Then that's at least three to five more guaranteed lunches here at Lula!" Stacey cheers.

Even though we four haven't gotten together for a meal in months, it's as though we were all here yesterday.

(Sidebar: We're the only non-hipster, non-fixie-riding, non-ironic-facial-haired patrons in the joint, as Stacey's neighborhood has basically morphed into Williamsburg, The Sequel. But we were here first and since Stacey finally convinced her old landlord to sell her the place she rented for the last twenty years—never doubt her ability to hold out for what she wants—I guarantee we'll be here long after they run off to the suburbs, having discovered the joys of free parking and riding lawn mowers.)

I want to say that lunch ends on a high note, but it doesn't. Right before Gina has to leave for an afternoon meeting, she receives a call that her friend's husband died from a cardiac event. He was forty-six years old.

Forty-six.

My age.

I'd actually met the man at a party back in the spring. He left an impression on me because he had such a beautiful wife and they seemed so happy together.

I hate that everything can be taken away in an instant.

I'm quietly reflective as I drive from the restaurant to my old neighborhood. Between the news of this good man's passing and wandering my old stomping grounds, I feel out of sorts, like everything's suddenly askew.

I mean, just look at Damen Avenue in Bucktown. What was once the bastion of coolness at the turn of the twenty-first century, with record shops and dive bars everywhere, has morphed into the Mall of America. We used to live around the corner from a guy who had a pet pig named Bacon. And this wasn't a pot-bellied pig; he was the real full-sized deal. Now there's nothing but Bugaboo strollers and black Labs. For crying out loud, there's a Marc Jacobs here now and the only free-range pork to be found is in the carnitas bowl at Chipotle.

While looking for a place to park by the tattoo shop, I pass my old building, which looks exactly the same as I left it twelve years ago. Except when I walked out those doors at that time, Fletch and I were newly married, unemployed, and terrified. We were desperately trying to figure out what we were going to do to survive. And suddenly, we weren't solely responsible for ourselves—we had a couple of little dogs, too. How were we going to feed Maisy and Loki when we weren't even sure how we'd take care of ourselves?

At that low point in my life, I never imagined I'd be surrounded by an incredible support network of friends who'd fulfill the roles of family in my life. I hadn't a clue as to how pet ownership would impact my every decision, starting with trying to become a writer so I could stay home with Maisy. I couldn't have guessed the kind of life Fletch and I would build for ourselves, and how we'd continue to grow together instead of falling apart in times of crisis.

Honestly, I'm glad I can't go back in time and tell myself it will all be okay, because I've needed to experience every high and low from the past decade to be not only where I am, but who I am, today.

Despite having had an anonymous Greek chorus in my ear for the past few years, telling me that I'm doing it all wrong, I realize I can't change anyone's perceptions and trying to do so would be fruitless.

All I can do is to find peace within myself and the surest path is to continue to eliminate that which I regret.

Each accomplishment on my bucket list has been inordinately

satisfactory, from the simple pleasure of finding a new backbeat when I drive with the top down, to connecting with the culture that's influenced me in so many ways. Even though I haven't yet gotten around to taking a self-defense class, that's still on my list and it's something I look forward to doing. Now, my world seems so much larger than it did a year ago. I've always feared growing older because I thought I'd run out of interests, but what this project has taught me is that I've barely scratched the surface of what I could try next. I can't possibly stagnate when everything feels brand-new and there's so much more to explore, especially with Fletcher beside me.

Plus, I have a new hobby that not only fulfills me, but also helps me cover unexpected expenses like buying Prozac for my weird little dog. (Yes, I do wonder exactly how funny the Italians would find the notion of dog therapists.) Discovering I have other marketable skills makes me less anxious for the future. So much regret is mitigated when there's an actionable plan in place. Couple this discovery with the realization that my things shouldn't own me and that life's meant to be lived, not displayed on Pinterest, and my sense is I've finally achieved something close to balance.

I feel excellent about actually having done more for others this year, rather than just posting status updates about how one could theoretically pursue service. And I'll definitely not regret taking a giant leap away from social media. I figure I was part of the first wave toward social networking, and I'm just as glad to be among the first to walk away.

Most of all, I'm so happy to have finally cracked my own code in terms of my health. I finally understand what drives me and I have a better grasp on how not to derail myself. I don't expect perfection; ergo, I won't be disappointed when I don't attain it. I've learned the importance of cutting myself a break, which is the most expedient path to a life lived without qualms, misgivings, and sorrow.

So I open the door to Vamoose, ready to begin to remove the tangible proof of so many poor choices and bad decisions.

Because regretting nothing is the new black.

ACKNOWLEDGMENTS

What's the opposite of regret? Welcome? Applaud? Because the following people are and have been instrumental in helping me mitigate my regrets, I both applaud and welcome you. (I know the welcome sounds weird—just go with it.)

For Tracy Bernstein, thank you for knowing what I mean even when I'm not even sure what I mean. I promise at some point I will learn the difference between "each other" and "one another" and also where to place the word "only" in a sentence. You are a saint and a scholar. For reals.

For Kara Welsh, thanks for taking a chance on a bitter ex-sorority girl all those years ago. Hope I've done you proud. And many thanks to Claire Zion, as well. You're my guiding lights.

Craig Burke, you're the best, even though we're about to be locked in an arms race over who can buy our dogs more costumes/sweaters. Jessica Butler, I'm your trial by fire, and you never cease to amaze with your firefighting prowess. There are many big things ahead, and I'm so excited for you!

For Sales, Marketing, Art, Audio, Speakers' Bureau, Production, and Contracting/Royalties—thanks for all you do. You are my village. (As in it takes a—get it?) And for Copyediting, I will always write out times, dollar amounts, and decades going forward. Swearsies. I make no promises on understanding the differences between further and farther, though—that shit is tricky.

For Scott Miller (and all the drummers from Spinal Tap), none of this happens without you. You go to eleven.

I don't know where I'd be without authors like Stacey Ballis, Karyn Bosnak, Quinn Cummings, Laurie Notaro, Sarah Pekkanen, Amy Hatvany, Beth Harbison, Emily Giffin, Jolene Siana, Jenny Mollen, Liz Fenton, Lisa Steinke, Jennifer Coburn, Jennifer Weiner, and Allie Larkin having my back. It's not trite to say "so blessed" when you really mean it. Really, for all the brilliant writers out there who inspire me to try harder, thank you. (And Amy Bromberg, we love you for being our biggest cheerleader!)

An extra-special thanks goes to Laurie Dolan, my rock, my sounding board, and my bestest Starbucks buddy. Life is better for knowing you, which means I will be relentless until you finish your own manuscript.

For Lisa Lampanelli and Luke McCollum, my spirit animals— I'll never miss another Annual Bitches at the Beach again. But at least we had Pageant!

For my girls Tracey and Gina, my family by choice—every day is Thanksgiving with you. For Joanna, Julia, Allison, and Alex—I swear on all that is porcine, we will have our sweet, sweet revenge. Count on it. (Remember, being bitter is what got me here in the first place.) Rachel and Trenna—thanks for Savannah, even if you all didn't make it there. (Still looking at you, United.) For Kathleen, Chris, and Finn, my fairy godson—you are tangible proof that faith plus patience equals dreams coming true.

For my boys Benjamin, Jon, and Jonathan—luff you! Never change.

For Kristin and Cecilia at Re-Invent—you give me hope for the next generation.

For everyone who should be thanked here but I've missed—I really need to start taking better notes. (Am old and I forget things now. My apologies.)

For Fletch, the only person I'd ever choose to sit next to for ten hours in Coach. Here's to twenty years and counting! I won't get squishy because you don't actually read my books (he says he doesn't have to because he lives them). Instead, I'll say this—sorry I'm not sorry about the three-wheeled bike. Thank you for being the best sport. And for the beasts—although I regret what you do to my floors every day, you're worth it. (But if you could stop peeing on the drapes in my office, I'd appreciate it.)

Finally, for the readers, the libraries, and the booksellers, thank you for always and forever.